The Role of Consciousness in Governance

Etta D. Jackson

All inquiries should be addressed to: Etta D. Jackson

Email: arcanum33@gmail.com

Phone: +1 917 667-8511

Website: http://www.ancientmysterybooks.com

Book editing: Jacqueline A. Routier-von Felbert

Library of Congress Control Number: 2008908887

International Standard Book No. 0-9746101-1-9

First Edition Published in the United States of America by Lapis Communications

Printed in the United States of America

ALSO BY ETTA D. JACKSON

Understanding Your Choice

Unveiling the Secrets of the Feminine Principle

E-Book: The Idea That Is the United States of America-Its Occult
Foundation

Dedication

This book is dedicated to my daughter, Jacqueline, who has been an incredible inspiration in my life. She has been my friend and my teacher. I often marvel at her courage, sense of adventure, brilliance, wisdom, and strength. You are the special gift I was given and you were equal to the challenges we faced, but what excitement and fun has characterized our lives. Thank you for being a wonderful friend and a precious daughter.

Table of Contents

Author's Note

The goal of this book is to introduce ideas regarding the trend in the evolution of human destiny as it relates to nations, the world in general, and to the effectiveness of the Spiritual Hierarchy. The Spiritual Hierarchy is a group of souls who have mastered the stages of spiritual unfoldment and live among us as the elder brothers and sisters of the race of Man. Their role is to guide the evolution of all life.

The responsibility and obligation of each government is to provide the environment for the citizens to develop each aspect of their personality vehicle, which is described as: the physical, emotional and mental bodies. The United States of America, as a nation, has a unique role to play in the evolution of conscious on our planet. World leaders and politicians make frequent references to the past as precedent for the way forward, however, they are realizing more and more that the past does not provide a good guidebook for the future. This is because are we are not only in a new age, but also in a new cosmic cycle, where the rules are very different. Leaders still continue to grope in the dark with little understanding of these fundamental facts; stumbling along in ignorance, and unfortunately the world population becomes the recipient of their illusion.

For the first time in the history of humanity, the public is educated and more informed than ever. No longer is the population dependent on a select group, made up of the rich, the intellectuals or the aristocrats to interpret complex information for them. Advances in technology have provided greater opportunities for the acquisition of knowledge by peoples in the remotest parts of the world for whom this information was before not accessible. The Spiritual Hierarchy has provided for the education of Humanity by establishing institutions of learning and culture in all countries. It is for this reason that an educational system of liberal arts and sciences was instituted in the

United States of America — the incubator for enlightenment, and an example to the world.

Every Mason knows that it is through the study of the Liberal Arts and Sciences, which includes: Rhetoric, Geometry, Grammar, Music, Logic, Astronomy and Arithmetic, which are the basic disciplines of education together with one's life experiences, that the individual is able to consciously embark on the journey to become a true citizen of the Fifth Kingdom who are those who have emerged out of the human race as a new race called *Homo Spiritualis*.

Leaders in both the private and public sectors have been given the opportunity to use their expertise and resources to make possible the Divine Plan for the liberation of humanity from educational and economic bondage. To lead effectively, one must be taught by his inner teacher. Our outer institutions alone cannot provide the kind of preparation needed to make one an agent of positive change in the new age. A government based on the principles of Brotherhood is one in which everyone is his brother's keeper, and where everyone makes a contribution to life and as the old hatreds are dying out, humanity is gradually coming together as one.

With the unfoldment of the mind, facilitated by the evolutionary process of physical, emotional and mental development, we are fast approaching the point when the united will of Humanity will be reached. This can only be realized when people are educated about the divine plan and made aware of the nature of the forces that control evolution, and the agencies directing those forces. The fact that a Hierarchy of Masters exists, must be made known to humanity, so that they can understand and appreciate the work being done, in love, on their behalf.

One World, with a New Order, is the divine plan that will be realized when all of the regions of the world come together. The expanded Federated States of Europe, now the European Union, modeled on the British Commonwealth of Nations, and the United States of America along with the steady spread of democracy in the former Soviet Union and Eastern bloc are giving impetus to this new emerging order in Asia and Africa. This speaks to the work being carried out behind the scenes by the Masters of Wisdom who are bringing this into manifestation.

Cicero says it best: "*To be civilized is to reach that state of personal and collective behavior in which men can live together constructively, in harmony and united for the betterment of all.*" By this definition, he says, "*We have never been civilized, but instead have existed in a state of cultured savagery.*"

Introduction

All systems of government were established to be a vehicle for the government above to become manifest on the earth below. The work of all earthly governments then, is to become a perfect reflection of the government above. The structure and function of all governments is to provide the appropriate conditions for its citizens to achieve full self-consciousness or initiation, resulting in self-governance, which is the ultimate form of government.

Through an examination of the government above we will come to understand the rationale for how and why the basic structure of all forms of governments on earth was designed. The *Hierarchy of Masters* has been steadily guiding Humanity and all governments along a path to this achievement. We will be using the Tree of Life as our structural model to look at how the Spirit, Soul, and Personality, taken together, the human body, are configured to deliver the plan of self-knowledge. The Tree of Life contains ten visible spheres of influence and operation. The first three spheres represent the three aspects of the godhead we commonly refer to as the Father, the Son, and Mother/Holy Spirit. These three aspects represent Knowledge, Wisdom and Understanding, respectively. The third aspect, the Mother/Holy Spirit, is the Creative Principle responsible for establishing the kingdom below on Earth. The process involves creating an intermediary through which the divine consciousness can manifest in a step-down process to deposit itself in a dense physical form, the personality vehicle, as it relates to the human being and similarly, in the government, as it relates to society.

The soul force is also represented on the Tree of Life as a triangular force to which is assigned the qualities of Mercy, Strength, and Beauty; the remaining four spheres represent the personality vehicle, or body, created to house the divine spark of spirit. The four centers of the personality vehicle correspond to Victory, Intellect, Foundation, and the Kingdom of Earth, respectively. The last seven of the ten spheres on the Tree of Life operate most directly in our etheric and physical spheres, and constitute the structures of government and the function of how spirit manifests on Earth. These seven spheres make up the three spiritual and causal levels of governance and the four departments through which the spiritual divine idea is made manifest in the physical lives of humanity. These ten cosmic forces mentioned above and represented on the Tree of Life are mirrored on the physical plane, since everything that transpires on the plane of matter is in response to an influence from above. Let us now look at each of these ten spheres to see what and how each contributes to the divine objective. The first sphere or Father, represents Will and Power and is associated with Government at all levels. Shamballah is the name used to represent the head center and the father aspect, which is the custodian of the Divine Plan and the place from which the plan is realized.

The second sphere or the Son, is associated with Love-Wisdom and represents the center of the Hierarchy. The Hierarchy is a group of spiritual beings on the inner planes of the solar system. They are the intelligent forces of nature that control the evolutionary processes, and are divided into twelve hierarchies. Within our planetary Earth scheme, there is a reflection of this hierarchy called the occult hierarchy, which consists of masters of wisdom, adepts, and initiates. The occult hierarchy works through their disciples to carry out the divine plan in the world.

The third, Active Intelligence, is most closely associated with Humanity, and is assigned to the Mother or Holy Spirit through whom everything in creation came into manifestation. Humanity as a whole is defined in the Ancient Wisdom teachings as the World Disciple. The city, state or nation are members of the world community and the family of man. The individual gradually grows to become conscious of his place in the world community. It is only when mankind collectively is able to think within wider international terms, as all great thinkers do, will the fusion of all men everywhere become possible. This awareness will ultimately facilitate true brotherhood and make *true humanity* a fact in the consciousness of everyone.

The control and maneuvering of these energies in the hands of the Master Architect and Grand Designer propel us forward to the building of a perfect structure of government where every race, gender and culture shares in the prosperity, the freedom, and the enlightenment which is their birthright. This is the reason for the establishment of every government and why the government of the United States of America was so meticulously constructed with its great esoteric constitution, because it is to be a model for the world. In fact, the Founding Fathers established the United States of America under the direction of the Masters of Wisdom in order to lead the country, and by extension the world, along a path of Initiation; the blueprint of which is provided through Masonry.

Today, a large percentage of people are both mentally and emotionally mature and evolved and able to respond adequately to the impulses of the Hierarchy. The ability of governments to recognize this maturity and accommodate greater involvement by their citizens, to provide them with a stronger voice and participation in their government is in itself a function of the evolution of the governments themselves. The ultimate task of every nation is to solve its own internal psychological problems by first recognizing that these problems exist; then working to mitigate national egotism and then take the steps necessary to establish unity in the life of its population. The next task of governments is to foster the spirit of right relations, which is accomplished through the recognition of the one world of which it is a part. Each nation must take the steps needed to enable it to enrich the whole world through its individual contribution. However, these two activities, one national and the other international, must proceed simultaneously and side by side.

CHAPTER ONE

The Governments Above and Below: Their Structure and Function

The Solar Trinity or Hierarchy consists of the Father, the Son and the Mother aspects, each representing the three aspects of the head of the government above in the unseen world, which is analogous to the three co-equal branches of government we see in the United States of America, i.e. the Executive, the Judicial and the Legislative. There are, in turn, the three constellations of the Great Bear, the Pleiades, and the sun Sirius from which streams of energies pour into the Earth. The three aspects of the government are in reality One and was designed to work as such in our Earth Scheme to carry out the Divine Will and Plan of establishing a reflection of itself on Earth.

The goal of life here is to evolve, to grow, and to know; since self-knowledge brings about the liberation of man from the bondage of ignorance. In other words, Man is to become fully conscious in his body, a state which occurs when the "germ of knowledge" expands in his human vehicle so that he becomes totally aware of him/herself as both god and man. In the same way, the government above reflects itself below.

The Father Aspect

The Father aspect of government is directly aligned with the constellation of the Great Bear and the spiritual center referred to as Shamballa, which is the custodian of the Divine Plan for our planet.

The Great Bear, also called Ursa Major, is a large northern constellation containing the seven conspicuous stars called Septentriones. The influence of the Great Bear conditions the Will aspect on Earth, and Will works downwards into form, bending the

1

Will consciously to Divine Purpose. The effect of the Great Bear therefore is as follows:

- To initiate
- To bring fulfillment
- To conquer death[1]

The Pole Star refers to the star Polaris or "North Star" and is currently aligned to the Earth's rotation and to the North Pole. It is the star of direction to Divine Will, Purpose and Plan. It is the end-star in the tail of Ursa Minor, which is the constellation of the Little Bear, and in which is located the Seven Sisters of the Pleiades. Apart from the Sun, it is regarded as the most important star in the sky, guiding sailors who navigate their way by the stars; also caravans of old, as they wind their way over the desert by night. The relationship and orientation of the two Pointers in the Great Bear to the Pole Star symbolizes the unavoidable, directed purpose and fulfillment of the Plan. The Seven Sisters of the Pleiades are referred to as the wives or sisters of the seven brothers, or stars of the Great Bear, and are the creative agents through which this plan is made manifest on Earth. As the shift in mans' consciousness continues, the interplay of forces in the universe will bring about a replacement of Polaris as the Pole Star. But the Pole Star, whatever its name may be, will forever be the "star of re-orientation", facilitating the recovery and the re-facing of that which is lost. Certain basic changes in the orientation of the Earth's axis are now taking place and our present Pole Star has not always held that position since it is continually moving toward the Celestial North Pole. But, at each of the great shifts in the Earth's axis, there is always upheaval and confusion, which precedes reconstruction, stabilization and relative quiet.[2]

The present world crises are a result of the cosmic and systemic influences, which occur at the end of each great cycle and are due to:

1. *The welling up of a magnetic force on Sirius which produces effects upon the earth.*

2. *A shift in the Earth's polarity due to the pull of a great cosmic*

center which is responsible for the earth's re-orientation, volcanic eruptions and earthquakes.

3. The great sweep of the Sun around the **greater zodiac** of 250,000 years, a complete round. This occurred two thousand years ago when the Sun entered the sign of Pisces.

4. The passing of the Sun out of the sign of Pisces into the sign of Aquarius, and the impact of the constellations in which these signs exist, are all producing the present confusion.

5. The increasing rapidity of the disintegration of the Moon, which given its relationship to the Earth, greatly affects terrestrial changes.[3]

The Pointer closest to the Pole Star guided Humanity on its in-volutionary path, while the Pointer furthest from the Pole Star is re-orienting Humanity back to the Hierarchy and to the Source. It is in this regard that the two pointers and with the Pole Star are mysteriously connected with the three aspects of the Spirit, Soul and Body of the incarnated Man. These three stars are the embodiments of the three aspects of Divine Will — Knowledge, Wisdom and Understanding. A great divine experiment was initiated on the Earth and the exoteric planet, Aries, is the vehicle for this experiment. The two esoteric planets of Vulcan and Pluto which are related to the two Pointers in the solar system become the vehicles through which the energy from the Great Bear is expressed. For the first time in this period of the Aryan race, mankind is showing reaction and response to the Spiritual Will.[4] The Great Bear is the source of the Seven Rays, which are the forces that condition all aspects of life. These seven Rays express in the following ways:

• The First Ray is the energy of Will or Power, also known as the Destroyer Ray. It destroys the concept of Death, which in reality is an illusion. The concept of death is part of the Great Illusion and causes limitation of the human consciousness as it is concerned with the brain. The concept of death is caused by a cleavage of the mind and is a figment of the mind. The First Ray is also what incites and produces Initiation.

- The Second Ray is that of Love-Wisdom, and relates to the Will to Unification; to Synthesis; to produce coherence and mutual attraction, and to establish relationships. It is through the forces of this Ray that the individual is able to see and to grasp the vision of what is to unfold.

- The Third Ray is the energy of Active Intelligence, which is the Will of Conditioned Purpose. This Ray is that which develops sensory perception into knowledge, then knowledge into wisdom, and finally wisdom into omniscience.

- The Fourth Ray is the energy of Harmony through Conflict, which is essentially the will to destroy limitation. It is the Ray of Illumined Will, which is intuition at its most basic level.

- The Fifth Ray is the energy of Concrete Science or Knowledge, and to understand this concept, it must be remembered that matter is spirit at its lowest point of manifestation and that spirit is matter at its highest. This aspect of will, therefore, produces concretion and is the point at which spirit and matter are balanced and co-equal. This Ray is the seed of liberation, and is therefore an aspect of destruction.

- The Sixth Ray is the energy of Devotion and Idealism and is the aspect of Will that embodies the ideas of the All; it provides the motivating power for working out whatever is the purpose of creation. The consciousness of the individual determines his ability to express the Will toward the Ideal in the mind of God and is related to the "creative urge".

- The Seventh Ray is the energy of Ceremonial Order, which is the expression of the Will and what drives through outer manifestation into **ritualistic synthesis**. It is the energy that embodies both the periphery and the center, expressing in a rhythmic and orderly manner. The 7th Ray can also be called the Principle of Order. [5]

Shamballah, which is the planetary and spiritual head center where the energies from the Great Bear are concentrated. From this center is manifested the Divine Purpose to condition the life of nations to establish esoteric politics and the determination of the Plan.[6] This sacred center, the place of the basic school of occultism, located in the higher physical ethers of our planet, is the residence of the Overlords of our planet. It is from here that the commands for the execution of the Plan for Humanity are issued. Here is where the Will of God is focused and from where Divine purposes are directed. From this place, Shamballah, or Shangri-Lha, great political movements and the destiny and progress of nations and races are determined. Those who incarnate from the spiritual center, Shamballa, hold immense power and the thread of their influence can be traced throughout history in great declarations and pronouncements such as:

- The Magna Charta
- The Declaration of Independence
- The Atlantic Charter

The Masters of the World, whether from Shamballah or from the Hierarchy are here for the guidance and release of humanity from bondage. They come in response to the strong desire and the demand of mankind and is due, in large part, to the spiritual interplay that exists between Humanity, the Hierarchy, and Shamballah. The messengers from the spiritual centers embody divine intention, and humanity's response to them is in direct relationship to the point of evolution attained by Man.

The Son Aspect

The second aspect of the Solar Trinity is that of the Son and is aligned with the Hierarchy and related to the Sun Sirius. The Son of Man, the Way-Shower, the Knower and Master Mason from the office of the Christ was given dominion over the Earth; earned by his journey into matter, his death, and his "raising". His overcoming qualifies him to show humanity the way out of the bondage of ignorance into the light of knowledge. The Hierarchy is the intermediary between Shamballah above and Humanity below. It is the center through which the Great Beings work to manifest the purpose and the plan for planetary evolution. It is a miniature replica of the greater synthesis of those Self-conscious entities that control, manipulate, and demonstrate through the Sun, and the seven sacred and other planets in our planetary scheme.

Our solar system is a part of this planetary scheme, and Jesus, the Christ, head of the Hierarchy, supervises four paramount lines of work:

1. **The Development of Self-Consciousness in All Beings**

   One of the ways to achieve this is by blending man's three higher aspects of spirit with his four lower etheric and physical aspects. Another is through the example set in service, renunciation, sacrifice and the constant stream of light it emanates The Hierarchy could be understood as the combined forces of the fifth kingdom in nature. One enters this fifth kingdom through the full development and control of the fifth principle of mind, which is the *higher human mind* and through which individualization begins; and through the full utilization of the faculty of discriminative love, which eventually transmutes into wisdom.[7]

2. **The Development of Consciousness in the Three Lower Kingdoms**.

   All these kingdoms—mineral, plant and animal—embody some kind of consciousness, and it is the responsibility of the Hierarchy to develop all these types to perfection; this is accomplished through the adjustment of the actions and reactions of force on the forms, which includes providing the right conditions for this to occur.[8]

The Five Kingdoms in Nature on an Evolution Arc, are:

- *The Mineral Kingdom.* A primary characteristic of all matter is activity of some kind, and the work of the Hierarchy in this kingdom is the development of discriminative and selective activity.

- *The Vegetable Kingdom.* To the faculty of discrimination developed in the mineral kingdom is added the response to sensation

- *The Animal Kingdom.* In this kingdom, rudimentary activity and sensation are increased and these symptoms can be described as the embryonic aspect of Will and Purpose.

- *The Human Kingdom.* Man is the macrocosm of the three lower kingdoms below him because the three lines of development are synthesized and come to full fruition in him as embryonic, dynamic and initiating will which becomes more fully developed after he enters the Fifth Kingdom.

- *The Spiritual Kingdom—God-Man.* What characterizes the fifth kingdom is the full flowering and consummation of the love-wisdom faculty in the adept. He first becomes a Master who works as part of the Hierarchy, then a Master of Compassion, and then a Lord of Love and then becomes God-Conscious.[9] They now tend the seed of self-consciousness in all beings. One of the great decisions made by these Beings is the inconceivable renunciation, which leads then to remain in our planetary scheme to carry out the plans of the Planetary Lord for the physical plane.

As such, they are:

3. **To Transmit the Will of the Planetary Lord.**

The plan of synthesizing fragmented Humanity and the establishment of the Brotherhood of Man is a primary goal of the Hierarchy. Mankind is beginning to understand his obligation to facilitate the goal of establishing the Brotherhood of Man. This is beginning to permeate his consciousness.[10]

4. **To Set An Example to Humanity**.

   The members of the Fifth Kingdom who make up the Spiritual Hierarchy are composed of men and women who have triumphed over matter and have achieved that goal by the same steps that each individual walks today. The advanced members of the Race of Man have all undergone the crucifixion of the personal self and know the reality of complete renunciation from all that humanity is engaged in at present. These adepts and masters have wrestled and fought for victory and mastery on the physical plane. They know the quintessence of pain and the depth of suffering and are qualified by those experiences; their methods can be adapted to the individual need of the aspirant.[11]

These Elder Brothers of humanity can be identified by a love that is enduring; a knowledge gained through millennia of lives in which they have worked their way from the bottom of life and the evolution path to the top; they are also distinguished by an experience that is based on time itself with all its many personality reactions and interactions; by a courage which is the result of that experience, which has produced ages of failures and successes, and ultimately triumph; by a courage used in the service of humanity; a purpose, which is enlightened, intelligent, co-operative, and always adjusting itself to the group and the hierarchical plan, and therefore fitting it to the purpose of the Planetary Lord. They speak when others are silent, and they are silent when others speak. Because these elder brothers know the divine plan so well, with their clear and illuminated vision, they bend their will steadfastly and firmly to the great work. Only when humanity has grasped these four facts and they are acknowledged as truths in the consciousness of the Race of Man, can we look forward to a cycle of peace, rest and righteousness.[12]

The Humanity/Mother Aspect

Humanity is the third major planetary center through which Active Intelligence expresses itself. The Divine Mother is associated with this center since she is the vehicle through which Humanity came into form, and whose obligation it is to liberate Him from the bondage of matter. Through Humanity, the three stages of the Plan, as they relate to the Head, the Heart, and the Throat centers in the body of the Great One and the Solar System are worked out. It is only through Humanity that the door on the physical plane can be opened to allow the light from the Lords of Liberation to make their activities possible on the planet. The potent, magnetic, in-drawing power of man is needed to pull the forces down not just to the mental plane, but further down into outer expression, power and manifestation. Humanity is a unit, just as the world is an entity and its misdeeds and sufferings are one. The goals of Humanity and the planet are, therefore, one and the same, and as humanity moves into the future, it must do so in a way that is disciplined, illumined, advised and with fusion. There are many among humanity who are unable to grasp this fact and will suffer greatly from non-participation in the evolution of the whole.

The esoteric goal before Humanity and the purpose for which He came into the kingdom of matter is to achieve enlightenment. Yes, this corresponds to the same tremendous event, which was acted out before humanity by the greatest of all the sons of God in his own body, and as the Master of all Masters — the Way-shower, the Christ.[13] Humanity is an expression of the life of God, and every human being came into form along one of seven rays of force. The nature of each soul is qualified or determined by the Ray of Life, which breathed him into life on the planet. This Ray Force colors the form he will assume during the cycle he experiences on the earth, and the quality of the race life he will occupy. The soul nature of this individual remains the same throughout a world period, but changes in each life cycle.

Humanity, which comprises the fourth kingdom in nature, is that group in which the emerging quality called **synthetic love** or understanding exists and is termed **intuition,** and which is a quality of mental matter. The development of mental matter is due to the inflow of energies from the fifth plane of mind or higher mind. It is an essential aspect of human evolution itself, and this is what is referred to as the development of **consciousness**. Man is the only entity who can be aware that he is aware and then becomes aware in varying degrees. His response mechanism makes him also aware of the kingdoms below him, and, in addition, to his becoming aware of himself. He is then able to respond, not only to external stimuli, but also to contacts from his own higher self, which emanate from within himself.

Man is a living soul and a conscious Son of God who occupies an animal body, and is the link between the kingdoms below him and the spiritual kingdoms above. He is the link between heaven and earth. He, therefore, unifies in himself the results of the evolutionary process as it occurred over all the past ages, and brings into this evolutionary process a new factor — an individual self-sustaining, self-knowing aspect. This aspect is what differentiates man from animals, and produces in humanity a consciousness of self-awareness, immortality, and self-centeredness that allows him to appear in the image of God. This same innate and hidden power gives man the capacity to suffer, but this power also confers upon him the ability to reap the benefits of that suffering in the realm of the intellect. He is then able to sense ideals, to register beauty, enjoy color and harmony, and react sensuously to music. This factor in man is what makes him the Prodigal Son who is torn between the desire for the worldly life, the possession of material things, and the pull of the attractive power of the home from which he came. This capacity for suffering in its embryonic form is what manifests itself in the animal kingdom as instinct.

Humanity is the custodian of the hidden mysteries of life; the dilemma he faces, however, is that the mysteries he conceals from the world, he also hides from himself because he does not know the awesomeness of what he preserves and nourishes.

A great Masonic secret is that Man is the treasure house of God, since only in humans can comprehension and full expression of the three divine qualities of the One Life take place. In Man is hidden the secret of life, God the Father; God the Son, which is the treasured secret of Love and Wisdom; and the Holy Spirit/ Divine Mother implanted in him the mystery of manifestation. Mankind stands at the midway point between heaven and earth with his feet planted firmly in the mud of material life and his head in the heavens. In most cases, he exists with his eyes closed and is unable to see the spiritual vision before him; however, when he catches a glimpse of that vision and the contrast between the spiritual values and the worldly reality, this vision initiates his struggle. This is also when the conflicted and distracted life of the aspirant begins in earnest. Man is given the task of lifting matter up into heaven, and the right to bring glory to form; he is able to do this through the conscious manifestation of his divine powers as he is the vehicle through the divine is manifest on earth. In order for the concept of God to be fully grasped intellectually, this idea must be known and revealed within the human heart and brain of Man.[14] The Ray Force of Harmony through Conflict influences the human kingdom, the fourth in nature, on the soul level, while on the level of his personality, the Fifth Ray of Concrete Knowledge or Science conditions his vehicle. Harmony through Conflict and the power to achieve knowledge through discriminating choices are the two major influences impacting humanity as a whole and driving it toward its divine destiny. This discriminating intelligence during his life experiences ultimately produces in the individual a sense of true values, a vision of the ideal, and the capacity to distinguish the reality behind the illusions.[15]

The Planetary Hierarchy-A Septentate Structure

Both the planetary hierarchy and government below are a reflection on the plane of matter of the spiritual or solar government above, which is characterized by Will, Love/Wisdom, and Active Intelligence. The solar government manifests as a septentate system with the first three divisions of operation corresponding to the Soul, the intermediate between the cosmic spiritual kingdom above, and the quaternary material division below, which it directs and develops.

The Three Major Planetary (Soul) Aspects and Department Heads

1. The name given to the Being who is largely concerned with the science of divine government, law, planetary politics, and with both foundation, direction and dissolution of racial types and forms is the Christ. He is also the ruler, forefather and chief of the human race, and is the Lord of civilization.

    This Being is responsible for the Will and Purpose, and for the causality of the planet. He knows and presides over the immediate objective for this cycle of evolution; He makes sure that this Will and Purpose become an accomplished fact on the planet and works closely and cooperatively with the heads of the other two departments of the Christ. He is the Ideal Man or Thinker who presided over the inception of the Aryan race over one hundred thousand years ago and set the race type and to which the department of the Christ is tasked. From this department is also responsible not only the setting of the race type but of segregating the groups out of which races will develop; of manipulating the forces which move the earth's crust, of raising and lowering continents, and of directing the minds of statesmen everywhere so that racial government will proceed as desired. The conditions then foster particular types along certain lines of energy and vibration. From the department of the Christ is produced the desired results through dynamic meditation and the flow

12

of energy between the cosmic and planetary head centers of each being and resulting in the perfect realization of what is to be visualized and accomplished. Through the power of sound, the Christ transmits the capacity for both creative and destructive energy to His assistants. This work is being carried out extensively, at this time, in North America, Europe and Australia.[16]

The energy of the first divine aspect of Will and Power, which is being scrupulously applied by Shamballah, is the concentration and power of the life in all beings that make contact with the **substance of humanity**. The Adept called El Morya is responsible for the true synthesis of the world of politics and government and in that regard, works with initiates and disciples to counteract wrong approaches to synthesis.

True synthesis is defined by the many aspects of basic and essential unity working to bring about eventual peace and understanding on earth. A peace that will preserve individual and national cultures, while at the same time subordinate these energies of synthesis and unity to the good of humanity, as a whole.[17]

The rulers in this department hold in their hands the reins of government for continents and nations, guiding them, in many cases, unknowingly, toward their destinies. They inspire and impress statesmen and rulers. They accomplish this by pouring mental energy into governing groups, to bring about the desired outcomes among **thinkers** wherever co-operation and receptive intuition is present.

2. The Presiding Head of the second department is the **World Teacher**, the Head of all religions of the world, who is also the Master of Masters of the angels. He is the Great Being whose consciousness has become intelligence. The Christians call Him the Christ. Those in the Orient know Him as the Lord Maitreya and as the Bodhisattva; and

to the Mohammedans, the Imam Madhi. This Being has presided over the guidance and destiny of humanity and the development and realization in Man that he is a Child of God and Son of the Most-High.[18]

The Archetypal Man or Manu is tasked with providing the type and form through which consciousness can evolve and gather experience in the deepest sense. The world teacher is tasked with directing that indwelling consciousness in its life and spirit aspect of humanity, seeking to energize this consciousness within the form of man, so that over time the form can be discarded and the liberated spirit can return to the Source. The Christ withdrew His presence from outer life two thousand years ago, just as the Bible stories indicate (except for the accuracy of the stories); however, the Christ never really left Humanity and has never been gone, though his appearance has changed, making Him visible only to those men with the ability to see Him. However, the light He pours outward stimulates the desires of humanity and propels them along the struggling path they must walk; nudging on the aspirant whose goal is to see the day when he will stand face to face with his initiator. An initiator of the sacred mysteries who has himself been lifted up in the occult sense, now draws all men to Himself.[19] The World Teacher directs the activities of different schools of thought in all the great world religions through the medium of a group of masters and initiates. The Master Jesus is director and inspirer of the Christian Churches, and He and the Master Kuthumi oversee this department of the World Teacher on the Physical Plane, bending the mind towards an occult understanding of Christ Principles.

His objective is to impact the field of education, thereby developing and unfolding consciousness in the student and the individual. At this time the primary concern of the Christ is the adjustment of present affairs through skillful action and with wise and understanding judgment to create the desired future. The Christ accomplishes this by establishing the platform upon which the new teaching must be founded and assessing the foundations upon which the structure of the incoming civilization must be instituted.[20]

3. The Head of the third great department of the Planetary Hierarchy is the Lord of Civilization and of the Principle of Active Intelligence. He is the embodiment of the intelligent aspect. His work is concerned with fostering and strengthening the relationship between spirit and matter, life and form, the self and not-self, the result of this is what we call civilization. He manipulates the forces of nature and is Himself the source of what we know as electric energy. They submit their plans to Him, and through Him, instructions are passed on to a large number of the deva agents.

This cooperation exemplifies Will, Love and Active Intelligence at work. In these three Lords, racial government, religion and civilization form a coherent whole. The closest possible cooperation and unity exists between these three Personalities with every move, plan, and event being a part of their united foreknowledge. These Beings are in touch with the Lord of the World at Shamballah on a daily basis, and the entire guidance of affairs rests in their hands.[21]

Under the direction of Master Rakoczi, also known as Count St. Germaine, head of this Department who presides over the seventh Ray of Organization, Alchemy and Ceremonial Order, the work of the Third Ray is now coming into prominence and manifestation. He is especially concerned with the future development of racial affairs in Europe, and the mental outgrowth in America and Australia. It is the task of this master to synthesize all parts of the divine plan on the physical plane.

He operates as the General Manager, carrying out the plans of the executive council of the Christ; and in that regard, He takes the plan as it is outlined in the inner Council Chamber and approximates it to what is possible.[22] When Humanity is able to stand with "massed intent", the Lord of Civilization can stimulate and prepare this center for right reception of the revitalizing, stimulating, and releasing of the force from the Center of God's Love — the Center of the Heart of the Christ. His task, in the spiritual development of humanity, is to end the present evil situation through the peculiar nature of his work with the Christ Center and the Manu.[23] The following four departments form the vehicle through which the three aspects of Spirit manifest the Divine plan on Earth.

The Minor Four Departments of Attributions

1. The Fourth Department is characterized by the energies of the Fourth Ray of Harmony through Conflict. The Fourth Ray is fundamentally responsible for the strains, stresses and the initial conflict between the major pair of opposites called spirit-matter.

   It is this Fourth Ray energy, which makes the distinction apparent between good and evil. The Age of Materialism came into emphasis during Atlantean times as a result of the decision made by the then leaders of men to place their focus on the matter aspects of life, cemented by their desires and emotions so characteristic of the essential duality of manifestation. The Age of Materialism expresses itself through its greed, hate, separateness, and aggression. It is this materialism, which led to the World Wars of the last century. However, the balance is now beginning to swing to the other side, to Spirit.

   Only when the Principle of Conflict, which is closely related to death, is properly evaluated as a spiritual necessity, will humanity be able to use this principle to emerge out of the control of matter and the three worlds — the physical, the emotional and the mental— to begin to function as soul-infused personalities. Man will then reject Maya, the all-inclusive effect of being immersed and overwhelmed by materialism. It is the Principle of Conflict latent in every atom of substance that initially produces conflict, to be followed by renunciation and finally emancipation.

This same principle, therefore, produces wars of all kinds, then rejection of those wars and finally, liberation. It demonstrates how Death, the great liberator, succeeds in releasing Spirit out of the imprisonment of matter. The principle of Harmony through Conflict is used by the Hierarchy to develop discriminative choice in man, which is the choice between good and evil, right and wrong, Spirit and Matter.

Man is then better able to:

1. perceive the plan;

2. participate in the purpose; and

3. prevent evil.

This principle is controlled by the influence of Love emanating from the office of the Christ and is based on active intelligence, given the development of conscious, intelligent love is always the goal. The country of Germany and the Jewish center, known as the center of Humanity, are both conditioned by the Fourth Ray influences of Harmony through Conflict, which condition the lives of individuals, groups, churches, families and nations who are being led from one renunciation to another, toward true sharing, and finally to the Great Renunciation from the slavery of materialism.[24]

2. The Fifth Department is aligned with the Fifth Ray of Concrete Knowledge and Science. It is the custodian of science, and of that which brings expression to the duality of spirit and matter.

Through the scientific use of energy, the world will be rebuilt and the factual nature of the Hierarchy will be proved. Under this Ray and within this department, the embryonic understanding of causes and conditions resulting from these causes are now emerging.

The energy of concrete knowledge is the substance of the mental plane and is the ***thought-form making energy***. All impressions from the physical, etheric, and astral planes force this energy into activity on the level of concrete knowledge, resulting in an array of thought forms. This spiritual energy produces pure thought, the thinker and thought-forms to produce the three categories of: science, philosophy, and psychology.[25]

The energy of concrete knowledge is being brought to maturity at this time in the form of active intelligence, which makes it possible for aspirants to be admitted into the mysteries of the Mind of God, thereby receiving the key to the universal mind.

A natural fusion of this energy with the energy of love occurs, becoming love-wisdom. All wisdom is knowledge gained by experience and implemented by love. This love-wisdom is a mental energy of the human being and a higher correspondence of the physical brain. The brain's existence is a result of the mind, which needs a brain as its focal point on the physical plane. The brain is responsive to impressions coming in from the spiritual triad, through the antakarana or rainbow bridge.

The brain receives varying energies from all these sources and is able to synthesizes them, to produce order out of them, and interpret them, we call this process the creating of "*commonsense*", and this is also how "*world thought*" is formulated. It is through this same process that divine ideas are transformed into ideals, and workable factors are produced in human evolution, cultures, and

18

civilizations. The Law of Cleavage operates in alignment with this energy, working within the human being to bring clearly to his attention the separateness which has made him unable to let go of the old cultures, old civilizations and the old order, which is rapidly passing away. The foundation for the New Order is being laid. This Aryan Race, the Fifth Life Wave, of which all humanity is a part, is naturally aligned with this Fifth Ray energy. This Aryan Age and Aryan Race expresses a state of mental consciousness and state of thinking that finds its advocates and race members in every nation without distinction or omission. The attainment in consciousness and the formulation of ideologies have given rise to the advancements in many schools of thought in the areas philosophy and psychology, while also giving rise to mental polarization by aspirants everywhere. In fact, everything is crystallizing in human consciousness, making Man aware of where he stands on the ladder of evolution, and of what is wrong and what is right. This realization allows for the transformation of the life of human being, his desires and ultimately revealing the reality that lies behind the human phenomenon.[26]

3. The Sixth Ray Energy of Devotion and Idealism is attributed to the sixth department of government above and below. This energy that was pre-dominant in the Age of Pisces that is now ending. This energy of idealism and devotion is called the ray of one-pointed determination and blind procedure. Under its influence, the individual or group sees only one aspect of reality at any one time.

    Because of Man's present position in his evolution, he was veiled from all else. His vision and horizon was therefore limited esoterically to one point of the compass. For the mass of humanity, the vision and reality for which they lived and died was: *the material world, material comfort, material possession and material enterprise.* The exception was a smaller group of humans who found the world of intelligence of greater importance; and the concrete mind, a more desirable ruler.

The impact of the long cycle of Pisces, which is now ending, but whose effects still linger, combined with the energies of Aquarius, the *water-carrier* these energies will bring about a potent transformation in the *watery realm* of the astral plane.

The Piscean Age, with its astral influence has fixed in the human consciousness the realization that *men are fishes, immersed in the sea of emotions*. The vortex of energy produced by the combination of the Piscean and Aquarian influences result in the person on the path of initiation undergoing the baptismal experience of fire and water, a process that produces cellular regeneration.

In summary, the Sixth Ray energy brings about an embryonic realization of the *will* aspect, which determines the true life of the initiate. It also creates a definite conflict between the lower and the higher self. This is reflective of the ancient struggle between the emotional nature and true realization. Under the continued influence of the Sixth Ray energy, humanity develops the tendency to clarify the atmosphere in the world and, in so doing, begins to release goodwill, which is the primary aspect of love toward his fellowmen.

As the tensions on the astral plane are generated, the emotional and ideological reactions will intensify; a crystallization of all thoughts will occur and a fanatical adherence to mass idealism will take place. These tendencies, however, are later transformed into spiritual devotion toward the welfare of humanity. It is this transformation that sets the stage for the Aquarian Age with its potent energies of purification and its qualities of synthesis and universality, which is necessary to make the New World Order possible.[27]

4. The Seventh Ray of Force, Ceremonial Order, Alchemy and Magic, on the seventh and final plane of manifestation, is the vehicle through which the energies of the solar trinity and the planetary hierarchy are expressed. This ray of attribute deals with the building of the forces of nature and is concerned with the intelligent utilization of form as it relates to the life aspect.

The seventh ray is primarily the ray of executive work, whose object is to build, coordinate and produce cohesion in the four kingdoms of nature. While this Seventh Ray energy is distinguished by ritual, it must not be viewed, however, in the narrow way in which we see Masonry, but rather should include the methods demonstrated in great business organizations, civilized communities, and the world of finance and commerce.

It is the influence of the ray, which brings opportunity to the occidental or western race, because through the medium of this life force of executive organization, of government by rule and order, of rhythm and ritual, the time will come when the western races with their active, concrete mind and vast business capacity will be able to take a major initiation.[28]

The Seventh Ray energies are clearly the medium of relationship; bringing together the two fundamental aspects of spirit and matter, relating soul and form, and also, as it relates to humanity, linking soul to personality.

During the first stage of the fusion of the soul and the personality, man becomes aware in his physical body, on the physical plane, of the emergence into manifestation of the *new man*. At this stage toward initiation, through the stimulation of the Seventh Ray energy, the personality of the candidate, and the hovering- over-shadowing soul are consciously brought together, and for the first time, the candidate knows that he is a soul-infused personality. His task is now to grow into the likeness of who he really is — God and Man. It is the function of the Seventh Ray energy to bring about this level of consciousness in the individual through the process of initiation. The effect on humanity is to bring about the birth of Christ-consciousness in the masses of intelligently aspired human beings, thereby setting in motion a new evolutionary process, which will transform humanity. The new initiate now sets about re-organizing world affairs, thereby inaugurating the New World Order.

From the perspective of the individual, it is the Seventh Ray energy, which restores order within the astral consciousness and on the mental plane, bringing together *within the head*, the lower and higher energies in such a way as to allow "the Christ to be born" in the initiate. This process involves the very important relationship that exists between the pituitary and the pineal glands in the head.[29]

Through the agencies of these seven centers and departments of energy, the Divine Plan is made manifest from the centers of power above to the agencies below, for the purpose of evolving consciousness in Man. The ultimate aim of the plan is that *the center which we call the race of men* will experience the potency of intelligence, as well as to bring to fruition the stirrings of the potency of *love* felt, and of *will* felt; and in the end, to transfer the energies of *love* and *will* to *knowing*. The implementation of this plan occurs through the radiating, dynamic, focused *will* at the heart of the Hierarchy, which, in fact, executes the Divine Plan.

CHAPTER TWO

The Divine Will and Plan

The Purpose for which the Divine Plan was formulated was for the Will of the One Life to be made manifest on Earth. And, to that end, the Will aspect is assigned to government, law and politics.

There is nothing but Spirit, and spiritual evolution and the liberation of humanity from the bondage of ignorance cannot be achieved outside the proper understanding of the true relationship between Spirit and Matter. A littleknown fact among most governments is that they exist for the sole purpose of carrying out the Divine Plan on Earth. However, in order to achieve this, knowledge of the ***Will of the Father*** must be known. The Will of the Father was anchored upon the Earth when in agony and despair, the Christ submerged His to the Will of the Father and was not so much by His death on the cross, but in the garden of Gethsemane. This was made clear when he uttered the words from Luke 22:42, KJV, and declared, Not my will, but thine, be done.

The Divine plan, which had been initiated since the beginning of time, was anchored there in the quiet garden of Gethsemane, and the new aspect of the plan began to unfold upon the Earth. Jesus, the Christ, as the representative of mankind, established the Father's Will and made it possible for intelligent humanity to carry it out. Prior to this, Will had been known only in the Father's House. The Hierarchy of Spiritual Masters, working under the leadership of the Christ, recognized and adapted the Will of the Father to meet the needs of the world by formulating the Divine Plan.

Because of what took place in Christ's moment of crisis thousands of years ago, the efforts, knowledge, and understanding of that crisis were added to the plan, and humanity became the beneficiary.

Christ, at this point, is now the direct line or thread of God's Will, which reaches from the highest to the lowest point of light. As the process of unfoldment takes place, this thread becomes a cable of ascension for humanity, and at the same time, a cable of descent for the merciful, loving spirit of God to Man. The ultimate purpose of the Will and the Plan is to lead humanity into Jerusalem, not into a Jewish city, but into **the place of peace**, which is the true meaning of the word *Jerusalem*.

In spite of the devastating conditions on the planet, the Christ will again *set his face to go up to Jerusalem,* and will again guide humanity into a civilization and a state of consciousness where the universal keynote will be right human relations and worldwide corporation for the good of all.[1]

For the Plan to be successful, the intellect of mankind must be reached, not just their hearts. This is crucial if the Will of God is to be intelligently carried out on earth. Thus, the major task of the Christ is to establish right human relations in every department of human living. The task is made more difficult, however, by the wrong intellectual emphasis of humanity.[2]

The Christ is being asked to again work in the world arena as the representative of the Love of God. He is again entering this arena at a time when His earlier messages of two thousand years ago have been negated, forgotten, or misinterpreted; unfortunately, hate and separateness are now the distinguishing marks of all men everywhere.[3] The logical question is: Of what purpose is the service of all who work fervently in the cause of humanity when everything seems so hopeless? The one thing that humanity must know is that there is a plan; that it is definitely working out through all of the happenings of world events, and that all the occurrences of both man's historical past and his present experiences are in line with the Divine Plan. It might be encouraging to know that the originators of this Plan are also responsible for its successful execution. From the perspective of the average human who thinks in terms of earthly happiness, the Plan should provide some joy and a way of achieving an easier material life. However, to those master souls who execute the Plan, it involves adjusting their lives to certain circumstances and arrangements to assist in raising and expanding the consciousness of mankind; this will enable the needed changes being made of their own free will, to produce the necessary improvements to the environment consistent with the unfolding spiritual requirements.[4] It is important to recognize that this plan can only be carried out by humanity, and so it is incumbent on us to look at what humanity's response to the inflowing streams of the light of the soul must be.

The different racial groups, with their special color, vibration and constitution, are essential to the achievement of humanity's true destiny since it is only through Humanity that the door to liberation on the physical plane can be opened. This opening will allow the consciousness of light in, bringing about a new era of peace, joy and spiritual synthesis, a synthesis called **Brotherhood**. For this to occur, the will of humanity must be aligned with the Will of the Father. Humanity is now reaching the point where the exercise of his personal will can be of great importance and in spite of the aggression, fear, terror, foreboding, and the numbness that comes from undue and ceaseless mental, emotional and physical pain aimed at suppressing and negating the free personal will of many sections of humanity.

Physical, mental, and emotional slavery, combined with the imposed and penalizing rule in many countries by their governments, are breaking the hearts of humanity, and causing deep distress and questioning among those whose hearts are not yet broken. The obligation of government is to provide the economic and educational environment, which ensures the safety, prosperity, and opportunity for reflection and spiritual unfoldment that eventually leads to self-rule and self-governance. For this kind of government to emerge, ideologies must go, old ideals must be relinquished, petty political, religious and social schemes must be discarded, and the one and only driving purpose, the sole outstanding determination, must be the release of humanity from the imposition of fear and unfair penalties.

Liberation for humanity can only come when the **so-called** good people, who are really most interested in saving their own souls, based on their high ideals, become more interested in the welfare of humanity. They must give up their pet theories and their beloved ideals, and grasp the important fact that if the Kingdom of Heaven and the New Age is to be entered into, it can only take place when mankind is truly loved and is selflessly served; when the true divine purpose is seen and understood, and when humanity fuses into one indivisible whole.

Then, and only then, will petty nationalism, religious differences, and selfish idealism be subordinated to human needs, the good of humanity, and the future happiness of humanity as a whole. These forces of evil on the planet are expressed through selfishness and material objectives, not toward the good and well-being of humanity. Their evil objectives with their distortions are imposed upon the world, eliciting the innate revolt we see among the citizens. At the same time, the forces of good are continually working to provide a counterbalance to the imposition of material selfishness, even though the problem does persist on the mental plane.

The potency and grasp of things material, and the unwavering and undivided focus on the physical plane, have given the forces of aggression much success on our planet. They have fused and blended together to form a group of seven souls that personify great and specific aspects of material forces, which are connected with the seven types of energy currently influencing our planet. These energies are of the lowest and most material expression and manifest as war, fear, and cruelty. The seven energies are united by one point of view, and one goal, which is responsible for their success. An example of this **seven** are: Hitler, von Ribbentrop, Goebbels, Goering, Hess, Himmler and Streicher of Germany. These seven are the dark and base parallel of the **seven** who lead humanity into light, and who are symbolized in the Seven Masons that constitute a true Lodge of Masons, and who have final control.[5] The hierarchy of spiritual masters are working with the souls on the planet who work tirelessly on the side of the forces of light and non-aggression to realize their goal. The goal of the spiritual masters must be seen by the advocates of light with equal clarity, and must be equally and uniformly united with the objective of ending aggression, oppression, and of freeing humanity. When this happens, we will see an embodiment of spiritual force, which will bring disaster to the potent seven. Once this necessary unification of objective and purpose becomes a reality, the force generated, and the power let loose upon the physical plane will be so stupendous that human liberation will occur rapidly.[6]

It must be borne in mind that the great battle of Armageddon is now in progress. This battle is fought where all wars begin--on the mental plane, between the pairs of opposites, and consequently this battle can only be won on the mental plane. It is the cleavage on the mental plane that was set up from the beginning of time, which is responsible for the ongoing conflict and over which victory must be achieved. It is through, and out of this battle that the Prince of Peace, who takes a definite part in this battle of Armageddon, will lead His triumphant cohorts through the *gates* to Jerusalem — the city of peace. But this will occur only when the free will of humanity is allowed a measure of expression on our planet.

Under the emerging New World Order, we are faced with a complex situation due in great part to the ideological regimes that have divided the world into opposing groups. What we now have are the great democracies, a few remaining monarchies, which they accommodate; and, the totalitarian powers in which ancient dictatorships and autocracies exist. In spite of the imperfect effectiveness of our democracies, within them lies the germ of something that is new, and the expression of an upward surge toward self-rule and self-mastery by humanity.

The Masters of Wisdom describe the communistic ideal as a curious blend of:

- Individualism
- Dictatorship
- The ancient conflict between labor and capital

- The Sermon on the Mount
- The worst aspects of revolution and exploitation. [7]

Behind the diversities of all our methods of government, the Divine Will and Plan for humanity is being executed. Clearer outlines of the Plan are now emerging, indicating that wider fusions are taking place, and a tendency toward the blending of the pairs of opposites, are occurring. The goal of the Spiritual Hierarchy is always to achieve a major synthesis between spirit and matter. It accomplishes this, in part, by facilitating the various basic trends of thought, which are rapidly appearing. The Hierarchy is committed to preserving the large, national and racial outlines in this process of synthesis. The secret of the Will lies in the recognition of the divine nature of man, which is the only means by which the true expression of the Will can evolve and which, in fact, evolves through the soul. The secret of the Will is also tied to the recognition of the unconquerable nature of goodness and to the inevitable triumph of good. This Will is not the result of a incited, stimulating, implacable focusing of energies to achieve triumph but an unrealized effort to understand and express the quality of Spiritual Will.

The Will is the manifestation of that divine energy, which makes the first divine aspect of Will, or Power, the distinctive feature of the force of the Kingdom Above/Shamballah. This force has such a peculiar quality that even the Christ Himself was unable to express it with facility and understanding. The significance of the episode in Gethsemane, in which Jesus acquiesced totally to the Will of the Father, lies in the fact that it makes clear beyond a shadow of a doubt, that *Man has no personal Will.*

The force of the first aspect of Will, which is a unifying and synthetic force, is always available for right usage. However, the power to express this force lies in the understanding of it, and the individual's stage of evolution. While Man is the only entity who can express this force effectively and who can manifest the Plan, to achieve this objective, he must make steady and regular progression toward unity and synthesis. The Hierarchy facilitates this process in

Man by penetrating the consciousness of the race, which allows the individual to begin to get in touch with the emerging ideas from the Hierarchy of Masters, and reveals the dim outlines of the Plan for liberation from the bondage of ignorance.

In order to have a better understanding of what is taking place today in relationship to the evolution of the consciousness of mankind, clarification must be sought from ancient sources. Modern academic literature reflects only a symbolic page of the vast and ancient historical records of our planetary life and the destiny of Man. This history, unfortunately, is not recognized by modern historians. The relevant information must be sought in the many world Scriptures, in ancient monuments, in the science of symbols, in racial myths, and in inherited and transmitted legends. Most importantly, this knowledge can be found in the study of the microcosmic, which is man himself, who holds the key to the study of human affairs in general.[8]

The three primary races carry key codes essential to the understanding and success of the divine plan. These three races are symbolized by the three primary colors — red, yellow and blue. Without the active and conscious participation of each racial group, including decision-making capacities in the development of policies that affect the lives of the world, suffering and pain will continue due to a lack of comprehensive knowledge of the family of man. Each group is constituted to integrate the ancient experiences, to make meaning of those experiences, and to interpret and communicate them for the benefit of all. However, each cultural and racial group must be respected, listened to and allowed to make the necessary contributions in alleviating world problems. Lack of respect and ignorance is responsible for the exclusion of valuable information, which informs better decision making. Additionally, the lack of proper education, as well as, inadequate development of the mind among minority groups, prevent them from making their needed contribution to the field of debate, and consequently, to the problems that face their people and the world.

The Red Race is identified as comprising the Indians of East India, and the Indians of North and South America, the Caribbean and Oceania, and is associated with the element of fire. They are generally known as the keepers of the earth and were a dominant race in the Atlantean civilization. They know the earth to be intelligent life and understand its vital contribution to the relationship of Matter and Spirit.

The Blue Race, largely the descendants of the continent of Africa, represents the element of water and the holders of the memory of all life and are known as the wisdom-keepers along with the earth peoples; they carrying the emotional memory.

The Yellow Race are the peoples of the Orient who represent the element of air and the agent responsible for combing the elements of water and fire through the mind to bring about a synthesis of thinking. This synthesis allows for an understanding of how the Divine Will and Plan can only be manifested through the vehicle of Humanity as an entity, and that only as each part of that entity becomes conscious of its relationship to each other and to the whole, can the Plan become a reality on the planet.

To this end, the Aquarian Age lends its vibration of synthesis and brotherhood as a vehicle and an integral part of the Divine plan. The United States of America was therefore, created with an Aquarian soul to best embody and unfold the Plan for the liberation of humanity. When the esoteric document called the United States Constitution is correctly understood and interpreted, it will be seen to contain the principles of unity, brotherhood and enlightenment, which are necessary to establish a government equal to the task of alleviating poverty, of educating all its citizens, and of providing an environment for correct spiritual understanding of the principles of Masonry, which will provide a vehicle for the enlightenment of its citizens.

Then, as a country, it will be qualified and able to appropriately become a beacon of light to the world. This is the Divine Will and Plan that is now being made manifest on Earth.

CHAPTER THREE

The Human Dilemma and Its Hope

Humanity is waiting with anxious anticipation for relief from the burdens they have carried for far too long. Those who are religious look to a Savior, whether that be in the form of the Christ, the Imam Mahadi, or the Maitreya; and those who are non-religious look to their governments or leaders and themselves. Interestingly, a combination of all three is relevant to experiencing the gifts of the present Age with its promises of peace, brotherhood and prosperity. To have a clearer and more adequate understanding of the issues faced by humanity, as a whole, a closer look must be given to man's origin, and to the impact of the cosmic, solar and planetary forces intermingled with the destiny of each individual and each nation which comprise the Center of Humanity. An understanding of the causes for the present restlessness and crises we are now witnessing might help to empower the reader instead allowing him to continue with a sense of helplessness. Ageless Wisdom teachings put forward the following reasons for the present world conditions:

1. The point reached by humanity is listed as one of the major and primary causes. Mankind is now at a unique point on his evolutionary path. He has just stepped through the gateway of the New Age of Aquarius, which will lead to the next step in his unfoldment, and includes drastic changes in *his* entire attitude to life and his worldview.

    It is important to note that man has brought himself to this point because of his own efforts; however, this has created certain tensions not only within himself, but within his brothers and, in all life. The principle of intelligence is now so strongly awakened in him that it cannot be arrested.

    Unfortunately, these same advances in Man's knowledge are at times dangerously and selfishly used, therefore mankind must learn to react to a higher and better sense of values as a safeguard against the lower aspects of himself.

Millions are now integrated enough individually to begin to function as a unit, in preparation for integration with humanity as a whole. The mind, the emotional body, and the brain are working together in unison to facilitate the more subtle and higher correspondences of wisdom, love and direction that will appear in physical manifestation.

An instinctive and mystical perception of the possibility that he can achieve these higher goals has developed in humanity. Therefore, the instinct to press forward and to search and enquire for better, has become very strong in him. The Hierarchy of Love is continually hastening the process of achievement, knowing always the risk of complication. A large number of souls, for the first time, are emerging out of the ***dead level of humanity***, meaning that these souls now stand above their fellow human beings; a position made possible through the process of personality-soul integration. These advanced souls are now able to influence the thought and life of the race of humanity toward what they know personally to be achievable.

Even though these illumined souls in the fields of government, science, religion, philosophy, economics and sociology impact the civilization in positive and not-so-positive ways, in the long run, the result will always be the awakening of the public consciousness.[1]

2. Another factor contributing to our planetary crisis is the emerging new racial type. This new, emerging race of every land across the globe are the members of the Fifth Life Wave who now make up the Kingdom of Spirit — the Fifth Kingdom.

This new racial type is more a state of consciousness and a state of mind, and less of physical form or a particular design of the body. One of the outstanding characteristics of this new racial type is their mystical and intuitive quality, which enables the understanding and control of energy, and its contribution to the development of the human being as well as the transmutation of selfish desire into group love.

The manifestation of this quality is reflected in the idealistic and nationalistic love and pride of leaders for their nation.[2]

3. A third factor impacting the life of humanity is the end of the Piscean Age. The conclusion of this Age is signified by the crystallization and, therefore, death of all the forms through which the Piscean ideals have molded. Those forms have served their purpose, accomplishing the necessary and important work for which they were created.[3]

Some of these ideals are:

- *The idea of authority*, which has led to the imposition of the many different forms of educational, religious, political, and social paternalism on humanity. This is evidenced by the way the privileged class tries to improve the lives of their dependents, and the overbearingly paternalistic, ecclesiastical authority in churches, religion and in education.[4]

- *The Idea of the Value of Sorrow and Pain*. Humanity is presently steeped in misery and an unhappy psychological acquiescence to sorrow and pain. This is due to the teachings of the guides of the race who taught the importance of detachment. They desired to orient mankind away from the material aspect of life and from matter. In so doing, however, it was overdone and what developed instead was a fearful, sorrowful and feeble expectancy and hope of some material reward in "heaven" to compensate for what he had to endure on

Earth. A correction in thinking, promised in this New Age, will prove to be the only hope for real joy.[5]

- *The Idea of Self-sacrifice:* The enforced submission to sacrifice by the stronger and more vocal in the society who failed in the realization that when self-sacrifice in the individual is not self-initiated, in the long run will serve to only delay the individualization of Man.[6]

- **The Idea of the Satisfaction of Desire:** The Piscean Age has been characterized by material production and commercial expansion, in which salesmanship is designed to influence and educate the public to believe that the acquisition of their product is essential to their happiness.

The Hierarchy of Wisdom has allowed these practices to continue in order to achieve satiation. We are beginning to see a revolt and Humanity is beginning to learn that the multiplication of material goods represents a handicap, and as a result, simplicity is rapidly gaining ground.[7]

4. *The emergence of the Aquarian Age*, whose characteristics are individual understanding and direct knowledge, is a major factor impacting humanity at present. The Piscean atoms in the bodies of individuals, nations and the planet are being abstracted or withdrawn, in an occult sense, as the Aquarian atoms are being stimulated and their vibratory activity is increased to be able to respond to the New Age tendencies and needs.

The Hierarchy of Wisdom depends on these steady, emerging influences to bring Humanity to its destined goal. The Piscean Age was seldom able to bring its ideals into the physical plane of manifestation, and so Mankind saw those ideals as two separate expressions --the ideals above and the plane below with the two never merging. Due to the established channel of contact between the soul and

34

the brain, made possible through the mind, the mind will be used to both penetrate the world of ideas and be the illuminator of life on the physical plane.

These factors will allow the ideals of the Piscean Age to finally be brought into manifestation, much to the delight of men and women of goodwill in every land, who have been frustrated by this fact.[8]

In the Age of Aquarius, also known as the Age of Synthesis, we will see the following become a reality:

- The fusion of mankind's differentiated spiritual aspirations, as expressed through many world religions, into the New World Religion—one that will be characterized by a conscious unified group approach to the world of spiritual values and the reaction that this naturally evokes from the Hierarchy.[9]

- The fusion of intellectual and philosophical thought, as put forth by some great intuitive. The emergence of ideals among the man on the street, evidenced by discussions with his fellowmen in the areas of politics, religion, science, sociology, philosophy, and psychology, etc.

This is leading to a spirit of inclusiveness and a trend toward Love-Wisdom, and represents a great step forward from the perspective of those who guide the evolution of mankind.

The New Age brings a synthesis, a fusion, a blending of mutual cooperation toward certain specific and envisioned ends. As this trend continues in the field of practical education, nations and individuals will develop the ideas which suit national and personal psychology, while recognizing the potency, usefulness and relevance of the points of view of other individuals and nations.[10]

Within the context of these **four** powerful cosmic influences, and the crises arising from them, an enormous opportunity for significant change is provided by the energies of Aquarius. These energies will permit the difficulties faced by humanity to be addressed with new vigor and greater insight. In view of the fact that the whole purpose of life on planet earth is to perfect the personality vehicle, it is my belief that the two most fundamental aids to this achievement are education and economic advancements. Let me take this opportunity to outline how mankind came to be in a state of physical, emotional, mental and spiritual poverty. Since the purpose of all my literary works is to decode the ancient mysteries, a correct interpretation of the "*Fall*" is essential here, since it is the starting point for an understanding of the illusion in which Man has been living.

The Fall, for many, has meant the expulsion from the Garden of Eden or Paradise by God, which thereby relegated Man to a life of sorrow, pain, toil and suffering. This is the result of the false messages humanity has given himself.

As a point of clarification, it is interesting to note that in Gematria, the number 358, representing the serpent, has come to be identified with the monstrous figure called the **Devil** who initiated Eve into the mystery of good and evil, and who took humanity on the involutionary journey into matter. This same number is synonymous with the word **Messiah**, and the name of the serpent is spelled with the same Hebrew letters used for the word **copper**, which is the metal of Venus.[11]

The psychological effects of being driven out of Paradise, cursed and left to fend for himself, has caused Man to be greatly immersed in, dependent on, and defined by, matter. One of the great benefits of the Aquarian Age, the Age of Occultism, is that the veil of secrecy will be removed and Man will come to **see** with his inner eye of wisdom and able to understand the laws of nature. He will come to know the truth that lies beneath the veil of illusion, to know and understand that he is, in fact, both the creator and the created. The adversarial relationship developed between the members of different groups, whether racial, economic, cultural, political, or religious, has intensified the level of separation and the need to be superior to others has left a chasm which can only be bridged by true knowledge. In fact, all our wars, hatreds, poverty, and prejudices have their origin in the separation which began in the Garden of Eden.

The following challenges are of major significance to the liberation of Humanity:

1. ***The Jewish Problem*** —the Jewish people are said to be representative of Humanity and, therefore, have become the clearing-house for the karmic debt that humanity must pay. It must be stated here that when I say Jewish, I am not speaking about a racial or religious group living in the Middle East. The true and esoteric meaning of the term, Jewish, relates to the three groups of Humanity within which the seeds of leadership exist.

They are:

1. The Semitic race or races of biblical and modern times. They include the Arabs, the Afghans, the Moors and the off-shoots and affiliations of these peoples including the Egyptians. They are all descended from the eldest of the three disciples.

2. The Latin peoples and their various branches throughout the world, as well as the Celtic races wherever found. These are descended from the second of the three disciples.

3. The Teutons, the Scandinavians and the Anglo-Saxons, who are the descendants of the third of the three disciples.[12]

The problems of the Jewish people are, therefore, those of Humanity. All of the positive and negative personality traits must be reconciled. The negatives we see in the exoteric group we call *Jews* must be transmuted; this transmutation must also be achieved in the wider group we call Israelites, which is another term for Humanity. Therefore, in all these racial groups lies the potential for transformation of the mind, which will lead to liberation from ignorance. The characteristics of the un-regenerated representative group we call the *Jews*, as it is with Humanity, are cruelty, hardness, materialism, pride, selfishness, ambition and egotism — characteristics symbolic of the Capricorn personality which also rules the knees. It is only when the aspirant has learned to bend his knees in humility before the Initiator to be allowed to pass through the gate of Initiation. He must pass through this gate on his knees, not standing up and demanding what he feels he deserves.[13]

The great lesson of these souls is brotherhood, which can only be achieved through the deepening love of nature. This great band of souls, the true remnants of Judah, who are of every race, ethnicity and nation, are the initiates who are called *Israel*, or *He who is like God*. The problems can only be solved when Jews, gentiles, blacks, whites, male and female come together and recognize the great contributions they have each made to the advancement of human life and freedom. Then, and only then, will we give birth to a new reality and peace on earth.

2. **Racial Minorities:** Under the law of evolution, every race of mankind differs in mental development, in physical stamina, in creative possibilities, in human perceptiveness, in understanding, and in its position on the ladder of civilization. However, this is temporary, since the same potential exists in everyone and every race without exception. These differences in abilities, which have set peoples apart, are rapidly dying out as peoples of all nations are being exposed to education, and the ability to read, to reason and to plan.

   The uniting, scientific discoveries are bringing humanity closer together by revealing the genetic oneness of mankind. Every nation and every race, as does every human being, passes through the evolutionary cycles of nature, which include the stages of childhood, adolescence, adulthood, maturity, decline, and disappearance. Behind every cycle is the triumphant spirit of Man, forever moving on from attainment to attainment and from height to height, always moving toward the goal of achieving the physical, emotional and mental development needed to ultimately attain Initiation.[14]

An international definition of the term *minority* might reveal that the majority nations are classified as such by their educational, economic, cultural and military achievements and prowess, and their ability to provide a high standard of living for their citizens. However, at the same time, all the smaller nations are clamoring for attention and equal recognition — this is a natural in Man. It is the obligation and responsibility of the more developed nations to assist developing nations to achieve the level of civilization they enjoy. The Hierarchy is monitoring them to see how well they steward the mental and physical resources given to them. It must be borne in mind that advanced souls exist in every race, culture and nation and so it should not be assumed that majority nations are the sole repositories of the souls who guide the development of Humanity behind the scenes, while wearing many different clothing of flesh.

The countries of Great Britain and its commonwealth of nations, the United States of America, Japan, Russia, Germany, France, Spain, and Canada are all characterized by a spirit of nationalism. Their developed culture their past and local traditions have conditioned their thinking and they are committed to hold on to these at all cost. They are bound together by what is called modern civilization, founded largely on materialism, not on unifying values which can bring their citizens together as true brothers.[15]

As the leading nations play politics and angle for place and position, the masses of humanity in every nation, small and great, are full of fear and questions. They are ravished by war, insecurity, are underfed and frightened as they look towards an uncertain future. They are tired, to the depths of their souls, of quarreling and fighting. They are weary of tyranny and of striking workmen. All they want is to live in safety, to acquire the necessities of existence, to raise their children in a place with a measure of

39

civilized culture, and to live in a country that is economically sound where they can practice their religions freely and access an adequate educational system. Those who we call minorities are the un-owned aspects of one's self. The Blue Man of Africa, the Yellow Man of the Orient, and the Red Man of India and South American, are the three aspects of the One Reality and when merged are the symbol of Absolute Unity.

Humanity's ignorance of this fact causes him to marginalize his brother and by extension himself. In- spite of the great sin of separateness seen in every country where the rich are organizing to control the finances of the world and religious groups are spreading dissention and seeking membership at the expense of other groups, there are those among mankind who continue to see the world as a whole and are working toward its unification.

They also know that the only true hope is an enlightened public opinion achieved through sound educational methods. It is only by the weight of public opinion that the principles of justice, fair play, and equal sharing of the world's economic resources can be enforced. These principles must be realized and the problems solved, if Humanity is to be liberated.[16]

3. *The Psychological Healing of Nations:* The psychological problems of every nation are rooted in their centuries-old background, are inherent in the souls of each individual nation, and have conditioned the minds of all its peoples. These problems fall into two general categories: (1) The internal, psychological problems of the individual nations and (2) World problems between nations, business, and the forces of labor. The eternal and intrinsic desire of every individual in every nation is to express the highest and most noble aspect of himself and to acquire for himself better material surroundings. The circumstances in the early stages of humanity's racial history was followed by man's desire for beauty, leisure and culture, and the need to work creatively. The urge for better human relations is also of primary importance.[17]

The evolution of the human intellect, which resulted in significant scientific achievements gives man the ability to see the world and humanity in far wider terms and with a broader perspective. The family is seen as a unit of the community; and the community as an integral and effective part of the city, state and nation. There are thinkers within each country whose perspective is international, and the eventual fusion of all peoples everywhere will result in the Brotherhood of Man. Nations tinged by hatreds and prejudices are split and divided among themselves by racial barriers, political party differences, and religious convictions; and these strongly held beliefs inevitably bring chaos and disaster. Most countries are distinguished by an intense assertive and boastful sense of nationalism, based on their culture and scientific achievements. These attitudes breed distrust and dislike among other peoples, and create poor human relations.[18]

Every nation has its own *thought-forms* with which it has been raised, and which has been created over centuries by the thinking, ambitions and goals of the people that have defined and conditioned its ideals as a nation. It is easy to recognize a Frenchman, a German, an American, or an Englishman based not only on appearance, intonation or habits, but more so, on the expressed mental attitude and general assertiveness. If the national thinking of each country has its basis in world unity, and a sense of equality, respect, and cooperativeness within its citizenry, these qualities would make for a positive contribution to the unity of the world.

On the contrary, if the citizen is arrogant, separative, critical of other nations and anti-social, this thinking and behavior is antagonistic to the peace of the world and contributes to international disruption. It is this type of thinking that has been responsible for the sense of separateness that has led to the exploitation and destruction of the economic life of weaker nations by a more powerful few.

The emphasis on material possessions, acquiring land and

of fighting to preserve them is actually not a sign of maturity. Humanity, however, has matured greatly and is demanding leadership that is reflective of that maturity.[19] Though ancient habits of mass thinking and reaction are difficult to overcome, we are now moving with great rapidity toward cooperation and sharing. This is due to the psychological adjustments nations are making within their own borders, as reform must begin at home.[20] The evolutionary process has prepared Humanity for Oneness, and the merging of countries and regions provides a vision of the world to come.

4. **The Problem of the Churches**: There is nothing in heaven or earth that can hinder the progress of the human soul on its long pilgrimage from darkness to light; from the unreal to the real, from death to immortality, and from ignorance to wisdom. Nothing can keep the spirit of Man from its source, and if the organized religious groups of churches in every country will not provide this assistance, humanity will find another way.[21]

The churches have failed humanity in two major ways:

1. By their narrow theological interpretations of the Scriptures and;

2. By their material and political ambitions.

Throughout the ages, there have been those who sought to impose their personal, religious interpretations of the truth of the scriptures and of God upon the masses, explaining their ideas through the filters of their own minds. It must be noted that theology is simply what men think is in the mind of God. In that regard, it appears that the more ancient the scripture, the greater the distortion of the doctrine. The presentation is that of a hateful, vengeful God filled with retribution, who is waiting to assign anyone who would dare use his mind to think independently, or be relegated to an everlasting hell. This is a doctrine Jesus the Christ knew nothing about. When men accept these dogma they are really accepting the infallibility of another human being. The key to truth lies in the unifying power of Comparative Religion. It becomes the obligation of theological seminaries to begin to teach and train the men and women they send out to minister to be individuals who think for themselves. The message the Christ taught was that God is love, that Christ is in every man, and that no man has ever been saved by theology, but only by the living Christ and through the awakened consciousness of the Christ within the heart of man.

Ultimately, it is Man's god-illumined mind that will search for truth and interpret it, thus liberating him from his bondage of ignorance. The voice of humanity is demanding security, peace, and light; some are seeking it from political and governmental lines in the hope that a leader will emerge. People everywhere are ready for the light and are expecting a new revelation and a new dispensation; this is due to significant mental, emotional and spiritual development, true values, and a sustained spiritual vision. Humanity is demanding not only physical, but spiritual food, and is feeling helpless and hopeless with nowhere to turn. However, the cries of humanity have reached the ears of those Christed Beings who watch over Man.[22]

Great opportunities now exist for the churches to respond to the needs and cries of a hungry and thirsty humanity in a meaningful way. Unfortunately, there has been no significant response to this appeal, nor are there any indications of any large-scale changes in the theological teachings or in the government of the churches. It is important for the church to recognize that the infant, Man, has now matured, and that adult humanity is capable of interpreting the ancient spiritual teachings without an intermediary. There is no finality in the presentation of truth, since it develops and grows to accommodate Man's evolving need for light. It is, therefore, time that churches let go of their old, outworn, erroneous interpretations and free the souls of their membership from their imposed authority to pursue individual relationships with God.[23] The time is fast approaching when all religions will be recognized as originating from one great spiritual source and from one root, and out of which a universal religion will emerge. The reality is of the Oneness of Humanity and that there is, in fact, no Jew, nor Gentile, Christian nor Heathen, but one great body of believers composed of all the current religions.

There are three basic unifying truths of all religions, which the church needs to present to mankind:

1. *The Fact that God is Both Immanent and Transcendent*, meaning that the immanent God exists in form as reflected in nature, in the heart of every man, and also exists in the person of the Christ who walked among us. God transcendent guarantees the Divine Plan for Humanity and the world, which becomes the purpose that conditions all lives, from the single-celled organism, through all the kingdoms of mature, to the God-Man.[24]

2. *The Fact of Immortality and Eternal Persistence*, which means that the human spirit never dies and does endure forever, persisting from stage to stage and point to point on the path of evolution; gradually, steadily and sequentially unfolding its divine aspects and attributes. The human Spirit always recognizes that this unfolding is taking place within the context of the Law of Rebirth, which we call Reincarnation, and through the Law of Cause and Effect, which is also referred to as the Law of Karma.

3. *The Fact of a Living, instead of a Dead Christ,* who dwells among mankind, has merit, and that the words: "*Lo I am with you always even unto the end of the world*", is a factual statement.

   And, that human beings with flesh and blood have achieved Christ consciousness and live among men, helping to guide humanity on the path of evolution, and carry out the Divine plan of humanity's liberation, is also a fact. In this regard, knowledge of the Spiritual Hierarchy of Masters, who can be contacted and who can explain the Plan to them, will be better known and understood.[25]

5. ***Education***— esoterically defined, is the intelligent training of an individual equipping him with the information necessary to function as a mature, sane, good citizen and a wise parent, able to intelligently connect with his environment. The Hierarchy does not recognize rich or poor, high or low, only that all men are brothers and that education, and more education is the primary solution to the problems facing humanity. Education will evolve along psychological lines, and since each individual has certain talents, he should be taught how to use them.

Educators should emphasize the following:

1. Development of mental control of the emotional nature.

2. Build the vision and the capacity to see beyond what is, and to see what might be.

3. Creating factual knowledge upon which it will be possible to superimpose the wisdom of the future.

4. Build capacity wisely to handle relationships and to recognize and assume responsibility.

5. Create the ability to use the mind in a ***commonsense*** way to analyze and synthesize information conveyed by the five senses, and to also use the mind as a searchlight to penetrate the world of ideas and abstract truth.[26]

Education should be concerned with the whole life, as well as, the details of daily individual life. Man should be trained to develop his reasoning powers, and to reason from cause to effect; knowledge comes from the ability to grasp and understand ideas implemented by curiosity and investigation.

There are six stages of mental development: *instinct, intellect, intuition, illumination, inspiration and identification.* Educators of the future will approach the development of the minds of the students from the angles of the first three — instinct, intellect, intuition—, these will become the keynotes of elementary, secondary and college or university education, respectively. Eventually, education will be given in the form of human interest, human achievement and human possibility, and will present the premise of the soul as the factor which produces all things beautiful, true and good.[27]

The aim of education, in general, has been to equip the child to compete with his fellow citizens in making a living, in the acquisition of material possessions, and in making a comfortable, successful living— a living characterized by separateness and nationalism, which communicates that he, his group, and his nation are superior to other people.[28] We now have a unique opportunity to re-direct the future by how well we educate our children and young people. They are the parents of future generations, the scientists, the engineers and the change agents who will produce the new civilization. They are the hope of the future.

6. *International Unity* — the kingdom above is in the process of being established below; one in which, politically speaking, Humanity, is far greater than any one nation. This new government will be the New World Order, built upon very different principles than those of the past. It will be one in which the spiritual visions will be carried into national governments, into economic planning, and into all areas of national life. The factors which have contributed to world unrest, poverty and insecurity are:

1. Leadership in the hands of the so-called powerful, reactionary, and conservative groups who have too much power, but no wisdom or vision.

2. Fanaticism among all political ideologies — democracy, fascism and communism.

3. The fact that the masses of humanity across the globe are only now beginning to learn the truth, which has been hidden from them for far too long.

The advent of the television, the internet, and other means of communication are lifting the veil of secrecy in government and empowering the people. Though there is no major war, there is also no peace, no real security nor economic freedom, and not too much progressive religious thinking.

It is difficult to think about international unity without having the United Nations come to mind. This organization was created under the direction of the Hierarchy of Masters to establish a major step in the Divine Plan for the Oneness of Humanity, and toward the creation of world peace. One of the primary objectives of the UN after World War II was to protect Germany from the threat of retribution, and to help that country attain the great destiny for which it came into manifestation.

Germany becomes a very important symbol because of its position in the family of Mankind; it is this seed group we called the Fifth Root Race, the Aryan Race, together with the Jewish seed group, who are among the first to help *root* the new developments of this Fifth Root Race into the consciousness of humanity.[29] This information is, therefore, relevant to understanding the establishment of world unity. Separateness is the underlying, destructive factor influencing the German people and Humanity. The main psychological problem of the German people is their inability to relate to all other people on equal terms, and the fact that they are easily conditioned and influenced negatively. Because the Fifth Root Race consists of all races and all groups throughout the planet, by extension, we are therefore talking about all Humanity. Until we are able to recognize that we are one people, and of one root, we delay our peace and liberation.

Like the Germans, the Jewish people and all humanity must begin to take responsibility for the role they play in the state of our world. Humanity must face the realities of life as they are, and become awakened to the understanding that it is their right to enjoy the bounties of life currently enjoyed by very few.

It is the mental acquiescence of humanity to the privileged few that has kept the masses in bondage. The masses have attributed far more greatness to leaders who are not deserving of that recognition and trust. When the masses are able to *see* that the personalities and characters of the few are not consistent with divine laws, the masses will begin to think for themselves, and consequently forge an agenda more akin to the needs of the disenfranchised. Nothing but a clear comprehension of the situation, as well as, the sources of the challenges will provide the impulse needed to take the required action. However, we are now seeing men and women at every level of society beginning to grasp the vision of the underlying issues, the remedies, and the steps that must be taken.

The economic problems can be solved by the realization that the oil, mineral, wheat, sugar, and grain resources of the world belong to everyone, not to any individual nation, who is only a steward, holding these resources in trust for its fellowmen. When the principle of sharing is substituted for grab and greed, the problems of humanity will be solved worldwide and in a very short time. Additionally, when nations become conscious of the fact that good and evil are two aspects of one reality, and that evil cannot be destroyed, but must be integrated, then military resources can be redirected to provide greater economic and educational resources for Humanity's freedom from want, and for the establishment of better human relations at home and abroad. Gross ignorance fueled by the erroneous, outdated dogmas and materialism of the churches have perpetuated the dismal condition of mankind.

The following steps by the United Nations, with robust support from each nation, have the potential to bring about the peace, alleviation from want, and adequate education that is now necessary:

1. The member nations of the United Nations must have a clear understanding and vision of what is needed, and its Assembly and Committees must be supported.

2. The citizens in every nation must be educated in right human relations, with the children and youth of the world being taught the true relationship of every race and culture to each other.

3. Adults and the youth alike must be taught that a new civilization is being built and that the patience necessary for the success of such an enormous feat must be exercised.

4. An intelligent and cooperative public opinion must be developed to communicate the spiritual impact of this effort.

5. A world economic council must be established to set the resources of the earth free for the use of humanity. However, this council must be independent of any connection to fraudulent politics, capitalistic influence, and devious scheming. Enlightened public opinion should make the decisions for the economic council; the aim being to replace greed and competition with cooperation and sharing.

6. When the above measures are implemented, greater freedom to travel within each country and across boundaries to every other country, to interact, to know and to appreciate the brothers and sisters who make up the family of Man in every land will be possible.

7. The future of humanity depends on the millions of men and women of goodwill in every land, including statesmen, professionals, scientists, educators, nurses, doctors, farmers, engineers and people of every group who have evolved in consciousness to understand their true relationship and obligation to each other. Once they are organized and mobilized, they represent a large sector of the thinking public and their work can be revolutionary.[30]

The momentum toward this new and unified world is now gathering. The nucleus and blueprint for this work already exists, and the technology provided by the new age makes it more possible than ever before for the execution of this urgently needed Plan.

CHAPTER FOUR

Jerusalem —Peace and Victory Defined

The New Jerusalem is the archetype of the perfect civilization. Most know of Jerusalem as a city in the Middle East, and have read or heard of its historic, political and religious significance. The city of Jerusalem, however, has a profound symbolic spiritual importance and significance to Humanity.

Ageless Wisdom defines Jerusalem as the ***Abode of Peace;*** the final destination of everyone who is consciously or un-consciously on the journey to this Holy Land in his quest for peace and longing to be free from strife. For many Christians, Jerusalem represents the place where a triumphant, returning Christ in His second coming from the clouds of heaven will come to reign for a thousand years. However, Ageless Wisdom agrees with this concept only in part, since the method and location of this return is incorrect as Jerusalem is not just a physical place in Palestine, but symbolizes a peaceful world created by the self-initiated efforts of Humanity itself. These efforts must result in a general quietude, the achievement of right human relations, and the attainment of a higher human consciousness.[1]

That the Christ will return as an omnipotent and triumphant warrior to lead his people has no basis in fact. A more accurate scenario is that the regenerated body of Humanity, which has achieved Christ consciousness, is now setting its face toward Jerusalem, ***The Abode of Peace***; one based on a secure foundation of divine laws and the principles of initiation. The twenty-first chapter of the Book of Revelation (KJV) speaks, in detail, about the New Jerusalem. The specifications for its foundation and structure are clearly given. We can also infer that this New Jerusalem implies the replacement of the Old Jerusalem. Those who are acquainted with the ancient mystery teachings, especially as it relates to the building to Solomon's Temple of which the New Jerusalem is a reference, know that the temple was destroyed twice and that the final temple is not a physical one, but is one *not made with hands, which are eternal in the heavens.*

St. John in his vision from the Isle of Patmos saw this Holy City descending out of Heaven with the glory of God, and the dimensions of the symbolic New Jerusalem described in very vivid details. She, as the city is described, is a fountain from which living waters will forever flow and whose light is like a most precious stone as that of jasper and is as clear as crystal. She has a great high wall with twelve gates, with twelve angels at each gate, and atop each of these gates is the name of each of the twelve tribes of Israel. This city also has twelve foundations on which are the names of the twelve apostles of the Lamb. These twelve names are none other than the twelve lines of the cube with the Eye of God in the center, and also the twelve signs of the zodiac with its corresponding tribes.

It further states that three gates lie in the east, three in the north, three in the south and three in the west. These allude to the cardinal, mutual and fixed triplicities of the twelve signs of the zodiac assigned to the four elements of fire, water, air and earth.

The city is laid out as a square with its length, width, and height being of the same measure. The wall of the city is 144 cubits, which is given as the measure of a Man, which is also that of an angel. The sum is the number nine (9), which is that of the Illuminated Man and symbolizes a Master Mason. This same Master Mason is the Christ, who also represents Hiram Abiff of the Masonic Legend. The twelve foundations of the city are adorned with the following twelve precious stones:—Jasper, Sapphire, Chalcedony, Emerald, Sardonyx, Sardius, Chrysolite, Beryl, Topaz, Chrysoprase, Jacinth and Amethyst. Each of the twelve gates is made of pearl, and the streets of the city made of pure gold and have the appearance of transparent glass. The pearl is a symbol associated with Venus and with the Divine Mother, and also with the metal gold, which is associated with the Sun—, the heart center in the body.

The twelve signs of the zodiac, the twelve tribes, and the twelve processes and stages of regeneration involved in the transformation of Old Jerusalem are the processes which change Jerusalem from the city of war to one of peace. The name, Jerusalem, has been assigned to the zodiacal sign of Pisces, a sign under which the emphasis on materialism and war, symbolic of Old Jerusalem, now prepares it to carry the mantle of peace in this the New Age of Aquarius. Pisces is also the sign under which the human body of Man is transmuted into full consciousness. The trunk of the body is said to be an oblong square and is the material upon which the alchemical work is performed.

The Masonic Craft suggests that the oblong square when divided equally produces two perfect cubes, which symbolize — one above (etheric), and the other below, the physical body. The alchemical work in which these forces of the zodiac are involved are the same forces involved in the making of alchemical gold, in which the dross of ignorance and fear are transmuted into knowledge and light, and the metal lead is transmuted into gold. An old axiom states: *"To make gold, one has to have gold."* This gold is the divine light; the divine spark present in every man.

The Twelve Signs of the Zodiac and the Stages of the Great Work

1. *Aries*, the cardinal and the initiating sign of the twelve gates, is where the two electric fiery bodies of Mars and the Sun are dominant and the work of Calcination takes place. It is assigned to the tribe of Gad. This is the first stage in the building of the temple where the currents of energy, which originate in the Mars center below the navel and the Sun center above and behind the heart, are activated. These two centers in the body — the Mars and the Sun centers assigned to the reproductive and heart centers, respectively, are key to producing this gold.

   The process of Calcination drives out of the consciousness in the body or matter, the volatile and changeable elements of emotion, personal bias, and erroneous opinion.

North-East is the place of the Earth, in the Masonic Temple and in the New Jerusalem where the candidate at this initial stage is placed. He receives his white lambskin apron, which is placed over the reproductive and Scorpio center of the body ruled by Mars. Lambskin, the material of which the apron is made, alludes to the sign of Aries. The color white refers to the purification of his consciousness, which he achieves through the process of Calcination; what is produced is the Stone of the Wise or Philosopher's Stone.

The placement of the apron is a reference to the need not to prevent daubing with "un-tempered mortar", meaning anything unsavory; vane; false; viscous or slimy. Seeing falsehood is seeing something that is not there, and is a kind of false vision.

Through the process of Calcination, the creation of a new generation is formed by virtue of the modification of the products of the gonads. The alchemical changes brought about in the blood, which is pumped by the heart through the body, always under the influence of the regenerated mind, and symbolized by Hermes, the Master Mason produces the ***Perfected Stone***. [2]

2. The second stage to which the next gate is assigned, is ***Taurus***, the zodiacal sign of the "Bull of Form". It is attributed to the cool, dry element of Earth and is assigned to the tribe of Ephraim, to the direction Southeast of the City of Jerusalem.

    Congelation is the regenerative process related to this stage of becoming the perfected stone. It is the act of changing from a fluid to a solid state through cooling or coagulation. The planets of Venus and the Moon are dominant at this stage. Venus, the planetary ruler of Taurus, is associated with the throat center, and with the pituitary body or Moon center in the body, assigned to the High Priestess. They make up the predominant forces at work in this second stage of Congelation. It is interesting to note that Venus, the dominant ruler of this second stage, is the complement of the Mars force of the first stage; the Moon, of this stage, is also the complement of the Sun in exaltation in the

Calcination process. The work of Calcination is primarily one of breaking down form through an analytic process, while the work of Congelation is that of building up form through a synthetic process.

An active principle of Congelation is creative imagination. To congeal, alchemically, is to work out patterns for the expression of the Life Power. However, these patterns must not be fixed, crystallized, or become solid like glass, on the contrary, they need to be like wax. The work of the inner teacher is active here. The process allows for the individual to know the reason or cause of the past, present, and future, and to understand that all these divisions are what the intellect uses to convey the eternal NOW. The process through which the individual makes union with the universal knower is what is called Alchemical Congelation. The flow of the mental substance of the sub-consciousness, as the Uniting Intelligence, connects the reasoning mind of the person who has made himself worthy; this is achieved by living a good and noble life characterized by a love of truth. This individual is also made worthy by a knowledge and virtue of one deserving of the gracious gift of uniting with the Universal Knower.

The Moon, which is related to memory, allows the aspirant to remember all that he has seen and experienced in our world as part of the One Life. Together with Venus, ruler of the throat center, which produces an alchemical change in the chemistry of the blood of the aspirant, he experiences a change in the emotional nature of the body. This change in the body allows the aspirant to change his attitude to everything and everyone in all kingdoms. He now understands that all things are part of the One Life. This gradual change in the aspirant's attitude is a result of the revelation of the Inner Voice or Universal Knower who reveals to the aspirant the essential spiritual quality of all things. This knowledge releases him from both attachment and repulsion. His filthy imaginations are now transformed into the pure gold of Truth.[3]

3. **Fixation** is the work associated with the third gate of the City. To the line East-Above of the cubic city is assigned the sign of **Gemini**, whose sole ruler is Mercury and which is related to the tribe of Simone. Fixation is the establishment in the aspirant's mind of a firm and immovable awareness of the true relations and functions of the three principles: Mercury, Sulphur, and Salt; they which are attributed to super-consciousness, self-consciousness and sub-consciousness, respectively. Fixation, which is the stability of perfect equilibrium, is the process whereby the relationship and perfect balance of these three principles become one in which none of the three has greater power than either of the others, and it is for this reason that the sign of Gemini, under which fixation occurs, has only one planetary ruler. This is all the work of the human self-consciousness as represented by Mercury. Self-consciousness is a symbol of the Masculine; the Alchemical Man; the Principle of Sulphur; the Mind, and the Sun.

Sub-consciousness is a symbol of the Feminine; the Alchemical Woman; the Moon; memory, and the Principle of Salt. Mercury is the element of Air, the symbol of the ONE SELF of which all three are aspects of the One Whole. It is the man (mind), says Ageless Wisdom, that must emancipate the woman (memory) by remembering that all Three Are One, and that none is greater than the other. Fixation is the symbol of the whole work, where the Great Work is accomplished by the Sun and the Moon with the aid of Concentration, represented by Mercury.[4]

4. The fourth gate is represented by the sign of **Cancer**, which is assigned to the tribe of Zebulon and to the process of **Separation** whose direction is the line East-Below in the cubical city. The two predominant planetary influences at this stage are that of the Moon, the natural ruler, and Jupiter, the planet in exaltation. Separation is related to occult speech; the formulation of a new language, a generally pictorial language, in the field of sub-consciousness, and is symbolized by the Moon. Separation is also involved in the establishment and formulation of the objective

of the special work in which the alchemist is directed. In every language, every word has its own specific vibration and geometric form.

The inner language is the true native tongue of every human being and it is only in this language that the spoken word has miraculous power. Regardless of one's language, when one has knowledge of this occult language, his style, diction, choice of phrases and synonyms will be life giving, vibrant and permeated with hidden power.

Sub-consciousness contains the record of this occult and magical language, and a record of it is written in the subtle, etheric center in the abdominal brain or solar plexus; that part of the human organism called the Jupiter Center.

This is where the entire history of the development of organic life and the story of the cycles of the Life-power's manifestation are written. The ability to read the information contained here is what supplies the clues, which lead to a true understanding of the total creative order.

Separation, therefore, is the making of new definitions and the recovery of the magical language. This comes about as the process distills and eliminates the sediment of error through bodily and mental stillness.

No one who deceives him/herself and others by the intentional or unintentional misuse of speech can accomplish the Great Work.

Our words are powerful and can be the cause of life or death. This explains why this stage, symbolized by the Chariot, is known as the House of Influence and is related to the stomach, the breast, and to nutrition. When perfected, this cubic personality vehicle becomes *A Pillar in the House of God* that will never be forever, and, is the means by which true Victory is achieved.[5]

5. The fifth gate of the City is symbolized by the sign of *Leo*, with the Sun as ruler and the planet Neptune in exaltation. To

this gate is assigned the tribe of Judah, as well as the work of Digestion, and the sense of taste. Digestion is a chemical process during which a substance is exposed to a liquid, and with the aid of heat, the soluble constituents are extracted, thus making fire and water essential to the process. This water is called cosmic, mental energy because it flows in streams, has currents, has tides, vibrates like waves, and is a reflector. Alchemical fire is that which takes form as solar radiance and heat, and is the electric vital force that breaks down and consumes the forms through which it manifests. This stage of activity is involved in the raising of the serpent power.

What results from the transformation of this reproductive force is a perfect comprehension of reality and the fulfillment of the desires that brought humanity into incarnation. The heart and the spine are the two centers in the body affected by this raised, alchemical fire, which turns passive natures into active ones by squaring the elements of water, fire, air and earth into the circle of Spirit.[6]

6. **Virgo** symbolizes the sixth gate, which is assigned to North-Below, to the tribe of Naphtali, and to the process of Distillation. It gives us an understanding of the workings needed by the inhabitants of the old city to manifest the New Jerusalem on earth. The ancient mystery teachings tell us that nothing can manifest on earth unless it comes through human beings, and so while many look to a benevolent God to come down and rescue humanity, the wisdom teachings do not support any such thinking. Humanity must create the civilization of peace that it hopes for. For this reason, an understanding of the process whereby this is achieved becomes mandatory. If not properly understood, man delays his liberation and Jerusalem continues to be a very distant destination to reach.

The process of Distillation is one which separates the volatile from less volatile compounds. It can be interpreted metaphysically as the release of the soul from the limitations of the body. This process of Distillation is what naturally takes place in the Virgo region, the small intestines of the body, that deal with absorption and assimilation. In the process of the Great Work, it can be considered alchemical distillation.

The inorganic substances in the form of food, water, air and light are transmuted and transformed into what alchemists call potable gold, also referred to as chyle, which contains the solar currents of Prana that is circulated throughout the body via the bloodstream. The more evolved in consciousness an individual is, the more of this potable gold is released into his blood. In this regard, an alchemical adept whose life is consciously under the guidance and rulership of the Higher Mind symbolized by Hermes or Mercury is able to more greatly influence the work of Distillation and the creation of larger amounts of chyle in his body.

These individuals eat, drink and breathe cosmic electricity, thereby charging the blood stream and nerves with radiant energy and living light. The Intelligence of Will is attributed to the sign of Virgo. Under this mode of consciousness, patterns of all bodies are formed; and by this same intelligence and ability to perceive, the Wisdom behind the whole process is discovered. Man, therefore, comes to know that all things in the universe are part of one, dynamic, living organism.[7]

7. The seventh stage of the work in building the City is assigned to the sign of *Libra*, to the tribe of **Asher**, to the process of *Sublimation*, to justice, faithful intelligence and to the line and direction, north-west of the cube. In chemistry, sublimation is defined as the process whereby a solid is converted to vapor by heat and when cooled then becomes a solid again. In psychology, sublimation is used to describe the diversion of undesirable natural trends or impulses through education into some more desirable type of activity or behavior to bring about a type of "exaltation."

Given that everyone on earth is under the Law of Karma or

the Law of Action and Reaction, an understanding of this stage becomes paramount to achieving liberation from the wheel of birth and death achieved through knowledge. There are those who dwell on earth, whose consciousness is limited to physical conditions, whose judgment is based on physical sensation, and whose expectations are based on past experiences. However, in every age, there are those who live in both heaven and earth. They are few in number but that number is increasing greatly. These few know the Faithful Intelligence to be absolute faith in the perfect law, so that even what seems like accidents are really links in a chain of cause and effect. The reality is that the inner life of Man is as much an expression of law as are the changing states in his environment. They know that all activities of one's personality are mathematical consequences of pre-existing causes, and that the controlling center behind every cause and effect is the I AM who is the one law maker.

The purpose of all practical work of occultism is to make the aspirant become aware of his relationship to this I AM. The aspirant can pay his karmic debt in cosmic currency by his work of alchemical sublimation. This is possible because of the operation of Venus, which is ruler of Libra, and Saturn, which is the planet in exaltation. These influences give him access to that treasure of all treasures, **memory**, and enables him to strike the balance without pain.

The sign of Libra rules the kidneys, the organ of elimination. A key aspect of this phase of the work is physical and mental elimination, which involves the excising of fear, doubt, and indecision, and replacing them with courage, confidence and decision.

In general, the individual eliminates whatever is wasteful to his power; this is achieved through the application of limitation and definitiveness, which is characteristic of Saturn. In this whole process of Sublimation, the changes which occur in the bloodstream create matrices of mental images that produce a change in thinking and, consequently, in the external conditions of his life, developing what can be regarded as not so **common sense**.[8]

8. **Scorpio**, a water sign, with its fiery planetary rulers of Mars, Pluto, and Uranus in exaltation, is the eighth gate of the city assigned to the tribe of **Dan**, to the line and direction of South-West, and to the process of **Putrefaction**.

Putrefaction is the decomposition and disintegration of a body into its elementary parts. It is the process that a seed undergoes in moist heat so it is able to multiply, and like all true alchemical work, it takes place inside the body and not in some external laboratory.

The action of the Mars force in this process breaks down, at the root level, the erroneous idea of a personal identity in the minds of most of humanity. Through alchemical putrefaction, the Mars force is re-directed to totally disintegrate the prior structures of false opinions, which involves a complete repudiation of one's ignorant interpretation of his selfhood. This work is said to produce black powder because the process brings the individual to the place that allows him to understand that no activity has its origin in his personality, but that all thoughts, action, and words are but expressions of the ONE LIFE. This awareness appears to the individual's intellect as utter darkness or no-thingness, also called radiant darkness. The individual must emerge out of this apparent darkness into the whiteness of knowledge. And when this light manifests it does so at the cellular level. This black powder is none other than gold and, this is true both physically and metaphysically, since the material worked upon by the alchemist is his own flesh and blood, as well as his etheric and astral counterparts.

Spiritual alchemy produces a regenerated heart and mind, which is golden and is a symbol of truth. It is Saturn, the ruler of the skeleton of Man, symbol of the grim reaper, with its center at the base of the spine, where the coiled up kundalini energy is located that stirs the Mars force into action.

Saturn precipitates self-denial and a loss of the old life, giving way to a new and regenerated life brought about by the mind's power to generate new images that deny the old conception of the self and the false interpretation of life which are essential to the unearthing of the true interpretation. What the individual loses is not only counterfeit and worthless, but is also the cause of all his miseries.[9]

9. The sign of **Sagittarius** represents the ninth gate, the line and direction, West-Above, and the tribe of **Benjamin**. Its process is Incineration in which the sole planetary ruler is Jupiter. Incineration is the residue which remains in sub-consciousness after the process of Putrefaction has burned to ashes the dross and refuse of the old ways of thinking. It is important to note that this process cannot be accomplished by the alchemist himself, but must be applied by a higher power. Latent tendencies that need to be purged do remain and the self-conscious cannot penetrate the depths of the sub-conscious. The alchemist comes to know that every circumstance of his life is God dealing with his soul through the process in the refiner's fire, where the Intelligence of probation or trial under fire, transmutes him into pure gold. The generative activity in the field, womb, or matrix of sub-consciousness brings about the finest silver and gold. Alchemical Incineration is, therefore, the process in which the secrets of the work of nature, allow the eyes of the alchemist to see firmly, and establishes knowledge in the consciousness of the alchemist.

10. Capricorn, the tenth gate. It is ruled by the planet Saturn with Mars in exaltation and belongs to the tribe of Issachar to which the line and direction is West-Below. Renewing Intelligence, and the stage of transformation called Fermentation are assigned to this stage.

On the physical level, the process of Fermentation refers to decomposition of a substance produced by living organisms.

The ancients, however, know that Fermentation is analogous to something higher. This process is concerned with: the eye as the organ of sight; to the visible part of an object, and to the surface, as well as the appearance of a thing.

Ageless Wisdom declares that what one **sees** with the natural eye is vastly different from what really is. The sages conclude that the world of appearances is not in itself one of deception, but that the tendency to take things at face value is the cause of delusion. In spite of this, however, the world around us provides intrigue, suspense, wonder, curiosity, excitement, puzzlement, and mystery, which for the normally constituted mind, it is what spurs humanity on toward growth and development. This need for discovery provides the scientist with the incentive to uncover that which is not evident to the average individual. While the unknown strikes terror and fear to the untrained eye and the undisciplined mind in every generation, there are a few persons who are prodded by the need to investigate what would be frightening to others.

It is for this reason that the ancients say, *"what we fear is what instructs us and sets our feet on the path toward liberation"*; and in that same context, they say, *"the Devil is God as He is misunderstood by the wicked"*. The One Life presents itself to Man as he conceives it; the Prince of Darkness is just an ignorant misunderstanding of the working of the power of light. The sacred books of all religions hint at this fact, and it is the responsibility of church leaders to assist their followers to unfold the hidden mysteries behind these realities. At this stage more than any other, the lower elements of personality are akin to the nature of beasts, thus calling into activity the force of Saturn to hinder, limit, and chain these desires.[11]

11. Aquarius is the eleventh gate of the City to which the tribe of **Manasseh**, the line and direction is South-Above are assigned. The stage of the Work called **Dissolution** or **Solution** and the planets Uranus and Saturn are attributed. Mathematically, the term solution is defined as the act of determining the answer to a problem. Chemically, it is the process whereby two or more substances are combined to form a single homogeneous solid or liquid. The ancient mystery teachings declare that all solids are liquefied gases, frozen liquids, and congealed fluids, and that all freezing points are points of crystallization, which vary according to the complexity of the elements involved. Man's dependable realities, which are all he knows, sees, feels, stands upon, builds, and relies upon are what he knows as true, real, and everlasting. They are a function of what Man has come to know as solid, determined by a temperature or point above which keeps ice solid.

Alchemical Congelation is the process, which reduces all solid bodies in man's experience into their elemental "water", or alchemical solution. Meditation, which is representative of this stage of transformation is a cosmic process and describes this reduction process. The process enables one who is proficient in it to change the consciousness of any solid into direct metaphysical awareness of that solid's essential spiritual substance. This spiritual substance is the first matter or alchemical water, which is the essential nature of all things in creation.

In truth, Man does not meditate, but in meditation, he is swept into a stream of cosmic, electric, and magnetic currents of the head and the heart in which the veil of secrecy, concerning the inner nature of anything concentrated upon, is revealed to him by Isis herself. The ability to transform any object is the ability to mold or build a matrix of that object with mental imagery, and to see the true fluidic substances of the forms perceived by his physical senses. This fluidic substance can then be cooled until it becomes an actual physical object in the alchemist's environment. Through this process of Meditation, which is a psychological process, the influence of the pairs of opposites can be overcome, since during meditation one becomes aware that every single thing is not only related to all other things, but that every single thing is composed of the same substance from which all other forms are built.

Meditation opens up the inner sensory centers to reveal the reality of this fact, and the inner natureof all things, by lifting the reservoirs of energy stored in sub-consciousness up to the surface, and into the field of conscious awareness. We can now see why Jesus instructed his disciples to go into Jerusalem where they would see a man carrying a Water Pot, symbol of the Aquarian Age; the age in which the feminine will be lifted up to her rightful position. The water-pot is a meaning and significance of the Divine Feminine and to Isis, symbol of the Age of Aquarius.[12]

12. *Pisces* is the twelfth stage and gate, and is the name given by the ancients to the City of Jerusalem in which the planets ***Jupiter*** and ***Neptune*** are rulers. It is the zodiacal sign to which the tribe ***Reuben***, the line and direction of the cube is South-Below, and the process of ***Multiplication*** are assigned. The Christ Consciousness in the initiate was born in the sign of Capricorn, which fulfilled the Law of Karma under Saturn. Venus then initiates the era of intelligent Brotherhood and assigns the Initiate to the role of World Server in Aquarius and World Savior in Pisces, thus completing the cycle of the zodiac.

Man is thus able to declare triumphantly: ***It Is finished***!

Multiplication is the act of increasing a number or quantity, and is the process whereby the alchemist, who has succeeded in Solution and the other stages of the Great Work, now expands his Elixir. Multiplication can, therefore, be compared to the fire from which all other fires may be kindled. This fire is the Alchemical Fire of the regenerated consciousness achieved by the alchemist. When the cubic stone is made in the pineal gland, as a result of the process of transformation, the whole body with its trillions of cells is tinged with the consciousness this process generates. This stage is related to Corporeal Intelligence because as the cells of the body become filled with light and the knowledge; Oneness becomes a reality in the body, and knowingness is achieved.

It is this same Intelligence which lies behind the formation of all bodies in all kingdoms and in all worlds. Under the Law of Creative Process, this same Intelligence builds a body appropriate to the Life-Power's expression. This happens by drawing from the atmosphere, and from the substance of the given planet, the materials needed to clothe that expression or divine idea. Corporeal Intelligence is assigned to sub-consciousness and to the function of sleep because it is during sleep that Multiplication takes places; a process that includes the building, repair, reproduction, and transformation of all vehicles in all worlds.

The perfected process of Multiplication precipitates change in the whole organism of the alchemist, making it possible for him to interrupt and change the rates of the Life- Power's electromagnetic vibration. His body is thus a perfect vehicle through which the Life-Power can project its ideas for the manifestation of the divine will and purpose for humanity's liberation. However, this ability to project can only be performed by the alchemist who has completed the Great Work and is able to mentally create matrices for the divine expressions. One of the great benefits of the process is the ability to transform the personality vehicle physically, mentally and morally. This helps the recipient to accomplish the stages of the Great Work with greater rapidity. It is in this way, also, that adepts influence the minds of souls to enable them to carry out certain tasks on our planet for the benefit of humanity, without them realizing that they are not the originators of the ideas they possess.13 The Great Work is the work of perfecting the personality vehicle, which is likened in ancient writings to that of a cube, just as is the Holy City, the New Jerusalem.

The transformation of the body, the personality vehicle, is the creation of Man by himself, and is accomplished by the total conquest of his faculties and his future. The aim of this Work must be the emancipation of the alchemist's will in preference to Universal Will. In this regard, the perfected vehicle facilitates the medium of the alchemist through which that Universal Will can be made manifest on Earth. In the Holy City, analogous to the Human Entity, there was no temple, and the light was not supplied by the Sun or Moon. Instead God, and the Lamb were both the Temple and the Light.

The gates of the city are open to the nations of the world, and their honor and glory will be a part of this city. Only those who are clean in their minds and heart are allowed in.

Manly P. Hall, in his book, The Secret Teachings of All Ages, indicates that the temple in Jerusalem is central to the city, and has been the cause of much conflict, which is cause by ignorance. We are told in the Book of Revelation that Man is synonymous to the Temple in Jerusalem, and it is the regeneration of this temple that renders the city fully lighted by the Sun and the Moon.

Solomon is said to be the Personification of Universal Wisdom, and it is the work of transformation and regeneration in Solomon's Temple, which produces the wisdom that lights the City of the New Jerusalem. The three syllables SOL-OM-ON relate to three temples or aspects of the temple and the three candidates of the Masonic Legend of Freemasonry, as well as to the Body, Mind and Spirit of Man. The three syllables also symbolize — light, glory and truth, collectively and respectively. The first aspect SOL means "the House of Everlasting Light", and its early symbol is the stone temple on the brow of Mount Moriah. It is the Grand House of the Universe where the SOL, the Sun, sits in the middle upon the golden throne where its three lights — stellar, solar and lunar — illuminate this Cosmic Temple.

The second, OM, is the Human body called the Little House made in the image of the Great Universal House, and the temple of God in which the Spirit of God dwells.

The third, ON, is the Solar House, an invisible structure which is the comprehensive representation of the Arcanum of Freemasonry. The mystery of this intangible edifice is concealed within the allegory of the Wedding Garment spoken of by St. Paul in the Robes of Glory of the High Priests of Israel; the Yellow Robes of the Buddhist Monks, and the Robes of Blue and Gold of the Royal Arch Degree in Freemasonry.[14]

The dimensions and elements of the New Jerusalem clarify the process and purpose involved in the construction of the New Jerusalem. This City, as the personality vehicle of the Human Being, is unfolded through the twelve stages of the Great Work in which the twelve signs of the zodiac constitute the twelve foundations and the twelve gates which aid in the process of regeneration and transformation. Each of the twelve signs of the zodiac is assigned to one of the twelve tribes of Israel. It is crucial to understand that the term, Israel, relates to Humanity because this city is one in which every member of Humanity is to become a citizen by virtue of being a member of the humanity family. The process whereby one becomes a citizen of this New Jerusalem, and does not remain a member of the Old Jerusalem, is a function of having undertaken the second birth, and its inhabitants are not qualified by physical birth. It is for this reason that the largest number of humanity who will be setting their face toward Jerusalem will be led by those who have experienced the second death that is synonymous with the destruction of the second temple of Solomon. This alludes to the destruction of the physical body and the soul that gives way to the erection of the Temple 'not made with hands eternal in the heavens.'

Manly P. Hall describes the process by saying that the soul is constructed from an invisible, fiery substance, a flaming golden metal, cast by Hiram Abiff, the Master Workman, into the mold of clay, the physical body, also called the Molten Sea. The temple of the human soul, he states, is built by three Master Masons personifying —Wisdom, Love and Service; and when constructed under the Law of Life, the Spirit of God dwells in this Holy Place. The Solar Temple is the true Everlasting House, and the individual who can raise this Solar Temple is indeed an Initiate or Master Mason. Hall further makes an analogy between the New Jerusalem and Atlantis by stating that the City of the Golden Gates, the capital of Atlantis as presented by Plato in the Timaeus, and presented by many religions as the archetype, is analogous to the New Jerusalem.[15]

The process and stages of the construction of the temple in Jerusalem are the same as those which allows the human being to be raised or regenerated and become a God-Man.

True peace cannot be achieved without the evolution of consciousness in which there is resolution and synthesis of the pairs of opposites; and victory is the liberation from ignorance concerning the pairs of opposites.

CHAPTER FIVE

The Role of the Major Nations in the Divine Plan

Every nation came into existence to serve its people, and the world, with its unique contribution. That contribution is being guided by its birth as a nation and the attendant astrological configuration designed for it to carry out its destiny in the Divine Plan. Like the organs of the human body, some countries have major roles and some minor roles, but each plays a part in successfully fulfilling the divine purpose. The history of almost every country is defined by a long past of battles, wars, changing frontiers, annexations of new territory, and the usual subjugation of the original inhabitants — many times beneficial, but through inexcusable methods.

For the most part, history concerns itself with the fiercely determined lines of distinction between countries, which define the culture, civilization and the type of rule each country develops.

The aim in the establishment and preservation of each nation is usually for selfish commercial profit, with international legislation further provided to ensure these nationalistic goals. What is usually not taken into consideration, however, is that these foster separateness. It is forgotten that all humanity is one, and all the resources of the earth belong to everyone.[1]

Almost all nations display the worst aspects of the spirit of nationalism with their sense of sovereignty; their selfish desires and aspirations seek to set one nation against another, which foster a sense of national superiority and a negative pride of race history. This attitude breeds arrogance, boastfulness, and contempt for other nation's civilizations and cultures, which is evil and degenerating. This also incites in its citizens a willingness to sacrifice the interests of others for their own, ignoring the truth that all men are created equal, are equally deserving, and equally entitled. No nation is exempt from this behavior, which is representative of the degree of blindness, cruelty, and lack of proportion that exists, with the result that humanity throughout the world paying a huge price. Nationalism does have a positive aspect when viewed from the regenerated minds of the enlightened. However, this view at present still remains a dream and a hope and not yet an effective and constructive reality in any nation. This new nationalism, while still fostering a sense of individual civilization, sees itself as contributing to the good of the whole. It seeks to improve and perfect its own way of life to benefit the world. Each country, consequently will become a living, spiritual, vital organism, instead of a selfish, material organization.[2]

Every country vibrates to a special note and tone with much to be contributed by each, beyond its commercial and political usefulness. These notes and tones must be brought into unison to expand the magnificent chorus from all the nations of the world. This will become a reality when pure religion and spiritual impetus are given free expression. All countries are closely related based on their history, deeds, and measures they have taken. This fact is most powerfully played out in the United States of America, where its people have come from all the known races. This makes the country international because the people of this great land are international by origin and background, allowing for isolationism to be defeated before it could rear its ugly head.[3] It is for this reason, among others, that the United States of America is referred to by many as the land of the New Jerusalem, in which the twelve tribes of Israel, plus one, exist. There has been a disruption of the old-world forms based on separation, brought about by the strengthening of the spiritual life of the center called Humanity. The appearance of the new world form is emerging, and is characterized by the creative life of the Spiritual Man and the One Spirit that is in every man and every nation.

The tasks of every nation are as follows:

1. To solve its own internal psychological problems. This can only be achieved when each country realizes the need to do so and curbs its national pride to allow for the establishment

of unity and the restoration of the tempo, flow and beauty of the nation.

2. To foster the spirit of oneness within and without each nation. This is accomplished by having its citizens become aware that their country is part of one world, and that they must enrich the world with their contribution. These national and international endeavors should be embarked upon simultaneously.[4]

Without exception, every country has its virtues and vices, determined by where it is in its evolution; by the measure of control of the forces impacting the physical, emotional, and mental bodies of the personality of the nation; the force controlling its soul, and the general focus of the nation. We are now at a point in the evolution of the consciousness of the citizens, which allows them to start seeing where their nation fits into the history of nations. It is interesting to note that every nation can be considered either positive and male, or negative and female. India, France, the United States of America, Russia and Brazil are considered feminine in their psychology, i.e. mystical, intuitive, alluring, beautiful, encapsulating, and containing the nurturing mother aspects, which also nurture ideas and civilization.

The negative aspects of the feminine are characterized by an over-emphasis on the material side of life, fondness of display, color, pageantry, possession of money and its equivalent symbol in form are also given expression. On the positive, masculine side are Great Britain, China, Germany and Italy — they are mental, political, governing, standardizing group consciousness, occult by inclination, aggressive, full of grandeur, interested in law and the placing of emphasis on race and empire. Interestingly, they also think in wider terms and are more inclusive than the feminine aspects of divine manifestation.[5]

There are seven forces of energy presented by Master Dujhl Kuhl and describes the influence these forces have on all organisms, from the one celled-organism to the lion in the jungle, to Man and

God-Man. These seven forces are identified as Rays of Energy and influence every nation in different ways. The Rays are the following and are described as follows:

1. Ray One: The energy of Will, Purpose or Power. It is called in Christian nations as the energy of the Will of God

2. Ray Two: The energy of Love-Wisdom and is called the Love of God

3. Ray Three: The energy of Active Intelligence, called the Mind of God

4. Ray Four: The energy of Harmony through Conflict, which significantly affects the human family

5. Ray Five: Concrete Knowledge or Science, which is very potent at this time.

6. Ray Six: The energy of Devotion or Idealism, which has produced the current ideologies

7. Ray Seven: The energy of Ceremonial Order, producing the new forms of civilization now emerging.[6]

Given the fact that a nation is a living organism, with a time of birth, adolescence, adulthood, maturity and decline, these forces influence the personality, the soul and spirit impacting the whole development of each nation. Each country has both positive and negative aspects and does not interfere with the free wills of the peoples of these nations. However, nations and races respond to them according to the mental and spiritual development of both. These seven forces are constantly affecting humanity and producing changes as they express through successive civilizations and cultures, thereby, conditioning and fashioning races and nations.

It might not be a well-known fact but humanity is not a free agent; his ideas come from a higher source and are imposed upon the racial mind, whether mankind wants them or not. However, when those ideas become ideals, Humanity then has the option to accept or reject them. How these ideas are used depends on the level of the mental and emotional development of humanity, who is now becoming more sensitive to the divine outflows designed to influence the evolution of the divine plan for planetary development.

Consequently, there are **five major ideas** influencing the world today:

1. The inherited and ancient ideas which have controlled the human race for centuries, which are primarily concerned with aggression for the sake of possession, and the domination of a group or church representing the State. This is expressed as selfish ambition and a violently imposed authority.

2. The idea that human beings can be easily sacrificed at any time for the good of the State or for the so-called general good.

3. The idea of democracy in which the people govern, and the government represents the will of the people.

4. The idea of a world state, divided into various great sections. This is the direction in which all humanity is headed, and is the dream of all inclusively-minded persons, though they are in the minority in-spite of the many antagonistic temporary ideologies which have emerged over time, this also includes democracy.

5. The idea of a Spiritual Hierarchy, which will govern the people throughout the world and embody in itself all the elements of the monarchial, democratic, totalitarian and communistic regimes. Latent in all these ideologies is much wisdom, beauty and strength with valuable contributions to make to humanity. We will see the best of these expressed under the control of the Hierarchy of the Lords of Compassion and Masters of Wisdom who have the knowledge and are directing and guiding Humanity.[7]

These five ideas are determining the trend of world affairs today and nothing can stop or impede their effect, irrespective of how much they are dismissed by those who do not agree with them. These ideas work through the five rays currently influencing humanity, namely, the first, second, third, sixth and seventh. We have now entered the Aquarian Age in which the Seventh Ray of Ceremonial Order and Alchemy will dominate, and we are at the turning point when the Sixth Ray energy of Devotion and Idealism is passing out of external expression. This cosmic event is largely responsible for the crisis playing out in religion. Of course, it is affecting all nations, and only a correct understanding of the causal level from which this emanates will ever bring about sustainable change. This Sixth Ray of Idealism and Devotion was the overarching and predominant influence not only for the last 2,160 years of the Age of Pisces now ending, but also the Grand Cosmic Piscean Cycle of 25, 920 years.

This explains why the turmoil we are experiencing is so turbulent and disturbing, especially coupled with the fact that leaders really have no accurate references for the way forward. The reason for this is that we are in a new paradigm where only an understanding of the divine plan for humanity and the planet can offer any adequate direction for the future.

The old ways are gone and no amount of reference to the past is going to substantially help. Only an understanding of the Piscean Age we have just left and the Aquarian Age we have now entered can help and/or provide a road map for the journey that lies ahead

These are the characteristics of the Age of Pisces:

1. One-pointed determination, and from only one perspective, with blind procedure; one in which the individual, group or humanity as a whole sees only one aspect of reality at any one time. Due to humanity's place in his evolution, he usually sees the least desirable aspect.

   The vision for which humanity lived and died was the material world, material comfort, material possessions, and material enterprises. Indisputable evidence of this exists both in the United Nations and the labor movement, and unfortunately, territorial possessions and material well-being have motivated all nations.[8]

2. Pisces highlighted the growing ideological tendencies and the unfoldment of mankind's mental principles during this Aryan Age, which forced desire in the form of great mass concepts.

3. Through the steadily growing influence of the soul, working out on the astral plane like leaven, the energy of Pisces has lifted desire out of its purely self-centered focus into a new unexpressed group of emotional consciousness. This fused the emotional nature of man into great ideological mass expression, which is the beginning of the understanding of the Brotherhood of Man.

4. It facilitated direct contact between the energy from Shamballah and Humanity for the first time. This produced an emotional vortex in which old ideals and institutions are seen more clearly thus permitting new and better ideologies to emerge in the consciousness of the race of Man. These factors are responsible for the emergence of the groups of thinkers and workers who are dedicated to the changing of the old order and the ending of separateness. Additionally, new technologies such as the radio, the airplane, the internet, and the telephone have all had a significant impact.

5. The development of a tendency on the mental nature toward the crystallization of thought, a reaction to imprisoning ideologies, and a fanatical mental adherence to mass ideals with no understanding of their relationship to the need of the time. Later, however, Pisces brings the Man to a place of spiritual devotion to human welfare and a one-pointed adherence to the Plan of the Spiritual Hierarchy. He will then be anchored in love, which streams from the soul and replaces the emotional reaction to the Hierarchy of Masters. However, with the dying out of this Piscean Age has come

the intensified fanaticism and emotional response we are now seeing.

6. The result of this long cycle of Pisces, also called the Sixth Ray Energy, is the impact it has on the Aquarian energy, which will potently transform the "watery realm" of the astral plane. The symbols used to describe this astral plane are— water, stormy, fluid, reflecting all impressions, the source of mist and fog — all of which are essential to human living. Fixed in the human consciousness is the realization that "men are fishes immersed in the sea of emotions." Lest we forget, the symbol for the sign of Aquarius is the "water-carrier."

7. This Sixth Ray Energy will bring together the above- named energies in time and space. All the energies of the Ray itself, the Piscean energy, the Aquarian energy, and the energy of the astral plane itself, are all producing a vortex of force, which invokes the mental energy. This controlling factor is plunging humanity into a tumultuous awareness of clashing ideologies, producing the present crises and points of tension that precipitate as a reflected vortex in the conflicts we are seeing worldwide. On the spiritual level, this causes a baptism experience, which is resulting in the largest number of humanity being prepared to take the next Initiation.[9]

No nation can proceed intelligently without an understanding of how these collective forces of the seven rays affect and condition his or her organism to position him to stand in his position. He must also know how the energies of the organism that is the nation he is called to serve are combined to produce the outcome destined under the divine plan for his life, and his country. We have entered a very awesome period in the life of humanity, the solar system, and the universe. We have simultaneously entered both the 25,920-year Grand Cosmic Cycle of Aquarius, and the 2,160 year period of the Age of Aquarius. The Age of Pisces, the maker of bodies, prepared the bodies of the planet, and of humanity, by evolving them to the point where they can now use the incoming energies from the place where the Will of God is known.

Mankind is, therefore, now poised to take this plan beyond any place it had every attained. I indicated above that not only is water an important symbol of the age we just left, but, also, it is now to be understood in an elevated manner, in this Age of Aquarius. Water is the substance of life, and is at the same time the foundation upon which all civilizations are built because it is a **liquid mineral** and functions, therefore, as both a liquid and a solid. To have an understanding of what is expected, we must look at the Aquarian characteristics, bearing in mind that the fundamental purpose of life on planet Earth is for Man to reconcile the pairs of opposites in his consciousness. The most significant of these is Spirit and Matter, and it is to this end, that the forces of this Age of Aquarius are dedicated.

Their characteristics of the Aquarian Age are:

1. The medium of relationship which brings together the fundamental aspects of Spirit and Matter, relating the soul to the personality, and initiating the individual to an understanding of the dual aspects of his own nature.

2. Its major aspect is to bring together the negative and positive aspects of all natural processes, and, therefore, governs the sex relationship of all forms, which is the underlying potency of all marriage relations. As this energy continues to unfold, we have the appearance of fundamental issues of sex problems, as it relates to — licenses, disturbances in marriage relations, and divorces, setting in motion a new attitude toward sex, and establishing those practices and moral perceptions which will govern the relationship between the sexes as dictated by the New Age.

3. The emergence of a cycle of an entirely new creative art, which expresses the Real versus the Unreal, which was so characteristic of the Piscean Age, resulting in ugliness and materialism being replaced by beauty and reality. On a large

scale, mankind is now being **led out of darkness into light**. This energy of Aquarius will create order out of chaos, and rhythm instead of disorder to construct the new world order for which humanity has long waited.

4. It will bring about the birth of Christ-consciousness among the masses of an intelligently aspiring humanity, who will set in motion new evolutionary processes that will transform humanity.

5. It will bring into being, on the mental plane, a widespread and recognized relationship between the soul and the mind.[10]

6. It will bring the emergence of Masonry, properly understood and integrated, into the public consciousness as the religion of this New Age. This new religion will rest upon a new and enlightened interpretation of Christianity, having no relation to theology and being universal in nature. At the same time its Jewish foundation will disappear.[11]

The nations of the world are the cups into which this new energy must flow, and to be receptive, they must empty themselves of the outmoded, outworn, erroneous ideas to which they still hold on. As stated before, these nations were created to carry out their unique destinies. They were not created to serve themselves in isolation of other nations. At this point, let us therefore briefly consider the major nations of the world — the United Kingdom, Germany, France, The United States and Russia.

1. **Great Britain**— astrologically, and on the inner or soul level of the nation, London, the capital and heart center of the country, is ruled by the sign of the Twins, Gemini. Gemini is also called the sign of **the forces in conflict** or the sign of the **quarrelling brothers**, and represents that aspect of the mind which expresses itself in intelligent government, based on just and loving understanding, and an ideal, it has not yet fully achieved.

The goal of this country is to live out its soul's purpose, which is to operate on the Love-Wisdom aspect, and which it is now beginning to do. Great Britain is the custodian of the Wisdom aspect of the Second Ray of Love-Wisdom energy of the Aryan Race. Through its vast experience with the British Empire and Commonwealth of nations, and having broken from war and its power politics to bring about harmony, its destiny is to fuse and blend men and races throughout the entire world.

Through the following centers of: London, Sydney, Johannesburg, Toronto, Vancouver, with subsidiary roles in Calcutta, Delhi, Singapore, Jamaica and Madras, the UK in conjunction with the United States and Russia, Great Britain is responsible for striking the keynote for humanity. It will be able to accomplish this, not due to their material resources or military might, but because they are fundamentally for the people and not selfish in their intent. They are visionaries, and have the capacity to fuse and blend many types.[12] Interestingly, Gemini is also the ruler of the United States of America, which is said to be the younger brother of the Twin, with Great Britain being the older brother.

This Gemini influence has led to the restlessness of the British people who cross and re-cross the oceans of the world to stage a constant going out, to the very ends of the earth, always to return to the center from which they came. The distrustful nature of Gemini has not escaped Great Britain due to the secret, subtle and devious diplomacy which has characterized its political activities. However, Great Britain is an ancient and experienced land and is quickly learning the lessons which it must master. Taurus, the personality or external ruler of Great Britain, is the First Ray of Will and Power, and has for ages influenced its imperialistic, material aims and its war-like conquests.[13]

Great Britain carries the sense of caste and class distinction into all its international relations. However, through the synthesizing aspect of this same energy of Will and Power operating through the Law of Synthesis, the city of London, center of this powerful empire, will play a crucial role in establishing a world order of intelligent justice and fair economic distribution. To Great Britain was given the responsibility of establishing the rule of law and fair play, and now that it is slowly gaining the confidence of the world, it is eager to ensure the good of the whole and is prepared to make the necessary sacrifices because its intentions are just and its will is focused on cooperation.[14]

2. **Germany,** astrologically, Aries, is one of the signs that influences this country, and its personality expresses on the First Ray of Will and Power. The German race is a very old one. It is the cup into which all the peoples of the world are poured, and out of which the transmuting power of the Law of Synthesis must work to bring about the Fourth Ray energies of Harmony through Conflict, which is the full realization of the soul destiny of this great land. However, her materialistic personality, with its focus manifesting through its emotional nature and not yet under the control of the soul, was greatly influenced by its need to seek power without the experience and wisdom of the soul. As a nation, Germany was too young, immature, lacking in wisdom, and filled with a sense of inferiority. This led it to use the ideal of power, which is a great spiritual responsibility, to try to synchronize the German race with the German nation.

It was this inexperience and childish ambition that set in motion the Principle of Conflict, and which operated violently to bring to an end the increasing nationalism in Germany and all the nations of the world. The peoples of this nation embody the strains of all the peoples of the world. In the past, its leaders have confused racial issues with national ambitions and the misuse of the forces from the First Ray of Will and Power, which emanate from the Cosmic Center through the Black Lodge. This in turn, produced the four veils of illusion, which began to condition the mental plane and made the distinction between truth and falsehood, good and evil, the left-hand path and the path of initiation blurred, except to those advanced souls and the Hierarchy of Masters.[15] The process of pain of the German people together with the point of tension brought about by the world wars, and through re-education and training in right human relations, the German people are now discovering their soul, and eventually, the soul-infused personality of this people will demonstrate to the world, in a unique way, the significance of Harmony.[16]

Germany will only recover if it does not allow itself to become a battleground, due to its strategic position in central Europe. The Life-Power brought five life waves into manifestation and the Indo-Germanic peoples were the first to help root the Fifth Life Wave into the consciousness of Humanity, and so, the full story of these people addresses Humanity's problems and opportunities. A full accounting can be researched in the manifesto of the Fama Fraternitatis, which recounts the story of the lad of German nobility who made his way across the desert from the West to the East, to Jerusalem, The Abode of Peace.[17] Because of the astral nature of the German people, they are very mediumistic, and consequently, very easily influenced and conditioned because of their negative thinking. Germany shares many qualities with Great Britain, and a close analysis will reveal certain racial lines of understanding between them which explains why Great Britain has been such a great help to that nation in establishing world peace. As the German people give up the notion of being a super-race, relinquish their futile efforts to preserve racial purity, and begin to realize their relationship to all people as equal members of the human family, the greatness of Germany will rise again. This is the nation that produced the great philosophers of Goethe and Schiller of the Middle Ages, and which gave the world some of the best music ever.[18]

3. **France** is astrologically constituted by a Piscean, the World Savior, has a Third Ray personality of Active Intelligence, which influences the development of the intellectual faculty and creative work. It is a force that will be dominant during this Age of Aquarius and will be characterized by the active,

speedy development in the intelligence of the race of man, and a grounding of the Christ principle in humanity. France's symbol, the fleur-de-lys, stands for the three divine aspects in manifestation. We will also see on the soul level, that the forces of Leo and the Fifth Ray of Science and Understanding influence it.

The soul of France ruled the most important and influential part of the Piscean Age, and with its Leo personality, colored the happenings in Europe for centuries during the Middle Ages. France mediated the Piscean qualities to the civilization of the then known world, and her Leo personality of self-confidence, self-centeredness, intelligence, and brilliant individualism, conditioned Europe. This self-centeredness, however, prevented France from expressing the Aquarian tendency toward universal consciousness or advancing the Piscean goal of saving the world. The lesson that France must learn today is that the goal of her Piscean soul is in the salvation of others and not just herself. Because Concrete Knowledge and Science condition the soul of France, it is reflected in the intellectual brilliance and scientific bias of its people.

The forces which condition the personality and soul of its capital, Paris, are Capricorn and Virgo, respectively. Here we see the interplay of the goal of initiation and the nurturing of the Christ consciousness. In these combinations of forces lie the hope of France, who is destined to bring a great soul or psychological revelation to world thought. When France finds both her spiritual soul and intellectual soul, she will prove to be the medium through which the revelation of the nature of the human soul will be known.[19] France staged the French Revolution, which resulted in the release of humanity from bondage, which can be attributed to its world savior characteristics. This is the similar effect realized with the signing of the Magna Charta. Thus, the recognition of the rights of humanity came to the world via France. This was indeed a high point in the evolution of the nation. Great Britain and France now have the opportunity to inaugurate an age of cooperation, understanding, and of a mutually shared responsibility. The question is if France will work for the peace and security of the whole in love and wisdom or selfishly in intellectual brilliance for herself alone.[20]

4. **The United States of America** astrologically is influenced by the Sixth Ray Gemini personality of Idealism and Devotion, and the Second Ray Aquarian Soul of Love-Wisdom. It is said that the United States is the younger twin to Great Britain and that together they share the attributes of Love and Wisdom, with Great Britain being the custodian of Wisdom, and, Love, the United States of America. Its capital, Washington D.C., is ruled by the signs of Cancer and Sagittarius. These influences cause it to carry its own house heavily on its back as crabs do, while at the same time potently one-pointed and determined in carrying out any decision it makes, as is typical of the Sagittarian archer.

Because of the impact of the Sixth Ray of Idealism and Devotion, it can become, at times fanatically blind to its ideals to the detriment of long-range vision. The United States is in a constant state of transition, and as it grows and becomes an adult nation, it will shift from a Cancerian influence to living out the full destiny of its Gemini personality and Aquarian soul, with balance. It is then that it will be a most powerful channel for human expression. Under these same astrological influences and the Law of Loving Understanding, Masonry will be re-interpreted and the concept of Brotherhood will be properly understood for the country and the world. A great future lies ahead for this vast nation, not based on its material power, its military power, or its commercial efficiency, but on a deeply spiritual, innate idealism, an enormous humanitarian potentiality, and because its original peoples come from peasants and a large middle-class.

The power of the government and the determination of practical ideologies are steadily passing into the hands of the people and out of the hands of the aristocracy and the so-called ruling class. The roots of the people of the United States are in other countries, with most of its original people coming from Germany, Great Britain, Finland, Italy, and in fact, from every other country. As a country, the United States can be likened to a young adult, still wrestling with many phases of life, considering every idea and experimenting with all relationships.[21]

As is the case with young adults, there is the tendency to feel superior to more mature nations; to feel that they have a saner and higher idealistic outlook, forgetting that the seemingly backward nation's ideals are just as high and their motives just as sound. They forget that, in fact, these other nations have a more mature and experienced approach to world problems. A period of great expansion and discovery awaits humanity, and under the influence of its Aquarian Soul and Gemini personality, the United States of America will fuse and blend with the nations and the peoples of the Americas, Central and Western Europe, and with the western hemisphere. As time goes on, it will become clear why the city of New York is home to the United Nations, and why the Beacon of Light, held by Lady Liberty, stands in her harbor.

5. **Russia** astrologically is ruled by the signs of Leo and Aquarius which rule its personality and soul, respectively, and respond to the Sixth Rays of Idealism and Devotion and the Seventh Ray of Ceremonial Order and Alchemy. Russia is still in its embryonic stage of development and world impact. Its territory covers a large part of Europe and of Asia, and, it is, itself, a synthesis of East and West. With its spiritual motto being: "I link two ways". This great country's task is to link the East with the West, with a leaning, however, more to the East. Russia is, at present, going through a great revolution to prepare it to collaborate with the rest of the world, though she wishes to do so on her own terms. She is gradually lifting her people from a condition of ignorance and poverty to one of knowledge and sufficiency, even though she is viewed with great mistrust by most of the world.

Russia is home to a germinating revelation of great spiritual value, of group significance, and of revelation to the world. Her potential for human service and her ability to impose her will on the world outpaces that of any other nation; this, in itself breeds distrust. As she matures and the energies of Aquarius, that of brotherhood and synthesis, control her soul, she will give to the world the true secret of brotherhood, even though, at present, she is just learning what that is within herself. Russia is destined to fulfill an ancient prophecy, which she will do as a result of the force of the great light precipitated by the fusion of the two spiritual centers of Humanity and the Hierarchy; and as this Light from the East radiates to the West, the whole world, will be flooded with the Sun of Righteousness.[22]

Russia's challenge is to give to other nations in the world an example of wise rule, free expression of individual purpose, and the use of an exclusive and sound education so that she becomes a model to other nations. At the same time, she will preserve her own cultural approach, her own self-chosen form of government, and her own mode of expressing brotherhood. At its core, Russia represents a new world consciousness, and through the fire of experiment and experience, this will gradually become apparent. This can only become a reality when she learns to rule without cruelty, and without infringing the free will of the individual, as she gains full confidence in the ideals she is developing.[23]

Every country makes an energetic contribution to the functioning of our planet, but like the systems of the body, some play major roles and others minor. It should be borne in mind that all the major nations are dealing with the Law of Cleavage, and only under the Law of Understanding will nations come to realize the brotherhood of all humanity and that all nations are held together by one common Oversoul. Every nation has a lot of house cleaning to do, in addition to outer efforts to create a better and more habitable world; a world consciously motivated by the idea of the general good of all, in which higher values as opposed to individual and national gain are emphasized. For this to occur, however, the citizens of each country must be trained in both national and international responsibility and citizenship. Success is already guaranteed by the fact that millions are now planning, and an equal number are talking about its possibility.

It is a historical fact that all ideas originating from the divine in man and nature eventually become ideals, and even though they appear distorted in the beginning, in the end they become the governing principles of the masses.[24]

CHAPTER SIX

Education and Economics— Keys to Freedom

The goal of education is enlightenment. Wishful thinking, the formulation of highly organized plans on paper, and visionary mystical hopes and dreams are only helpful in as much as they indicate a real sense of interest, responsibility and clear objectives. However, unless there is a clear grasp of the magnitude, need, possibilities, willingness, and compromises necessary to lay the foundation for the successful work of education, it is all for naught. There has not been much success in bridging the education of today with the needs of the future. To be successful, education must prepare and equip students by mentally training them to make that bridge, to be cooperative citizens. Every youth should be trained to be successfully integrated into the world community and to be in keeping with this new civilization we are in the process of creating.

Now is the time when those who are highly developed mentally, along with the practical mystics with spiritual vision, to take the place of the impractical visionary idealists who have refused to compromise. These impractical idealists are responsible for slowing the progress of humanity, and for which mankind has paid a very high price. Our educational systems have failed to adequately train the minds of our children for right living, by not inculcating in them the methods of thinking that will lead to happiness, true success, and a full experience in whatever area of human endeavor they choose to serve. It could be argued that if children were educated in right human relations and the oneness of all humanity, we could have avoided the world wars of the twentieth century.[1]

The old civilization has passed away, and to be able to establish the new, innovating ways of thinking must be forged and established. For some, the old ways are comfortable and so they resent and try to overthrow the efforts of those who are establishing the new systems of education and general living. The concept of education is a spiritual enterprise designed to facilitate the evolution of the whole Man. If the student is subjected to crystallized, theological thinking and the academic philosophies of the churches and other religious organizations, it could pose a threat to the expansion of their consciousness. Once we can accept that there is no hope for the future of our world without humanity, we can begin to build a new foundation for peace and prosperity. It must be understood that his divinity and Christ consciousness, rejects man-made interpretations of this Jesus who is central to his future. Instead, this future, full of promise, must be built on the foundation of the authority of the human soul.

Humanity has an innate and inherent characteristic of mystical perception, which allows him not only to recognize a vision of the nature of the universe, but also gives him the ability to make contact through his soul. It is this ability that enables the philosopher to appreciate the world of meaning, and through this perception able to touch Reality. This ability constitutes the power of love, enabling the individual to move outward to that which is beyond the self. It gives one the ability to grasp ideas, given that the history of humanity is, in fact, the history of the growth of ideas; ideas that facilitate the development in the individual of the capacity to sense the unknown, to believe in that which is not yet proven, and to seek and demand revelations that are hidden and undiscovered.

This determined and demanding spirit of investigation has initiated new revelations. Throughout the ages, this innate spiritual faculty within our scientists, artists, philosophers, and all spiritual people and humanitarians, has produced the great Sons of God who love and have sacrificed for their fellowmen. Our new educators must establish a foundation on these premises, in order to, design a new world.[2]

The primary requirement of our time is the rapid education of people about the divine plan, the nature of the forces controlling evolution, and the agencies through which they are directed.

Every nation and every member of the human family is a part of this Fifth Life Wave we call the Aryan Race of mankind; and the corresponding Fifth Ray Energy of Concrete Knowledge and Science is the conditioning force, which is impacting humanity.

For the Divine Will to become manifest on Earth and the Divine Plan to be understood, it is essential that the abstract emotional feeling of awareness of the Divine and of Nature be grounded or anchored into matter. Regardless of their initial capacity of the individual, he has the ability to be trained in the science of right human relations, which is the major objective of all future educational systems. The process of education should be one in which the youth and adult are taught to reason from cause to effect, and to understand why certain actions are inevitably bound to produce certain results, as well as why the outcomes are as they are.

The new education will take into consideration man's social position, which is to determine his exposure to the different kinds of information, heredity, national conditioning, his environment, and his mental and emotional equipment. Given that the true meaning of the word **education** is to **lead him out**, the educational process should be designed to open mankind up to the entire world and free him from any limiting condition. He should be trained to think in terms of constructive world citizenship, and as such, future educators will teach from the perspective of instinct for the early grades, intellect for the secondary students, and intuition for the college or university students. The objective of the new educational methods must be to focus public attention on cultural unfoldment, mental development, and the steps needed to achieve them in the context of understanding that fundamental to any education is the spiritual unfoldment of the individual. As used here, the word **spiritual** is not synonymous with religion, but describes all the activities that drive the human being forward toward emotional, mental, intuitive, or social development, since the perpetual, enduring spirit of Man is always progressing along the Path of Evolution.[3]

This emerging education is the result of the precipitation

of the thought-waves that penetrated the mental atmosphere of humanity, leading to the initiation of new ways of living. All things in manifestation begin on the mental plane and filter down to the physical plane, giving clarity to the statement, *as a man thinketh, so is he*. Our present educational premise concentrates on synthesizing past history and past achievements in human thought with past scientific evolution, which is what presently constitutes human knowledge. This, it must be admitted, is undoubtedly backward looking. Education has concerned itself with the organization of the lower mind, and the child's abilities are then determined by how well he is able to accumulate, collate, and collect the information given to him. He is then expected to digest and arrange this information so as to equip him to compete with the information other students possess. Fortunately, this system is ending. To date, education has been mostly about memory training, which includes assimilating the facts the nation or race believes to be true and, which, through its own tests, have found to be perfectly adequate.

However, each Age has a new standard for adequacy, and in the Piscean Age, the emphasis on sensed ideals was significant. This resulted in a history and geography driven by economics, and other necessities of racial achievement. This also involved methods whereby tribes acquired national status through aggression, war and conquest. Scientific achievement by nations and races followed similar lines. Therefore, conquests in science, territory, and nations are all indicative of the Piscean methods, characterized by its idealism, militancy, and separateness in the fields of politics, religion, and economics. Thankfully, in this age of synthesis — the Age of Aquarius— the new education of inclusiveness is now gently penetrating the human aura. While it is important for the student to study and know past history, education involves more than the investigation of a subject leading to conclusions and more hypotheses. It is more appropriate for mankind to be educated to be a good citizen, a commercial asset, to make his life enjoyable by achieving culture and by participating with interest in the world of human affairs.

Education should have three major objectives:

1. It must make the individual an intelligent citizen, a wise parent, and a controlled personality, able to play his part in the work of the world, and also be fit to live in peace with his neighbors.

2. It must prepare the student to bridge the gap between various aspects of his own mental nature, including the following three aspects of the mind:

    *   *The lower concrete receptive mind; which is the reasoning principle, and is the aspect of the individual our educational process and psychologists claim to work with;*

    *   *The Soul, which is the intelligent principle; and*

    *   *The higher abstract, illuminating mind; the custodian of ideas and the conveyor of illumination to the lower mind once the lower mind is en rapport with the soul.*[4]

3. To bridge of the gap between the lower mind and the soul.

Humanity, on an intuitive level, has always known that the gap between the lower mind and the soul had to be bridged, and why Man speaks about **achieving attainment**, **at-one-ment**, and **achieving unity**; these are all intuitive attempts at expressing this truth. The previous Age of Pisces has prepared humanity and made him ready, for the first time in his history, to bring about the bridging of the soul and the lower mind, to result in a soul-infused personality. Ultimately, education is the science of what is called the antahkarana, which is the science of expressing the truth of the whole bridging process. It is a bridge that man builds through understanding, meditation, and the alchemical creative work of the soul, in which the work that takes place is between the three aspects of the nature of the mind.

This bridging, therefore, produces alignment between the

mind and the brain, through a correct understanding of the inner constitution of man, and especially of that which exists between the etheric body and the seven chakras. It constructs a bridge between the brain-mind-soul, producing the soul-infused personality, a process that steadily develops the expression of the indwelling soul, resulting in the achievement of illumination; this constitutes the completion of the bridge which unites the lower mind, the soul, and the higher mind.

In the end, true education is the science of integrating the many parts of man, connecting him to his environment, and then to the greater whole with which he interacts. The challenge of every educator therefore, is to identify and gauge the focus of the student's attention and to observe where his consciousness is centered to be able to shift the focus from the lower aspect to the higher.

The personality vehicle is only an instrument of the process, and becomes secondary to the process whose primary emphasis is always the will and purpose of that which is higher than itself. Similarly, if the emotional or astral body is the focus, the educational objective must, therefore, be to bring that emotional body under the control of the mind; if the mind is the focus then the soul must be the controlling influence. This is the ladder that must be built so that man can tread on the Path back to Oneness. The paradox of the occult path is that the mind, which is the healer, must also be the builder of the bridge that takes humanity across the abyss back home, and makes clear the maxim that *before a man can tread the Path, he must become that Path itself.* Man does this by constructing the staircase, step by step and stage by stage, just as a spider spins its thread to build his web, and is one out of which he evolves to find his way home. The practical applications of these principles should lead educators to train students to respond intelligently to impulses coming into the brain through their sense apparatus, and create thought-forms in response to those impulses. These impulses stir emotional reactions, set in motion by the feeling-desire nature, and also respond to impulses coming from the world of thought in the environment.

These emotional and mental impulses are designed to orient the student/individual spiritually; leading him from a place of potentiality to one of active participation in governance. The educator must also take into account the cycles that control the development of individuals, nations, and the planets, which are usually seven, and ten-year cycles. The first ten years of a child's life are the ones in which the child should be taught to deal with information coming into his brain via his senses, emphasizing observation, quick response, and physical coordination. The child should be taught to hear, see, make contact, and use his judgment. His fingers must then respond to those creative impulses to produce and create what he sees and hears through the avenues of the arts, craft, music and drawing. In the second ten-year period of the child's life, the training of the mind must have dominant focus. He must be taught to rationalize the emotional and desire impulses coming into his being, and to discriminate between right and wrong; the desirable and the undesirable; the essential and the non-essential.

These concepts and a sense of values and right standards can be taught and established through the lens of the history of his country, and his place in it. During this period of training, he should also be taught the difference between memorizing and thinking, between the bodies of facts established by thinkers and written in books and the application of those facts as they relate to the objective world.

The student begins to understand that there is a direct relationship between the subjective, causal ideas and the world of reality, of which the phenomenal world is but a symbol.

By the age of seventeen, the child should be able to strike his own note and determine the pattern in which his life impulses will run. At this time, he should also be introduced to the study of psychology and the relation of the individual soul to the World Soul. Meditation, defined by the Hindu psychologist, Patanjali, as **an unbroken flow of knowledge in a particular object**, should be added to his curriculum, not along religious lines, but as a means of deep thinking on a given subject, like mathematics, biology, physics, etc. Young people fall into two groups — the mystical, which includes those interested in groups of subjects classified as religious, and the artistic, or those drawn toward the more impractical tendencies or the occult, which includes the intellectual, scientific and mental types.[5]

As the Age of Aquarius progresses and the new educational system unfolds, children will be assessed and evaluated along the following lines:

- Astrology — esoteric astrology should be employed to determine the forces impacting the student's physical, emotional and mental bodies. A careful record should be kept of the exact moment of birth or first breath, which is usually aligned with the first cry. Careful analysis made every seven years would allow educators, who should be wise guides and friends to the youth, to understand and determine any particular problem of the soul, its tendencies, the child's pre-disposition to its soul-purpose, and then take the necessary steps to hasten the child's unfoldment along correct lines.[6]

- Psychology — the physical, vital, emotional, and mental nature of boys and girls should be carefully investigated, and their unconnected life purposes re-directed along right lines. They will be taught to see themselves as persons who see, act, feel and think. In this regard, the central occupant of his body, the "I", will be taught. This understanding will change the way the youth of the world sees himself, his fellowmen, and his part in the world.[7]

- Medical — special attention should be paid to the endocrine system, and other physiological issues such as eyes, teeth, ears, etc.

- Vocational — this type of training should not be emphasized until the later years of the educational process, when their gifts and capacities will find the fullest expression, and they are capable of fulfilling their obligations to the world.[8]

- Spiritual — the age of the soul should be studied to determine the place of the student on the ladder of evolution and his mystical and introspective tendencies, as well as any lack noted. The proper coordination of the brain, the mind and the soul as these relate to the individual itself and his own apparatus, to his environment, and to world thought are all essential. The entire equipment, latent or developed, must function as a unified whole.[9]

The Seven Ray Forces of: Will and Purpose; Love and Wisdom; Active Intelligence; Harmony through Conflict; Concrete Knowledge or Science; Devotion and Idealism, and Ceremonial Order and Alchemy, will greatly influence and direct the lines of the new education in the following ways:

1. **Will and Purpose** — the direction to Will should be of major concern to all educators as they direct the youth toward a conscious spiritual purpose and an orientation to **reality**, which will lead to the will-to-good, the will-to-beauty, and the will-to-serve.[10]

2. **Love-Wisdom** — in education, this force represents the development of the student in the consciousness of the whole. The first stage of this is the awareness of self-consciousness, which is the realization of the soul, and that man is the three-in-one and the one-in-three, and that he is the embodiment of the three aspects of the Divine. As the group consciousness begins to build, the concept of love begins to unfold — love of self, love of those around him, and love of the whole (self-consciousness, group consciousness, and God-consciousness).[11]

3. **Active Intelligence**— the creative nature of the conscious spiritual man should be every educator's objective. This training should include the understanding of the nature of

ideas, the methods of intuiting those ideas, and the laws that govern all creative work.[12]

4. **Harmony through Conflict** — this energy relates to the eventual power of creation, which is latent in all forms. It is the innate urge or discontent which leads man to struggle, progress, and evolve in order to finally make union with his soul. The educator will assist the student in knowing that it is the consciousness of harmony and beauty that drives the individual on the path of evolution back to his emanating Source.[13]

5. **Concrete Knowledge or Science** — The dissatisfaction generated by the previous stage of conflict must now be directed by the educator to enable the student to concretize his concepts, and to build the appropriate thought-forms that allow the student to materialize his visions and dreams, and thus bring his ideas into physical manifestation. The mind of the lower man must be trained in the art of discrimination, in the power of choice, and to become sensitive to his vision, all of which lead to an understanding of the underlying purpose of his being, and the right use of the mind.[14]

6. **Devotion and Idealism** — Devotion is the result of dissatisfaction coupled with the faculty of choice. The depth of man's discontent leads him along many stages of searching to find the ideal, which eventually leads him into full union with the Self. The educator's task, therefore, is to lead the student from one realized goal to another, but this must be done within the context of achieving the soul's purpose, and not within the context of national educational standards.[15]

7. **Ceremonial Order and Alchemy** — this is the energy dominating the New Age of Aquarius and the new education. The standardized, ritualistic rhythm imposed autocratically on public life in all countries is the established rhythm through which the innate faculty to function under direct purpose

98

and ritual operates. Educators will work to make this innate instinct to ordered rhythm more creatively constructive, which will lead to the revelation of the powers of the soul.[16]

Economics

It can be easily concluded that all world problems are based on economics. The cause of most global unrest and world conflict that inflict misery on humanity can largely be attributed to a selfish group with materialistic purposes, who have for centuries exploited the masses and used the labor of mankind for their selfish objectives. The economic problem, however, is really not a difficult one to solve, since all the natural and human resources needed for everyone on our planet to live a decent quality of life is readily available. We have the mineral wealth of the world, the oil, the produce of the fields, the contribution of the animal kingdom, the riches of the sea, and the fruits and that flowers, all of which offer themselves to humanity.[17]

Once we recognize that all resources belong to everyone, not just to a few groups, nations or races, it will significantly shift the dynamics needed to initiate global economic transformation. Under a wise system of distribution and a regenerated heart and mind, these resources could rapidly be made available around the globe, given the advancement in transportation. This current state of affairs can be justly attributed to the use of incorrect educational methodologies, which have emphasized competition and facilitated the exploitation of the weak and the helpless. It is, therefore, urgent that a new system of education be instituted, which trains the youth in the need to share, and to know that each individual has an obligation to assist in the betterment of his brother. At present, we are experiencing a climax of extreme poverty and of great luxury, a gross over-feeding of the few, and a starvation of the many, all in the face of the centralization of the world's produce and its control by a few people in each country.

Here are three suggestions for ending this condition:

1. The recognition that there is enough oil, fuel, minerals, and

food to satisfy the needs of the entire world population, and that the fundamental problem is distribution;

2. Given that all the resources needed on the planet are now available, it must be accepted that the supplies, essential to health, security and the happiness of mankind must be made available;

3. The establishment of an *economic league of nations* in which all nations, having knowledge of their country's resources, needs and how much each can contribute to the family of nations, should have a place;

The general good of humanity is the premise on which this whole project must be based. The general misery of humanity can be attributed largely to the attitudes and behaviors of the interrelated groups of businessmen, bankers, executives of international cartels, monopolies, trusts, and the directors of huge corporations. We are seeing the emergence of a war of sorts, which is initiating the dawning of a new economic age. This war is between the selfish, monied interests, and the mass of humanity who demand fair play and an appropriate share in the world's wealth. It must be added that this universal spirit of selfishness can be seen not only in the practice of big business, but at the corner grocer, by the plumber, and by the dry cleaner, all of whom deceive their customers and exploit their employees.

Within these capitalistic systems, there are humanitarians who seek to do good on behalf of their fellowmen, but due to the existing rules of the game, their hands are tied. There are those able to read the signs of the time, which clearly indicate that these practices cannot continue for too much longer, due to the emerging spiritual consciousness and humanity's rising demands. Unfortunately, however, many of these changes are still motivated by selfish reasons.[18]Fundamental to this economic dilemma is the notion that the greatest sin of all is *separateness*, which is responsible for the full gamut of human evils. It engenders a destructive sense of superiority in nations, which leads to the malicious and destructive doctrine of superior and inferior races and nations. This mind-set produces economic selfishness, and the consequent economic exploitation of human beings; trade barriers, territorial possessiveness, and the extremes of poverty and riches. The distrust and hatred among peoples around the world, which have led to cruel and destructive wars, are a result of the emphasis upon material acquisition, on the establishment of geographic boundaries, and the dangerous doctrine of national sovereignty, with all that these selfish attitudes engender.[19] One thing is now blatantly clear, the old order of economic governance has not worked, and a period of adjustment, when all nations will have to contribute to settling the economic and humanitarian needs of humanity along very different lines, is sorely needed. The new economic order must bring the disciplines of politics, religion, economics, philanthropy, education and science to the forefront of human aspiration.[20]

The hope of the world lies with the intelligentsia, and the influential middle class will be the catalyzing force that initiates the intelligent changes needed to affect every human being. Goodwill, the basic aspect of love, and not peace as the word is usually interpreted, is the element needed to bring about this change. For most, the word "*peace*" implies enforced pacifism and cessation from war. The cultivation of a spirit of goodwill is what must work itself out into the fabric of the life of the nation and the people. I am sure that Unity, Peace, and Plenty, each sequentially leading to the other, is the underlying principle in the thinking of everyone who holds a prominent position and who appreciates world peace and international order, as well as interracial and religious understanding; all the factors leading to economic interdependence, stability and universal goodwill.

CHAPTER SEVEN

Governance in the Aquarian Age

The keywords of the Aquarian Age are:

1. Service

2. Synthesis

3. Brotherhood

4. The Feminine — her restoration to equal power and rulership

5. Masonry — the religion of the 21st century

Service

The symbol for service in the Aquarian Age is that of a man carrying a jar of water on his shoulders. The jar is so full that the water is pouring out and overflowing but is still not diminished. The symbol for the Law of Service is one in which a man with outstretched arms in the form of a cross stands perfectly balanced with a water pot on his head. The significant difference of these two symbols is that the water jar on the shoulder signifies the burden of service, which is never easy. With great poise, balance and equilibrium the man on the cross with outstretched arms has held the jar of water on his head for a very long time, and though this has become natural to him, this symbol must now disappear.

Through the understanding of the Law of Magnetic Impulse and the Law of Polar Union, the originator of the sign for the constellation Libra, which is the symbol of balance and service, these two forces will determine the objective of this New Age. To carry out the mission of this age, the new local, national and international leaders must become educated in the true spiritual and esoteric meaning of service, as well as all the other objectives of this age since none is up for debate. Service has traditionally been viewed as what the busy, overactive person who wants to bring people together around a point of view does to change the conditions of the poor, distressed, afflicted, diseased and unhappy because the plight of the under-privileged has made him uncomfortable and he needs to return to a place of comfort in himself.

Service can also be the result of a fanatical desire to follow in the footsteps of the Christ, the Son of God who went about doing good. However, though the idea is right and admirable, the motive behind it is not always good. For many, service gives them a sense of power, the need for group activity, and in a worldly sense, brings more attention to the server than to the served, however, despite these motives, humanity is being served.[1] When the act of service is clearly understood, however, and the heart and mind are properly conditioned and re-oriented, we will see a remarkable change not only in the delivery of service, but in the outcomes. The statistics from the United Nations and other data collecting institutions seem to indicate that in-spite of the increased financial contributions of individuals and philanthropic organizations to the alleviation of poverty in the world, the rate of decline is unimpressive.[2] This is because sustainable change can only be achieved through a consciousness which understands how poverty originates on all levels — physical, emotional, mental and spiritual. Many of those offering service are oftentimes in even greater poverty on the higher levels than those they serve. We are reminded by Ageless Wisdom that one cannot manifest anything that he is not, himself. So, if one is poor, he cannot manifest wealth in the life of another, and so the efforts result in muted success. In the chain of transmitting energies, Humanity is now on its way to a correct understanding of service, as it becomes responsive to the new Law of Service and learns to react to the steady imposing Will of the Great Life of the planet.

As we become receptive to the incoming energies of this new age, the idea of service is now the major concept we need to grasp as these streams of energies are now subjecting humanity to the following three realities:

1. The awakening heart center in all aspirants;

2. The enabling of emotionally polarized humanity to become more focused intelligently in the mind;

3. The transfer of the energies of the solar plexus to the heart.[3]

This is leading to the development of true feeling or *the consciousness of the heart*, which is the first step toward group awareness. The impact of these new Aquarian energies is being registered in the astral or emotional body, and being worked out through the solar plexus of those who serve. This phenomenon is responsible for the emotional nature of the service being rendered and the generally unsatisfactory response of those being served, who sometimes display great hatred and lay blame at the feet of those who are delivering this service. This response is prompted by the reality that the delivery of service is not coming from the soul. Once the service being rendered is based on a mental response to humanity's need, the whole world will be lifted out of the veil of illusion and the valley of world delusion, and a happier more successful demonstration of service will be seen when the impulses for this service originate from the heart, and not from the solar plexus.

There is a group of souls in incarnation who have a highly developed understanding and because of their point of evolution, their stage of unfoldment, and their idea of the Divine Plan, they work out the Plan to evoke a response in the human consciousness. These souls come in under the impulse to help this sorrowing planet. These are the key people with the essential psychological facilities who, in any historical period, set the pace, and do the pioneering work. They are both hated and loved by humanity, and they carry this knowledge within their being, because they know they are both the Builders and the Destroyers. They bear the scars of their battles and, at the same time, the assurance that they have advanced the task to which they have been assigned. During the last century, this category of beings has been greatly enlarged, and it for this reason we are seeing a rapid development in the characteristics of the now Aquarian Age.[4]

Service looked at within the context of the Seven Ray Forces will express in the following ways:

1. The individual who functions as a soul type of the First Ray of Will, Power and Purpose, and as a trained aspirant, works in the capacity to impose the Will of God on the minds of men, by impacting ideas and emphasizing the governing principles behind those ideas. This work necessitates the destruction of old thinking and forms to make way for the ideas of the current New Age.[5]

2. The Second Ray type works with the energies of Love-Wisdom, and through magnetic, sympathetic understanding, and slow action based on love. He serves by pondering and meditating on the ideas associated with the Plan; then by the power of attractive love, he draws to him those who have reached the point in their evolution that can respond to the rhythm and measure of the Plan. Given the fact that the work of the Hierarchy of Wisdom is primarily associated with ideas, he is the one who can carry the ideas of the Plan deeper into the masses of humanity.[6]

3. The special function of the server on the Ray of Active Intelligence is to stimulate the intellect of humanity, by sharpening and inspiring the intellect. His work focuses on manipulating the ideas, so that intelligent men and women whose intuition is not yet awakened can more easily comprehend them, and in turn these ideas are communicated to the masses.[7]

4. The server on the Ray of Harmony through Conflict has the role of harmonizing the new ideas with those of the old, so that there is no dangerous gap. This is accomplished by the creation of a "righteous compromise" in which the bridging

process of the old to the new, the true pattern, is preserved. These souls are truly intuitive, have the capacity for the art of synthesis, and can portray a true presentation of the Divine picture.[8]

5. The server of Concrete Knowledge and Science is increasingly and rapidly coming into prominence; they are those who investigate the form to find its hidden idea and its motivating power, to prove these ideas true or false through scientific investigation. The many expressions of this Ray give credence to the fact that all things in manifestation express spiritual ideas, that inventions are materialized ideas, and that the law exemplifies the Plan. These servers are preparing a new world in which humanity will live a more deeply spiritual life, and are leading humanity into a world of meaning where their discoveries will eventually end unemployment, change the human condition, and hasten an era of peace and leisure.[9]

6. The goal of the workers who has served on the Ray of Devotion and Idealism over the last two thousand years, has been to train humanity to recognize ideals, (which are the blueprint of ideas), and to assist them in avoiding the disaster of fanaticism and superficial desires. Many of these individuals have incarnated now and they should be handled carefully, since they tend not only to be one-pointed in thinking, but also to follow their personal desires, lack wisdom, and respond to ideas long the path of least resistance. However, this Ray is indispensable for materializing ideals, and with the facility of this Ray, workers can teach men to recognize the truth within the framework of the ideal and restrain them from becoming too energetic or fanatical.[10]

7. This worker is able to bring a group together around an idea, and produce group idealism, focalizing it into definite form without the dominance of any one individual. The Seventh

Ray is specific to the Aquarian Age, and those who serve must lead an organized movement around certain Words of Power and be able to bend all energies toward the note and tone of the Age. The sensitivity of the worker to the Aquarian influence is essential; he must be willing to work in a group without any idea of personal ambition or of being a leader, since any such need automatically disqualifies him. Always striving to be harmless, his dedication to the service of humanity requires that he holds back nothing which can be rightly given.[11]

Synthesis

The Age of Aquarius is predominantly the age of synthesis and light. In this age, the light of day will bring the physical world to the point where the healing of the nations is accomplished through the rising of the Son/Sun of Mind. It is critical, at this point, to note the distinction between synthesis and unity. Synthesis emerges as one directs him/herself and life toward the Way of Higher Evolution and should be understood as an "*is-ness*." Unity on the other hand, is a product of achievement and the reward of action and effort.[12] As oneness is already a reality, man's task is to unfold his consciousness, which will bring him into the knowingness of that fact. On the physical plane, the avatar of synthesis, along with initiates and disciples, work to express the concept of synthesis in the world of politics and government, with the goal of counterbalancing incorrect approaches to synthesis and preserving freedom in unity. They work towards subjective synthesis, which expresses itself in an outer differentiation, defining the many aspects of the essential basic unity, and is enabled through the stimulation of the energy of synthesis. This is the way to achieve eventual peace and understanding on earth and to preserve individual and national cultures, both of which will be subordinate to the good of humanity.[13]

Those working in the field of science are greatly allied with the Seventh Ray group who are working through an alchemical technique, to produce synthesis between the three aspects of Divinity — Knowledge, Love-Wisdom, and Understanding, on the physical plane, as well as between the solar and lunar forces. These workers will penetrate beyond the outer form to the energy that motivates that form, and under alchemical law, create new forms, which express as the inflowing life. This group's workers will focus on closely studying the problem of evil, on how to bring about a better understanding of the purpose that exists in substance or matter, and the inflowing different, enlightened purpose of the soul aspect. It is synthesis which dictates the evolutionary process that works to achieve larger blocs, global planning, international relationships, brotherhood, economic fusion, fellowship of faiths, the free flow of commodities everywhere, and interdependence. This concept of synthesis will be taught in the new esoteric schools to prepare the builders of the new world through this interior training.

Synthesis can be summed up by the following mystical declaration:

"I take a body. That body is alive. I know its life. I therefore know my mother. "I use a body. That body is not me. I serve the group and in this serving live within the body, detached, a Son of God. I know my Self".

"I infuse a body. I am its life, and in that life, shall see life. That life is known as love. I am the love of God. I know the Father, and know His life is love. I am the body and its loving life. I am the Self, whose quality is love. I am the life of God Himself. The Mother-Father-Son Am I."

"Behind these three there stands the unknown God. That God Am I."[14]

Brotherhood

One can become aware through contemplation of the knower in himself, which is identical to the soul within the form. This knowledge of the two being one can be cultivated in a practical way between human beings, with recognition of the contact being possible between two individuals who can see, hear, and touch each other. At a higher stage of evolution, the individual passes behind the form and comes to a place where he can touch the quality of his brother's life, the nature of his plans, his aspirations, hopes and purposes, by touching that aspect of the consciousness which is analogous to his own. The better he knows himself and his own soul, the better and deeper the knowledge of his brother will become, because he knows and feels what his brother knows and feels. It is that identification of the Christ with Humanity that allowed the apostle John to utter the occult statement: '*we shall be like Him for we shall see Him as He is.*'[15]

As a prelude to the establishment of Brotherhood, the intelligentsia must recognize humanity through the breaking down of the mental barriers that exist between races, nations and types, and the disregard of all racial and national differences. These actions will carry the life of mankind forward. Men everywhere will be brought to an understanding of the fundamental ideals that govern the new age through both the impression and expression of certain great ideas. The true Brotherhood of man is based on the one divine life working through the one soul and expressing itself through the one Humanity, and recognition of the relationship between the divine life within the world and mankind itself.

As the mystery of Brotherhood unfolds through this new age, the universal brotherhood and our essential immortality will be proven as a fact of nature.[16]

The Feminine — her restoration to equal power and rulership will be one of the primary accomplishments of the Aquarian Age. In Qabalistic Tarot, the pictorial symbol for the Age of Aquarius is that of a nude woman kneeling by a pool with one foot on the water and the other on dry land, holding two vases as she transfers water from one to the other. This symbol is identified as the Egyptian goddess, Isis, who is the bringer of the new age. Both this symbol and that of the man carrying a water-pot on his shoulder further elucidate the importance of this feminine element, Water, with its imaginative and creative emphasis in the Aquarian Age.

Ageless Wisdom declares that the sole goal of the regeneration of man is the return of the feminine creative principle to her role as co-ruler of our planet, and that the liberation of humanity cannot be achieved without knowing her as the Regent Mother of the world. Without the balance which the feminine brings to any perspective, the premise of every policy decision must be faulty and the outcome by extension must also be faulty. Isis, as a symbol of the Feminine, represents truth and is in fact, Truth herself. No correct understanding of the world and the elements in it can be accurately grasped without understanding the Divine Feminine, who is the creative principle behind all things in manifestation. She, is the Woman spoken of in the *Book of Revelations*, with a crown of twelve stars on her head and the moon under her feet, who is the holder of the scepter of power equal to her male counterpart, with whom she will wield equal power in the Age of Aquarius. It is she who holds the secrets of life and who must unveil and reveal them to humanity, since no man can lift her veil to reveal what she has held hidden for eons. She alone, who is life itself, can teach humanity how to quench its thirst and hunger with the waters and bread of life.

The knowledge that the masculine and the feminine, male and female, good and evil, and all pairs of opposites are two aspects of one reality is essential to grasp as a premise of understanding the concept of synthesis. She, we are told by Ageless Wisdom, is the keeper of the occult mysteries of the truth about mankind, regarding his constitution, his origin, and destiny. Her rightful place in the cosmic, solar and planetary order of things is as the one who gave birth to all living things, including the Sun.

In every culture and every religion she is known by different names but her attributes are the same. She is the representation of all aspects of the feminine — mother, daughter, whore, virgin, queen, and beggar woman. She is the dark maid of Jerusalem, who is symbolic of receptive Nature and the watery, maternal principle, which creates all things out of Herself after impregnation has been achieved by the virility of the Sun.[17]

Masonry — the spiritualization of form is the primary objective of this Seventh Ray Energy of Ceremonial Ritual and Alchemy. And because of the legends and rituals of Masonry, many regard it as the religion of the 21st century. As the concept of oneness is more fully understood, political and national unselfishness will be established and international synthesis will take hold. This synthesis will manifest as a recognition that all formulations of truth and belief are only partial in time and space, and temporarily suited to the temperaments and conditions of the age and race. As the Ray of Devotion and Idealism moves out and Mankind experiences Divinity from a mental perspective, he will come to know that his task is to lift matter up to heaven and glorify the form by his conscious manifestation of divine powers.

Humanity is the custodian of the hidden mysteries. His dilemma is this: that which man hides from the world, he simultaneously hides from himself because he does not yet know the wonder he is, he hides and nourishes. He is the treasure house of God and, in fact, this is the great Masonic secret. It is only in the human kingdom that the three divine qualities are found, nurtured, and brought to full flowering. In Mankind, God the Father has hidden the secret of Life; in Mankind, God the Son has secreted the treasures of Wisdom and Love; and in Mankind, God the Holy Spirit (Mother) has implanted the mystery of manifestation. Man is indeed the great mystery, and it is he alone who can reveal the nature of the Godhead and of eternal life. It is to Man who is given the privilege of revealing the nature of divine consciousness and of portraying before every eye what has been hidden in the Mind of God.

Man stands mid-way between heaven and earth, with his feet in the mud of material life and his head in the heavens. Too often, however, are his eyes fixed on the mud and slime in which his feet are covered but once his eyes are opened, even for a moment and he catches a glimpse of the heavenly vision, like the Prodigal Son, torn between desire for the world of matter, experience, and possessions and the call of that attractive power at his center, the home from which he came, propels him on.[18]

The mind of man must, therefore, be conditioned to be like the mind that dwells in God, and it is to this task that the mental evolution of humanity is dedicated in the Aquarian Age, with the principles and structure of the Masonic knowledge offering much understanding to this end.

All leaders should seek, through education and economics, to create the environment where the soul is brought into active cooperation with the inner plan of the divine in accordance with the goal of the Hierarchy. This goal is to express the activity of the mind that has been initiated into purpose by the universal mind.

CHAPTER EIGHT

The Idea That is the United States of America

The Adepts Who Shaped the Vision

The New World Order as described by Dr. Paul Foster Case in his book: ***The True and Invisible Rosicrucian Order***, is an order of immortals, whose nucleus is now on this planet. It is composed of the new creatures that constitute a new species of organic life. This chapter gives the context for how this emerging New Order of the Ages as the next step in the unfoldment of the Divine Plan for Humanity and the World, puts the United States of America at the center of the establishment of the kingdom above on Earth.

It all began with the rise of a democratic dream in Europe, which prompted the beginning of western civilization, and so those in search of a Promised Land looked west to a virgin continent populated by Indian tribes — a vast continent suitable for the establishment of a democratic commonwealth.

It was well known that in this New Land, now the United States, one could experience freedom from tyranny, intolerance, and enforced poverty, and so by the nineteenth century, the hope of a better life drew streams of immigrants from almost every nation on earth. Here, there were opportunities for education, free enterprise, and a life lived according to the dictates of hope and conscience. Consequently, in a relatively short time, the races had met and mingled, and a new race — the American race, — was born, a race determined and set apart by a conviction; a conviction that human beings are created free and equal, and are entitled to equal opportunities for perfecting their life, their liberty and the pursuit of their happiness, which is not determined by an analysis of one's blood or the proportions of one's cranium.

We have also discovered that the race of democracy is distributed throughout the world among men and women of all nations and all races who share this conviction, and because they do, they too are of the American race. This realization is the mark of the beginning of a world democracy. The old philosophers taught that physical birth was an accident since men and women born of different nationalities and races were born under the law of generation. The ancients believed that wise men were of a separate race, born through the second birth, which they achieved by the mind having been developed, through proper intent, to a state of enlightened intelligence. Through this second birth, the individual emerged out of any particular race or nation into an international race and an international nation, which is the larger race and nation that will eventually inherit the earth.[1]

Egypt's Connection to the American Ideal

It is to this international race and nation that Akhenaton, the first democratic leader, who was a child of the second birth, belonged. Akhenaton, the very young Priest-King and Pharaoh of ancient Egypt, is described as the first man in recorded history to exemplify social consciousness in the administration of a great nation. He saw every living thing as having a Divine right to live well, to hope, and to aspire in a world governed by brotherly love.[2] Described as the first pacifist, the first realist, the first monotheist, the first democrat, the first heretic, the first humanitarian, the first internationalist, and the first person known to attempt the *founding* of a religion, he was born several thousand years before his time.[3] To Akhenaton, Aton (God) was not a mighty warrior ruling over Egypt, speaking through the oracles of priests, nor some Supreme Being flying through the air in a chariot leading armies of destruction. To him, Aton was a gentle father who loved all his children, of every nation and race, who desired that they live together in peace and comradeship, and who felt that the social problems faced by humanity were related to religion. He knew that the Aton created all things — from the smallest to the mightiest; that he had fashioned them in his wisdom,

116

and preserved them with his love and tenderness. So, this Pharaoh traveled alone through the countryside, meeting the peasants, conversing with slaves, and sharing the simple food of the poor.[4]

He listened with great respect, because in each of his subjects he sought and found the life of Aton. He witnessed the Universe shining through the eyes of little children, and he beheld the beauty of Aton in the bodies of the men who worked in the fields. He could not understand why others failed to see God in everything, as he did. Nor could he accept the inequalities of birth, wealth, or physical estate as justification for men exploiting or persecuting each other. He saw it as his duty, and that of every ruler, to protect the beauty in the hearts of his people, to nourish it and to provide every possible opportunity for its expression and perfection.[5] From his perspective, religious intolerance was impossible among those who worshipped the true Aton, and there was no room for political intolerance in a world governed by the laws of brotherly love since each person became the protector and comforter of everyone else, always cherishing the dreams of others equally as he did his own.

In his personal life, Akhenaton emerged as the first man in history to bring dignity and gentle beauty to the management of his home. He was completely devoted to his seven daughters and his wife Queen Nefertiti, whom he always referred to as his beloved wife. When he died at the age of thirty-six, it was written of him that the spirit with which he died had never been before, and he was indeed, "The beautiful child of the Aton, whose name shall live forever and ever." This story might help to explain why the capstone, or fire triangle, that the Egyptians call "The Light" appears twice on the reverse of the Seal of the United States of America as the unfinished pyramid; and a radiant triangle, enclosing the all-seeing eye, is another piece of evidence that the structure of government intended by the founders of the American Republic presented itself to their minds as a piece of Egyptian Masonry, as well as the vision and democratic philosophy of the first conscious leader, Akhanaton.[6]

The Greeks also knew of the wisdom with which ancient Egypt

under Akhanaton flourished, and they wanted to have this influence in the way they governed, so Solon their lawmaker traveled to Egypt to gather information. In ***The Secret Destiny of America***, Manly P. Hall tells the story of this great Athenian leader, Solon, who visited Egypt in search of the wisdom of Akhenaton. In response to his search, the High Priest of the Shrine of Sais, who served the Goddess Isis, took him through the long passageways of the temple that led down stone stairs, rutted by time and lit only by flaming torches, to long subterranean chambers hewn out of living rock. A river flowed through the chambers and the High Priest told Solon that this was the sacred Nile which flowed from Egypt through the underworld to water the fields of the immortals.

Accompanied by the Priest and the torchbearers, Solon was rowed out over the dark water in a small black boat that was waiting on the bank of the underground stream. The boat was then anchored on the shores of a tiny island far underground. Two tall columns made of strange metal, which neither rusted nor deteriorated with age, and which were covered with curious writing in an unknown language, glistened in the light from the torches. The High Priest explained the mystery of the columns to an astonished Solon, by pointing a golden rod at the pillars. He said that a lost people, who had vanished from the earth, had placed the columns on the island thousands of years ago. He went on to explain that a long time ago a vast empire, whose power extended to every corner of the world, had existed on our planet. Great fleets of merchant ships sailed the seven seas and brought their wealth to its fabulous City of the Golden Gate — the capital of Atlantis. This empire was ruled over by seven kings, descendants of Neptune, the God of the Seas. In this great land there were schools for the study of the mysteries of Nature, towers for the examination of the stars, and, beneath the earth, were mines from which an abundance of precious metals were extracted. Then came the fatal day, when in disobedience to the laws of the gods, the seven kings of the Islands of the west resolved to conquer the whole earth. Prior to this there had been no strife among men, but it was out of this act that war came into being. Coming in great ships from the west, approximately 9000 years before the siege of Troy, the seven kings led an army against the ancient Greeks and invaded Europe.

But before Atlantis sank, its spiritually illumined Initiates, who realized that the land was doomed because it had departed from the path of Light, withdrew from the ill-fated continent, carrying the sacred and secret doctrine with them to Egypt, where they set themselves up as the first Divine Rulers. The world received its heritage of arts, crafts, philosophy, ethics and religion, as well as its heritage of war, perversion and strife as a result. It has been said that through the instigation of the first war, all subsequent wars have been fought in a fruitless effort to justify the first one, and to right the wrong which it caused.[7]

This act by the seven kings greatly angered the gods who caused a great earthquake to occur, and the great islands of the West to be submerged into the sea as a result. Sixty million human beings are reputed to have perished because they disobeyed the laws of heaven, and over time even the name of the Atlantic Empire was forgotten, as was the memory of all those who, regardless of their power or wealth, had disobeyed the gods. The High Priest continued to explain: *"From these ancient columns, we have read the laws that were given in olden times for the government of nations. These laws are not made by men, but are the will of Eternal Nature. Upon these laws enduring states must be built. To depart from these laws is to die and so perished the nations of the elder world."*[8]

These are the pillars of Hercules to which Francis Bacon referred in Novum Organum when he indicated that between them runs the path which leads upward from the uncertainties of earth to that perfect order, which is established in the sphere of the enlightened. In Freemasonry, the two pillars also represent Jachin and Boaz, between which the World Virgin, Isis, — symbol of Nature, — sits; and it also alludes to the fact that Nature attains productivity by means of productivity and that She is the Mother of all productions. As the personification of Wisdom, Isis stands between the pillars of opposites, demonstrating that understanding is always found at the point of equilibrium, and that truth is often crucified between two thieves of apparent contradiction[9] Solon returned to Greece with the intention of developing the story of the Atlantic Empire into an epic poem, but due to the responsibilities of the State and the infirmity of age, he failed to do so. However, he told the story to his friend Dropis, who in turn told it to his son Critias. And so, in his 90th year, Critias told the story to his grandson of the same name, who became a disciple of Socrates, which is how the story came to be part of the Platonic dialogues of the same name.

Plato was, first and foremost, a philosopher, and he considered philosophy to be the greatest good ever imparted to man by Divinity. He therefore saw in the account of the fall of Atlantis, the opportunity to summarize his convictions concerning government and politics. Thus, in the Critias, he describes the blessed state of the Atlantean people under the benevolent rulership of ten kings, who were bound together in a league — The Ancient League of Nations. These kings were the monarchs of the seven islands and the three great continents of Europe, Asia and Africa. The ten were said to have been philosopher kings endowed with all virtues, who were wise guardians of the public good, and who obeyed the laws of the Divine Father, Poseidon, — God of the Seas. [10]

Atlantis the Prototype of the American Government

On one of the columns of the law, it was written that the ten kings of Atlantis should never take up arms against each other for any reason, and that should one break this law, the other nine would unite against him to preserve the peace. Moreover, in all matters relating to the public good, the ten kings were to deliberate together, each being mindful of the just needs of the other. Qabalists attribute this structure and function to the Tree of Life with its ten spheres of Divine emanations, which function as a whole unit, and represent the glyph of Divine Man. This description of the Atlantean government is a description of the government of the Golden Age, in which men on earth lived according to the laws of heaven. The league of the ten kings is the cooperative commonwealth of mankind; it is the natural and proper form of human government, which is the archetype or pattern of the right government that existed in ancient days, but was destroyed by the selfishness and ignorance of men.

The Critias described how in the beginning of the Atlantean days, wealth and prosperity grew as a result of friendship and sharing, but as the Divine portion of consciousness in them faded away, their souls became diluted with a mortal admixture, and things changed. In the end, as man departed from the perfect pattern and conduct, he denied the very truths which were the foundations of his strength. He lost his spiritual perception, his material ambitions increased, and the desire for conquest was born; as men yearned after that which they had not earned, and gazed with covetous eyes upon the goods of others. Cooperation, Plato states, is natural to the wise, while competition is natural to the ignorant.[11]

Ambition and selfishness caused the dissolution of the league; war came into being, and with it, tyranny, which brought with it oppression, despotism, and the exploitation of people, until finally, the ten kings of Atlantis decided to use their collective power to enslave all the peoples of the earth.[12]

Plato's image of the ideal king is a wise man perfected in the virtues, who is a benevolent ruler of those less informed than himself. This king is a descendant of a Divine Race, belonging to the Order of the Illumined — those who come to a state of wisdom and belong to the family of perfected human beings.[13]

The story of Plato's Atlantis ends with Zeus, — the Ancient of Days, also called Jupiter, God of the thunderbolts, — hurling a thunderbolt against the empire of the sea, shaking it with earthquakes, and destroying it by horrible combustion. The only remaining records were that of vague traditions, and the two columns set up under the temple of Sais, in tribute to Isis.[14]

The Fate of Atlantis

The destruction of Atlantis can be interpreted, politically, as the breaking up of the ideal pattern of government. So complete was the destruction that in mankind's memory there is no remembrance of a better way of life, and he has therefore accepted the evils of war, crime, and poverty as inevitable. Lost, also, is the world's sense of its own unity. Under a deluge of politics, the perfect state disappeared, and the priest of Poseidon gave way to the priesthood of materialism. Plato's political vision, then, if human beings are to be preserved from their total self-destruction, is for the restoration of the old ways of the Gods, and of the Empire of the Golden Age. Hence, the establishment of the university of Athens —the first school of formal education. At this school men were taught great truths of religion, philosophy, science, and politics, all of which were designed to restore to their minds the vision of the perfect State. Although old Atlantis was dissolved in a sea of doubts, a philosophic empire would return as a democracy of wise men.

Francis Bacon's Implementation of the Plan for New Atlantis

Two thousand years later, Francis Bacon restated this vision of a philosophic empire in his book, New Atlantis, which describes the model of a college he named "Solomon's House", or the college of the six days work, a thinly veiled reference to the perfection of nature through art. The six days are the days of creation, as given in the account of Genesis, during which God symbolically created the Universe and brought the natural world into existence. Likewise, Man, through art, which is philosophy, must create the conditions of his own perfection by means of six philosophic steps. This school is a secret school, the wise man's house in which all arts and sciences are taught according to the Divine understanding of causes, not according to materialistic interpretation.

The college of Solomon's House was comprised of a Society of unknown Philosophers who dwelt together in a gentle commonwealth of scientific and philosophic learning that included the study of medicine, plants and music. It consisted of laboratories, observatories, mines, hospitals and various engines and inventions by which the elements could be controlled and the secrets of nature discovered. In this philosophical city, everyone was employed according to his taste and ability, — each contributing in his own way to the totality of useful knowledge.[15]

In John Heydon's Holy Guide, he reprints the New Atlantis as an alchemical allegory, connecting the book of the Rosicrucian Mysteries, by inference, with the symbols of Freemasonry. Bacon writes about "the sons of peace, or of the ladder" as the philosophic empire, called Bensalem, which existed in the mysterious institution called Solomon's House. Any discerning Mason should be able to see that this Temple or House is that of an order of men and women of universal wisdom and education, all of whom are united in the quest for universal realities. There is every indication that Bacon's dream was for the college of the six days, **Solomon's House**, to be erected in America. He strongly felt that this was an area set aside by nature for the perfection of philosophy and the sciences, for the investigation of the laws of life and the mysteries of the universe.[16] The Ancients believed that religion, science, and philosophy are the three parts of essential learning and that any government based on only one or even two of these parts must ultimately degenerate into a tyranny of either men or of opinion.

These three areas comprise the unity of knowledge, and are called: "The Order of the Quest." In this order, religion, which is the quest for truth by means of the mystical powers latent in the consciousness of man, is the spiritual part of learning; philosophy, the quest for truth by the extension of the intellectual powers toward the substance of reality, is the mental part of learning; and the sciences, a quest for truth by the study of anatomy and physiology and the body of truth, as revealed in the material creation, is the physical part of learning. Together, these three can bring about the perfection of man through the discovery of the Plan for man, because the nature of man is a composite of the spiritual, mental, and physical, which manifests in his daily living. Therefore, if he is to be self-governing, man must become equally informed in all the parts of his nature. The great philosophers of the past were great because they approached the problems of life as priests/philosophers/scientists, knowing that the great secrets of antiquity were the realization of the unity of knowledge. The plan was that an ideal university, — a college of the six-day work, would be established in which mankind would learn that the sciences are as sacred as the theologies, and that philosophies are as practical as craft and trades, so that those mystical extra-sensory perceptions viewed with suspicion by the materialists would then be developed according to the disciplines of the sciences. All learning would then be consecrated to the supreme end of men becoming like gods, and knowing good and evil [17]

Philosophy sets up its house in the world to free men by liberating them from their own excessive desires and ambitions; it saw selfishness as natural to all who are untutored and as the greatest crime against the common good; teaching the completion of the great work of social regeneration, which must be accomplished in man, not in society. Bacon taught that the democratic commonwealth can never be legislated into existence, nor can it result from formal treaties or conferences, and the Ancient League of Nations was a clear example of this. We saw that the nations which comprised the League, lacked the courage of high conviction, and, therefore, failed the very institution they had established. Bacon believed that permanent progress results from education and not from legislation since the true purpose of education is to inform the mind in basic truths concerning conduct, as well as the consequences of that conduct. It should also be clearly understood here that the lesser part of learning is definitely not befitting of the individual to deal with the problems of economic survival, but instead learning to deal with the intangibles of right motivation and right use, which is the greater part of learning.[18]

In all learning, the fact that the supreme human purpose is the

124

perfection of Man must come first. When this end has been achieved, all good things inevitably follow. No human being, Bacon continues, who is moved to action through wrong motivation or who misuses the privileges of his times, can be considered educated, regardless of the amount of schooling he has received. A human being is established in knowledge through the examples set by leaders and by the personal experiences of living and not by the reading of books alone.

The Baconian system therefore established that there were three sources of learning, namely:

- Learning by tradition, which may be derived from books;

- Learning by observation, which we learn from the actions of each other;

- Learning by experimentation — a study of causes and consequences brought about by personal conduct.

Only an enlightened citizenry can sustain enlightened leadership, for only the wise can recognize and reward wisdom; as such, in a democracy, the very survival of the State depends upon the intelligent cooperation of its people.[19] Solon, the Greek law-giver, declared that an ideal State has few simple laws because they are derived from certainties. By direct contrast, in a corrupt State the laws are many and confused because they are derived from uncertainties, and, like the web of a spider, they catch small insects, while allowing the break-through and escape of the stronger creatures. It was established that where there are too many laws there is lawlessness, and the people come to despise and ridicule the restraints imposed on them. Thus, the degeneration of democracy and the loss of liberty occur when already corrupt laws are amended by further inadequate legislation, revealing the general ignorance of right and wrong.

Half-truths, he explained, are the most dangerous form of lies, simply because they can be defended in part by incontestable logic; and since our body of learning has been broken up, those fragments have become partial truths, so that what we are now experiencing is the consequences of division, which must be remedied.[20]

125

It is a remarkable, fascinating and little-known fact that two thousand years before the democracy of 1776, even before the white man arrived, the first American democracy characterized by the spirit of human equality, human cooperation, and freedom of worship, existed and flourished. That democracy was the first League of Nations, created among the Great Lakes Indians of the American Northeast.

Civilization after civilization has been built by human courage and destroyed by human ignorance. We are now at the beginning of a New Age and on the threshold of a day of reckoning. It must be remembered that when humanity willfully ignores the Universal Laws which govern his destiny, Nature has unique and devious ways of pressing home the lessons.[21]

The Order of the Quest—the Adepts Behind the Plan

In every age, as in this, there are enlightened humans with the intellectual and the spiritual perceptions that are united in what might be termed the Order of the Quest. It has been revealed to them that civilization has a Secret Destiny — one whose high purpose is not realized by the great mass of people since they have no knowledge that they are part of a Universal Motion in time and space. Thousands of years before the beginning of the Christian era, many enlightened thinkers from Egypt, Greece, India, and China discovered that the Will of God is expressed through nature, in the affairs of men. These philosophers knew that world democracy was the secret dream of the great sages, philosophers, seers and mystics like Aristotle, Pythagoras, Buddha, Jesus, Lao Tse, Mohammed, and Quetzalcoatl. In the pursuit of accomplishing this greatest of human ends, they outlined programs of education, religion, and social conduct directed to ultimately achieve a practical and universal Brotherhood, of which current Masonry is but a faint reflection. As far back as two thousand years B.C., the mystical orders of Egypt were aware of the existence of the great Western Continent called America, and decided that it should be the site of this philosophic

126

empire[22] It was also Bacon's conviction that the Order of the Quest should be set up in the divinely assigned land America, which he called the New Atlantis, and that the vision and philosophy of the Quest was to be the foundation upon which the American Republic should be built.

In Search of the Promised Land

The desire to pillage the treasures of the New World was the overarching motivation of those who sought to colonize the Western Hemisphere; their goal being to amass hordes of gold, and silver, and to build palaces encrusted with jewels. With this in mind, large self-financed expeditions, and others subsidized by the State, set out to exploit the New Land. Spain seemed to have profited the most and so it became clear very early on that only sober colonization would yield the results of a Higher Order. The western hemisphere was also virgin soil for the Christian faith, whose priests eagerly accompanied the Conquistadores in order to convert pagan tribes and nations to the faith of the old world.

Under the guise of holy inquisition, tens of thousands of Indians were killed, and the Mayans' libraries with all their historical records were destroyed. Over time, the explorers and adventurers brought back reasonably accurate accounts of the natural advantages of the resources of the Americas.[23]

The French and the Dutch set up territories along the Atlantic seaboard, but Sir Francis Bacon, who had given up hope of bringing his dream to fruition in his own country of England, set up the Secret Order in America in the middle of the 17th century. The Divine assignment was entrusted to him and his genius gave purpose to the whole enterprise. Membership in Bacon's Secret Society was not limited to England, and was most powerful in Germany, France, and the Netherlands. It included most of the leading European thinkers of the time who were involved in the vast pattern of Bacon's purpose. This mystic empire of the wise had no national boundaries, with a citizenry of Alchemists, Qabalists, Rosicrucians, and Mystics of every land who had migrated to the new colony during the early stages of the colonization and set up their organizations in places they found to be suitable. Paul Foster Case, in his book *The Great Seal of the United States*, indicates that in the design of the Seal by the first committee, was a coat of arms in six quarters, with emblems representing the countries of: England, Scotland, Ireland, France, Germany, and Holland (The Netherlands), representative of the countries from which the new nation was originally peopled.[24]

Bacon very quickly realized that this new land provided the ideal environment for the establishment and accomplishment of the dream of the philosophic empire. However, he was not alone in this endeavor. He was the head of a secret society, which included in its membership men of high rank and broad influence, who were the most brilliant intellectuals of his day. Bound together by the common oath of labor and the cause of world democracy, they devised the colonization scheme. Bacon made sure that the American colonists were indoctrinated in the principles of religious tolerance, political democracy and social equality, carefully appointing representatives for a democratic machinery, which was in place for over a hundred years before the Revolutionary War.[25]

Some of the colonizers were of the *Order of the Quest*, but many were not, and so it was not long before religious strife broke out in the colonies, as much of the intolerance of the old world came over with them to plague the new civilization. It is well known that people do not change their natures merely by changing their place of habitation, and it soon became clear to Bacon and his *Secret Society* that not only were they still pioneering in the areas of right thinking and right living, but that much work needed to be done before the philosophic empire would emerge in America. The country saw many changes in social and political life; cities sprung up and trade flourished, as did most of the important secret societies of Europe and England since with the American organizations under European sovereignty, membership in the two hemispheres were bound together by understanding and sympathy. The plan Bacon outlined was working out on schedule; quietly and industriously, America was being conditioned to fulfill its destiny of leadership in the free world.

No account of the work of the Secret Societies in America can be complete without highlighting the input of Dr. Benjamin Franklin, a quiet, dignified, scholarly and gentle man who, despite having never been the country's President or a military general, stands out as one of the country's most important figures in the struggle for American independence. Even though he was not a law maker, because of the enormous psychological influence he had on colonial politics, his words became law. Few knew that the source of his power was the secret society to which he belonged, and for which he was the appointed spokesperson. His profound wisdom was reflected in the Almanac he wrote under the penname, **Poor Richard**. He understood the farmer and the philosopher, and knew the languages of both. Franklin spoke for *The Order of the Quest* both at home and abroad, especially in France where he received many honors. He watched the New Atlantis take shape, as well as the plan set out by Francis Bacon one hundred and fifty years before.[26] There have been numerous prophetic statements made throughout the centuries foreshadowing the emergence of this great empire. The first president, George Washington, the Flag, and the Great Seal of the United States, could all be seen as emblematic expressions of that profound esoteric document, the *Declaration of Independence*. Ancient writings are prolific with the sense of destiny which surrounded this New Land.

Among these were predictions made public in 1732 by Sir William Hope, deputy governor of Edinburgh Castle in his little book on fencing written forty-four years before the Revolutionary War and the United States Declaration of Independence. In it, he foretells the destiny of the United States, and more specifically the awesome responsibility and obligation America has to achieve its liberation and in turn becoming a beacon of light to the world. At this time the then thirteen colonies had not devised a plan for independence, and George Washington had just been born in Virginia. Of the fifty-six men who signed the Declaration of Independence, twenty were but small boys, and eighteen were not yet born at the time of his telling.

Little is known of Sir Hope except that his writings seem to reflect some knowledge of Cabala and Astrology, as well as the specific mention of four men— George Washington, Abraham Lincoln, Benjamin Harris, and William McKinley, and the significant occurrences in their lives. Reference is made to the contributions these presidents would make to the United States as well as to the two tombs where George Washington would be buried and the 555-foot monument to be erected in his honor — the tallest memorial ever constructed to the memory of a man. The story is told of the committee for the design of the Flag, chaired by Dr. Franklin, which met in Cambridge Massachusetts at the home of the host. Described as a man beyond seventy years old, still in the prime of his life who ate no meat, fish nor fowl, but whose diet was comprised of nuts, ripened fruits, tea, honey and molasses, he was referred to as the **Professor**, who spent his time reading ancient manuscripts and pondering over rare books. With the approval of George Washington, the Professor completed the committee of signers, as the seventh person to do so. After a preamble, it was suggested by Franklin, that the entire committee listen to remarks by this new found and honorable friend who stated:

> *The sun of our political air, like the sun in the heavens, is very low in the horizon — just now approaching the winter solstice, which it will reach very soon. But, as the sun rises from his grave in Capricorn, mounts its resurrection in Aries, and passes onward and upward to his glorious culmination in Cancer, so will our political sun rise and continue to increase in power, in light, and in glory; and the exalted sun of summer will not have gained his full strength of heat and power in the starry Lion until our Colonial Sun will be, in its glorious exaltation, demanding a place in the governmental firmaments alongside of, coordinate with, and in no wise subordinate to, any other sun of any other nation upon earth.* [27]

He also added that over time the gradual modification of the

Flag would be made in order to reflect the new nation gestating in the womb of time. In Cambridge, on January 2, 1776, in the presence of the army, George Washington, with his own hands, raised the newly made flag on a tall, specially made pine, liberty tree pole. The British Army was just as pleased as the Colonies, and gave an official salute of thirteen guns in honor of the new standard.[28]

Thomas Paine, a Quaker and Englishman by birth, came to America at the suggestion of Benjamin Franklin, and became a great champion in the cause of freedom for the colonies. And it is said that he did more to win the independence of the colonies with his pen, than George Washington accomplished with his sword. The vision he had for the country would require a complete re-organization of the government, religion, and education from its present status. Most people believed that He assisted Thomas Jefferson in the writing of the Declaration of Independence, while others believe that he composed the entire document, and then submitted it to Jefferson who edited and revised it. A free thinker, and a radical pamphleteer, he was considered to be born before his time. However, by his very birth and the nature of his energy, he was able to change the face of time. He emphasized the separation of church and state in his book, *The Age of Reason*, and believed that when the clergy involved itself in the political conspiracies of the State, it descended to the level of self-interest; he believed that when their spiritual powers were prostituted they would lose all public respect. He witnessed the conniving, plotting, and counter-plotting of religious leaders who had cast their lot in with the aristocracy against the long suffering and exploited citizens. He felt that it was bad enough for government to burden the people with extravagancies, but even worse for the church to preach that men should accept this load as coming from God as being designed to purify their souls through the practice of patience and humility.[29]

Paine was correct in his assessment. As we know, political experience and wisdom lead one to realize that the possibilities of public office are limited and good things are brought about slowly.

However, when the dream of world democracy is finally realized, Paine's name and memory will undoubtedly be immortalized. On July 4th, 1776, fifty-six patriotic men gathered in the old State House in Philadelphia for the solemn purpose of proclaiming the liberty of the American colonies. The names of men such as: Benjamin Franklin, John Adams, Thomas Jefferson, John Hancock and a few others are readily recognized, but the majority was unknown men, and to write their history would be to write that of the **Order of the Quest.** Among the unknowns was the Professor who assisted in designing the Flag.

It can be said that it is the mysterious and obscure persons — those who receive little or no credit for the part they play, that further almost all great causes; and in this case, these men were from many nations and cultures. An old book of rules used by the brothers of the Secret Orders reveals the following: "Our brothers shall wear the dress and practice the customs of those nations to which they travel, so that they shall not be conspicuous or convey any appearance that is different or unusual. Under no condition shall they reveal their true identity, or the work which they have come to accomplish, but shall accomplish all things secretly and without violating the laws or statutes of the countries in which they work."[30]

The Role of Rosicrucians in the Founding of the United States of America

The Declaration of Independence set forth the veiled principles of Rosicrucianism with careful phrases from the *Fama Fraternitatis,* a manifesto created in Europe circa 1610 by the Rosicrucian Order. It stated that the coming of: the strong child of Europe who, once it had attained its growth on the American continent, would be the channel of Freemasonry, and that essentially Rosicrucian ideas would be made the first principles of the **New Order of the Ages** as stated in the American **Declaration of Independence**.[31]

In secrecy and anonymity, well ordered aid was given to the Universal Plan in the struggle for human equity and justice that has been America's destiny throughout the past, and into our present time. This destiny will continue to be served by the unknowns until the Platonic empire is established on the earth, and the two towers of the *New Atlantis* rise from the ruins of a materialistic and selfish world.[32] The Rosicrucians left the Great Seal of the United States of America as an imperishable reminder of their secret activities. Late in the afternoon of July 4th, 1776, the Continental Congress resolved that Dr. Franklin, Mr. J. Adams, and Mr. Jefferson were to form a committee to devise a Seal for the United States of America. This was the same committee, except for Robert R. Livingstone and Roger Sherman, which had drawn up the *Declaration of Independence* that had been signed at about 2 pm that very afternoon.

The Great Seal— Decoding Its Symbols

The Congress assembled after dinner, desirous of completing the evidence of the independence of the United States by formally adopting an official sign of sovereignty and a national coat of arms. It was understood by each successive committee that the coat of arms and the seal would be one and the same. On the 20th of June 1782, the secretary for the third committee delivered a report describing the Seal, which read as follows:

> **ARMS:** *Paleways of thirteen pieces, argent and glues; a chief, azure; the escutcheon on the breast of the American Eagle displayed proper, holding in his dexter talon, an olive branch, and in his sinister, a bundle of thirteen arrows, all proper, and in his beak a scroll, inscribed with the motto,* **E Pluribus Unum.**[33]

> For the **CREST**: *Over the head of the eagle, which appears above the escutcheon, a glory, or, breaking through a cloud, proper, and surrounding thirteen stars, forming a constellation, argent, on an azure field.*[34]

> **REVERSE**: *A pyramid unfinished. In the zenith, an eye in a triangle, surrounded with a glory proper. Over the eye these words,* "**Annuit Coeptis**." *On the base of the pyramid the numerical letters*

MDCCLXXVI. And underneath the following motto: **Novous Ordo Seclorum**.[35]

The remarks and explanation are as follows:

The Esucutcheon is composed of the chief and pale, the two most honourable ordinaries. The pale pieces represent the Several States all joined in one entire solid compact, supporting a Chief which unites the whole and represents Congress. The Motto alludes to this union. The pales in the arms are kept closely united by the chief and the chief depends upon that Union and the strength resulting from it for its support to denote the Confederacy of the United States of America and the preservation of their Union through Congress. The colours of the pales are those used in the flag of the United States of America: White signifies purity and innocence, Red, hardiness & Valour, and Blue, the colour of the Chief, signifies Vigilance, Perseverance & Justice. The Olive branch and the arrows denote the power of peace & war, which is exclusively vested in Congress. The Constellation denotes a new State taking its place and rank among other sovereign powers. The Escutcheon is born on the breast of an American Eagle without any other supporters, to denote that the United States of America ought to rely on their own Virtue.[36]

Reverse: *The pyramid signifies Strength and Duration: the Eye over it & the Motto allude to the many signal interpositions of Providence in favour of the American cause. The date underneath it signifies the beginning of the New American Era, which commences from that date.*

The concepts for the American government, adopted in 1776, are all set forth in detail in the lectures, dramatized in the rituals, and summarized in the symbols of Freemasonry; prior to this date, the lodges in England and America were the only places where the principles of liberty, equality, and fraternity were explained and practiced. Freemasonry taught that all men were brothers, and, as such, all Masons met as equals, and learned from the many experiences and practical helpfulness each to the other, but most of all it taught the great truth, that all men are brothers. The founders of the nation drew their inspiration from the doctrines of Pythagoras, Plato, the Egyptian schools in Alexandria, the Qabalists, the Rosicrucians, and the Hebrew and Christian scriptures.

Symbolism of the Obverse

There are many esoteric interpretations of the Seal. Paul Foster Case in his book **The Great Seal of the United States**, gives his interpretation of the observe side in which he describes the eagle as an ancient symbol of spiritual vision and the only bird capable of looking directly into the sun. He further states that it is connected with the sign of Scorpio, which is the ascendant or rising sign of the United States. In astrology, the sign of Scorpio is said to rule the physical forces and functions in the human body that relate to the reproductive system. These energies must be controlled, re-directed and sublimated before the individual can develop true, higher vision. The eagle suggests, then, that spiritual vision is essential to true Americanism, and exemplifies how that vision can be attained.[37]

In the eagle's dexter talon is an olive branch, — a symbol of peace, — with thirteen leaves and thirteen berries. These numbers added together result in the number twenty-six, which in Freemasonry and Qabalistic thought relates to Jehovah. It must be noted that the eagles of the monarchies which preceded the United States carried the symbols of war on the dexter side, and by extension be concluded that the national arms proclaim the principle that the primary aim of the United States shall be to establish peace. And so, it is for this reason that the eagle faces the olive branch, denoting the idea that any nation which dedicates itself to the establishment of peace dedicates itself to the quest for an ever-increasing knowledge of God, or Jehovah.[38]

The arrows in the eagle's left talon represent the power of war. However, arrows are more than emblems of war; they are also symbols of aim denoting purpose, will, and intention. The number thirteen in Hebrew is related to "love" and "unity", and when all these ideas are combined, we could conclude that the cardinal principle of true

Americanism is that recourse to arms should be for no other purpose than the maintenance of a just cause, having for its objective the establishment and preservation of unity and love.

The colors red, white, and blue, Qabalistically yield the number 103; and the interpretation of the **stone of Adam** or **The Perfect Red Stone**, which in Freemasonry, relates to the perfect ashlar or squared stone, — symbolic of perfected humanity. This number, which relates to the colors in both the flag and the shield, is a number considered to be related to the Ancient of Days, and refers to the Divine protection, under which the country exists. It also signifies "builders", or "masons" and therefore the national colors spell out, by Goematria, the name of the fraternity, which did so much for the American Cause. Case further states that the dexter wing of the eagle has thirty-two feathers, which is the number for the Paths of Wisdom, and is the summary of the Qabalistic philosophy, as well as the number of ordinary degrees in Scottish Rite Freemasonry.[39] The sinister wing has thirty-three feathers, and corresponds to the thirty-third degree of the same, conferred on Masons for outstanding service.

The total number of feathers is sixty-five, which means **together in unity**, and is the expression used in the first degree of the Masonic ritual. These are the same ideas expressed by the motto: "**E Pluribus Unum**", which also contains thirteen letters, and suggests that true Americanism cannot be understood to mean rule by the many, as a false definition of democracy implies. Such a rule is but tyranny of the mob, and it is for that reason that the motto indicates a move away form the hydra-headed multifariousness of clashing opinions and toward a singleness of purpose and effort based on real knowledge of the One, from which all things proceed, in other words — a movement of the mind away from the many-ness of external appearance towards the idea of Oneness. This idea has been rejected by academics in the fields of science and philosophy, but today the field of physics accepts this postulate, a concept that has always been an assumption of Qabalistic and Hermetic thought, and which has been the source for the ideals of the founders of the United States — that all things are from One Reality.[40]

The crest over the eagle's head includes a golden glory, an azure field, and thirteen silver stars. Gold represents the Sun; azure the sky-father, the god of thunder and Jupiter who is the Master of the Lodge above. The constellation of silver refers to the letter "G", seen in most Masonic temples, and refers to the Hebrew word, Gimel, which represents the High Priestess, who sits between the two pillars of Solomon's temple. The constellation of thirteen stars is composed of pentagrams arranged in such a way to form a hexagram, — a symbol of **Solomon's Seal**, known throughout eternity to represent the forces of the macrocosm, or the "kingdom of the heavens." These forces influence all things in manifestation and all the cycles in and through which they manifest. The pentagram is another symbol of the perfected ashlar, or perfected man, whose mind in this state has dominion over the elements.

Surrounding the constellation is a golden glory divided into twenty-four equal parts, a Masonic reference to the twenty-four-inch gauge, emblematic of the twenty-four-hour day, which is divided in three equal parts of eight hours each. This is the number of Jesus or Joshua, who succeeded Moses in liberating the children of Israel from Pharaoh and from the bondage to form, or matter.[41]

Behind the azure background are twenty-six horizontal lines, the number name of Jehovah, another reference to the master of the Lodge above. Around the glory are nineteen clouds, a reference to Eve, who all major religions know as the cause of form that brought Spirit into Matter, and through veiling the One Light, manifests it into matter. The right foundation by which one becomes a doer is symbolized on the obverse Seal by the nine feathers of the eagle's tail. The number nine represents Basis, Foundation or Yesod, which adds to eighty, and is also the number of the tower, a symbol of Mars, the ruler of the sign of Scorpio, the ascendant of the United Sates, and the energy which must be transmuted so that the United States can grasp a higher vision of its destiny. The number nine also refers to the control of the Martian forces necessary to accomplish the goal.[42]

The combination of the numbers comprising the nineteen clouds, the nine tail feathers, and the twenty-four divisions of the glory, total fifty-two (4x13), which is the number of "ben", the Son, the Christos or Jesus. This is the Mystical Son and universal light-energy made flesh, the one who dwells among us, and is the central point of illumination personified as Horus in the Egyptian rituals. He is the Word or Logos made flesh and the power whereby all things are made possible. Today, this truth is a fundamental postulate of science and one which Qabalists, Hermeticists, Rosicrucians, and Freemasons in the eighteenth century understood as that single energy, like light in its essential nature, which is the underlying power expressed in every kind of vital activity.[43]

The **Declaration of Independence** implies what the Seal symbolizes Qabalistically and Hermetically, that the basis of what the founding fathers fought for, is truth. That truth is that the underlying law of the universe is the law of liberty. Mankind is at present enslaved to materialism, but the hour is striking when a revolution greater than that of 1176 is at hand. This revolution will not involve armies, but will be one of consciousness, involving the human soul, a revolution where the shackles of hateful servitude will be thrown off and the false standards of value will be overturned. Prophets have foreseen this time, but their visions have been ignored, misunderstood, and disregarded. However, the perfect law of liberty is now being more and more greatly realized in the affairs of men.[44]

In *The Secret Destiny of America by* Manly P. Hall insists that the bird drawn by the designers was the Phoenix. This selection could be understood to reflect the evolutionary process of the United States, as it rises out of the ashes of its transformation, since, as with everyone who passes through the gates of initiation, one must die and become twice born. This bird of ancient symbolism is the same in size and shape as the eagle and is described as having a body of glossy purple feathers, with the plumes in the tail being alternately red and blue. The head is light in color with a circlet of golden plumage, and a crest of feathers of brilliant colors at the back of the head. Its home is reputed to be in the distant parts of Arabia, in a nest of frankincense and myrrh. It is said that at any given time only one of these birds is alive and that it lives for 500 years, with its body opening up at death, thus allowing for the emergence of the newborn Phoenix. For this reason, the Phoenix is considered to be representative of immortality and resurrection. It is one of those symbols with a tangible origin, and is one of the signs of the secret order of the ancient world, especially of the initiates of those orders who are considered twice-born.

The wisdom conferred by the process of Initiation constitutes a new life. The Phoenix, as a symbol, is emblematic of royalty, power, superiority and immortality, and, in meaning is identical to the Phoenix in China, Egypt, and Greece as well as to the Thunder Bird of the American Indians. But, whatever the bird on the obverse side of the seal is, it is nevertheless clearly the stamp of the **Order of the Quest**, and in that same context, the reverse of the Seal is irrefutably even more so related to the Ancient Mysteries.[45]

Symbolism of the Reverse

This side of the seal displays the Pyramid of Gizah, believed by the Egyptians to be a shrine to the gods Thoth and Hermes, personifications of Universal Wisdom. It is composed of thirteen courses of masonry, showing seventy-two stones, and is without a capstone. Its upper platform floats a triangle containing the All-Seeing Eye, surrounded by rays of light. The thirty-foot square platform shows no evidence of ever containing a capstone. This is an appropriate symbol since it is representative of human society itself, i.e. unfinished and incomplete. The converging, ascending angles and faces of the pyramid represent the common aspiration of humanity; the radiant triangle with its All-Seeing Eye that floats above is the symbol of the esoteric orders. The triangle is in the shape of the Greek letter Delta, the first letter of the name of God, who is the

Divine part of nature that completes the works of men. The Pyramid could, therefore, be called the Universal House with its unfinished apex or — the Great Architect of the Universe.

In the legend of old Atlantis it is said that a great University stood in its center in the shape of an immense Pyramid, with an observatory at the top of it, for the study of the stars. This temple is shadowed in the seal of the New Atlantis. The question then is: was it the old philosophers who sealed the new nation with the eternal emblems, so that all nations might know the purpose for which the new country was founded?[46] Case describes the symbolic statement of the reverse seal as displaying the essentials of true Americanism and as a marvel of ingenuity. The upper motto: Annuit Coeptis, like E Pluribus Unum, of the Observe, contains thirteen letters. The date on the lower course of masonry of the pyramid contains nine letters and is in the same position as the nine tail feathers of the bird on the Obverse side of the Seal. The motto: **Novus Ordo Seclorum**, meaning the **New World Order**, contains seventeen letters, and these three together total thirty-nine, or 13 x 3. Qabalistically, the numbers, words and names repeatedly speak to the Divine destiny for which this great nation was brought into manifestation. A further comprehensive look at the esoteric interpretations of the reverse seal can be found in Paul Foster Case's treatise, **The Great Seal of the United States**.

The motto: **Novous Ordo Sseclorum — The New World Order** — is represented by the capstone, which completes the unfinished structure depicted on the seal; and the foundation of the work, which will complete and perfect the New World Order, must be the recognition of the Christos in every human heart. This work must proceed from the principle summed up in the meaning of the name Jesus, the nature of reality is to liberate. The New World Order must begin with the principle set forth in the words of the Declaration of Independence, which states that the laws of Nature, and of God, are but variations of the one basic law of liberty. In the end, the real nature of the New World Order at the bottom of the reverse seal is that the wise men, who established the republic, knew the time would come when the work of the men represented by the unfinished pyramid, would have to be completed by a power higher than that possessed by ordinary men.

It is only when the individual "stones" of the temple of government, the persons composing the body politic, awaken to the truths so clearly set out in the Declaration of Independence and in the symbolism of the Seal, that we shall see the completion of the structure began in 1776.[47]

America is in great need of a vision of its purpose! As each age comes into manifestation, it brings with it definite philosophic revelations of thought designed to solve the problems peculiar to that age, and to help bridge the ethical intervals between generations. This age demands a doctrine of synthesis and a government founded on the philosophy of mutual understanding, where the black and white, the Jew and the gentile, the Chinese and the Turk have a fundamental premise of one denominator on which all can agree. Humanity has become so advanced and strong that it would be dangerous to allow its parts to remain fragmented. We can no longer maintain our position of isolated individualism without endangering the rights of all men. Democracy is the realization of the unity of life, and in this realization, all competitive standards of civilization which are based on the erroneous assumption that one part of life can survive without, or at the expense of the other, is shattered, because it is upon the basis of competition that the whole structure of human sorrow is erected.[48] The destiny and plan devised in secrecy so long ago in far places, upon and above the earth, were brought into manifestation to be fulfilled openly as the greatest wonder born out of time.

CHAPTER NINE

Freemasonry and Governance

As we move into the New Age, no governance can be successful or effective without those in positions of influence over the minds of the public having a clear understanding of the fact that Man is a spiritual being; and a being who has been immersed in the illusion of matter and is seeking the way to regain his sense of wholeness. Without a philosophical understanding of his origin and destiny, in which the mind is trained and made able to grasp the truth of his life, he, the individual, and humanity in general, linger in poverty of spirit with little hope of finding liberation from the bondage of ignorance in which he is entangled. It should be the goal of every government that its citizens become self-governing, since this is the divine plan and purpose for humanity. Interestingly, each earthly system of government is designed for the explicit purpose of accomplishing this plan. It is for this reason, I have chosen to devote an entire chapter to the relevance of Masonry in Governance, and to present a system put in place from the beginning of time, which was designed to accomplish the physical, emotional, and mental development needed to achieve the goal of liberation from ignorance. Masonry is a veiled and mysterious expression of the difficult science of spiritual life; the understanding of which, requires special and informed guidance on the one hand and the genuine and earnest desire for knowledge on the other, as well as a great capacity for spiritual perception on the part of those seeking to be instructed.[1]

Masonry is a modern externalization of great systems of initiation that existed for spiritual instruction of men and women in all parts of the world since the beginning of time. The great world-religions, which are two-fold in their purpose, have been established to teach in their respective manners the same truths as the mystery systems have taught. There has always been an external, elementary

143

popular doctrine, which has served for the instruction of the masses who are insufficiently prepared for deeper teaching; and concurrently, an interior, advanced doctrine, a more secret knowledge, preserved for more mature minds and into which only proficient and properly prepared candidates voluntarily seek to participate. This is true of all peoples of every race and culture whether we are referring to India, Europe, Mexico, Africa, Asia, the Druids, Egypt, Italy or Greece. Temples of initiation have always existed for the discipline of body and mind to enable the acquisition of the secret knowledge and to develop the spiritual faculties through experimental processes of initiation, of which the present systems are but faint reflections.[2]

The Philosophy of Masonry

For those with any discernment inside and outside of the Masonic Order, it is becoming clear that the system of masonry contains something deeper than a code of elementary morality. Candidates begin to recognize that there is no virtue in continuing to imitate the customs of ancient trade-guilds just for its own sake, or for the maintenance of social and philanthropic organizations when many other organizations are fully capable of doing so. An examination of the Third Degree, which is the great central legend of the Craft, and is the climax of the Craft System, reveals that the work of the Order is to initiate candidates into certain secrets and mysteries as they pass through the requisite stages of development and unfoldment and in which there is an increase in the understanding of the mysteries.

The meaning of Masonry is not noticeable at once, and unless the mind is properly prepared and the understanding carefully trained, the individual is unlikely to ever participate in the real inner secrets and mysteries of Masonry. The theory of Masonic progress dictates that every member admitted to the Order enters in a state of darkness and ignorance and as he progresses, he is brought into light and knowledge. In other words, he enters the Lodge as a rough ashlar, and it is his responsibility to develop his character and understanding, which will ultimately make him a finished and perfect cube because of what he has learned and practiced.[3] The first stage and genesis concerns the surface-value of the doctrine and an acquaintance with the literal side of the knowledge imparted, which the candidate acquires upon entering the Order. Unfortunately, the majority of those who enter the Order never progress beyond this first stage. At this stage of knowledge, the Craft is regarded as a social, semi-public, semi-secret community, and participation is viewed as agreeable and advantageous for sociable or even ulterior purposes; and the goal and ambition of the Mason is to attain to office, high advancement, and to wear a breast full of decorations. He takes a literal, superficial and historic view of the subject-matter of the doctrine. To him, the height of Masonic proficiency becomes the ability to perform ceremonial work with dignity and effectiveness, to know the instruction catechisms by heart so that not one syllable is wrongly rendered, — all qualities that belong to the rough ashlar stage of Masonic conception, through which most must pass.[4] The Craft, in general, struggles to attain the goal, of becoming the "perfected cube," and, to accomplish this, it is incumbent on every thoughtful man to ask and receive answers to the following questions:

1. Who am I?
2. Where did I come from?
3. What am I here to do?
4. Where am I going?[5]

In the quiet moments of everyone's life, it might be safe to say he asks these questions, and it becomes the paramount wish of every heart to find the answers to these questions. It is presumed that the Masonic candidate enters the Order in search of light on these subjects, which he was unable to find elsewhere. If the motive for becoming a candidate is driven by any other impulse than a genuine desire for knowledge about these problems and a sincere desire to be of service to all creatures, his candidature is a less than a worthy one. In this regard, no one should be solicited to join the Order since these matters of sacred and critical importance should be contemplated within the context of the first impulses that originated within the candidate's own heart, which is always the first place of preparation.

It must be the cry and knocking of his inward need that provides the motive that allows the door to the mysteries to be opened and the seeker to find the help he seeks. As the candidate proceeds on his quest, he learns from his superior brethren at a certain stage that he, like them is in search of something that is lost, and now has some hope of finding; this is the whole purpose of Masonry, the quest after this lost *something*. It is also the motive behind all systems of religion and philosophy within Orders of Initiation, past and present. In the reflective moments of every individual, he realizes the sense of moral imperfection, of ignorance, and of restricted knowledge about himself and his surroundings. He is aware of some radical deficiency in his constitution, which, if it were found and made good, would satisfy this craving for information, completeness and perfection, and would **lead him from darkness to light**, placing him beyond ignorance and the touch of many illnesses of the flesh.[6]

The reference made to '*the fall of man*' is of a doctrine that forms the philosophic basis of all systems of religion and of all the great systems of the mysteries, and of initiation. Throughout the history of humanity, this event has been recounted in parables, allegories, myths and legends. However, the single meaning is that humanity has fallen away from its original parent source and place, where Man is imbedded in the eternal center of life. Man has been projected from this center to the circumference, and because of this, he is undergoing a period of restriction, ignorance, discipline and experience in this world, which will ultimately return him to the center from which he came, and to which he rightfully belongs. The story of *Paradise Lost* by Milton, which emphasizes this fact and the sense of loss, is the theme of Masonry.[7]

Beneath a veil of allegory, which describes the intention to build a certain temple whose completion was hindered by an untimely disaster, Masonry implies that Humanity is the real temple whose building was obstructed. It is, Humanity, who is both the builder (craftsman) and at the same time, the building material; and this is what is intended to be an unparalleled structure. Owing to a certain unhappy event, *The Fall,* mankind is living in this world under conditions where the genuine and full secrets of his nature are, for the time being, lost to him. During this time, the full powers of the soul of man are curtailed by the limitations of physical life, and during his apprenticeship of probation and discipline, he must endure substituted knowledge derived through his limited and fallible senses. The greatest virtue and purpose of the initiatory process is the method by which both the candidate and Humanity can regain what is lost. It holds the promise that with divine assistance, and the diligent, patient, and persevering work of the individual, he will be made worthy to participate in the genuine realities instead of the imperfect shadows that are part of his present experience. This subject of emerging from darkness into light is mirrored in the craft ceremonial. The East of the lodge is designated as the symbolic center and the source of Light, and is the place of the throne of the Master of all Life. On the other hand, the West, is the place of the disappearing sun, and is this world of imperfection and darkness from which the divine spiritual light is, in large measure, withdrawn and shines only by reflection.

The ceremonies the candidate passes through are symbolic of the stages of progress every man, formally or informally makes on his way to self-purification and self-building, until he at last dies to his present natural self. He is then raised out of a state of imperfection and emerged once again into perfect union with his divine self and glory into whose image he is shaped and conformed. It is, in this sense, that Masonry becomes a working philosophy for those sincerely inquiring into the purpose and destiny of human life. For those who feel that their lives and their path have been a series of missteps and irregular steps made haphazardly, and under hoodwinked conditions, it provides the means of being initiated into reliable knowledge.[8] Masonry contains many invaluable secrets, which are not those formally communicated ceremonially in symbolic signs, tokens and words to candidates. Instead, those secrets are the deep and hidden things of the soul, which are instinctively kept locked up in the recesses and safe repository of every heart, and can only be communicated to those who share the common sympathetic interests in the deeper problems and mysteries of life.[9]

Masonry's Sirius Origin

The ancient markers and the ancient mysteries, so well preserved by the Masonic tradition and securely preserved in the Masonic ritual, await the day of resurrection. Humanity also waits and looks forward to the return of Atlantean days when God Himself walked among men. Divinity was present in physical form because the members of the hierarchy guided and directed the affairs of Humanity to the degree that free will permitted. We know without any shadow of doubt that these Masters of Wisdom still walk among men. My hope in going into depth with this information is to help dismiss the many fallacies regarding this most profound subject of Masonry, which is so essential to humanity's evolution.

Technically, everyone is a Freemason, since everyone's goal is to build a perfected temple of light in which his spirit can dwell, permanently. Similarly, planet Earth is also a Lodge, one in which the rituals of life are being enacted. This individual temple or lodge is the personality vehicle, consisting of the physical, emotional and mental bodies, in which the movements of time and space are gradually bringing each individual to a point of self-knowledge, and it is for this reason that the Lodge rituals exist.[10]

A history of Masonry reveals an influence of the Star system Sirius, which dates way back to the very dawn of time, even before the Jewish dispensation. Its purpose is closely related to the restoration of the mysteries, which have held the clue to the platform upon which the restored teaching can be based. In the structure of Masonry can be seen expressed in powerful ritual, and organized detailed rites, the history of Man's forward movement upon the Path of Return through the process of Initiation. The ancient mysteries I write about were originally given to Humanity by the Hierarchy of Masters, who received them from the Great White Lodge on Sirius. These members of the Hierarchy on Earth are the Custodians of the Mysteries and will give these secrets openly to Man when his mind and his will-to-good become closely aligned to condition human behavior. Only then will Humanity be able to grasp these imminent revelations and be trusted with these secrets. Both Masonry and the Churches have failed humanity in their divinely assigned task.[11] However, a new form of Masonry will emerge in the New Age and its foundation will be a newly interpreted and enlightened Christianity, having relation to theology and being universal in nature— this will be the religion of the Age of Aquarius. The Jewish foundation on which present Masonry rests is over five thousand years old and must disappear. As Mankind merges back into spirit due to the influence which is proceeding from Sirius, he will increasingly pull away from an obsession with form or matter.[12]

The History of Modern Masonry

Manly P. Hall in his book **Lectures on Ancient Philosophy** gives a robust account of the history of Masonry in which he reveals that the secret doctrine which runs through Masonic symbols, and in whose continuation the invisible body is dedicated, has its source in three ancient and exalted orders— the Dionysiac artificers, the Roman Collegia, and the Arabian Rosicrucians. Hall states that the Dionysians were the master builders of the ancient world. This order was originally founded to design and erect the theatres of Dionysus in which tragic dramas of rituals were enacted. Eventually, the order was elevated by popular demand to greater dignity, until finally it was entrusted with the planning and construction of all public edifices concerned with the commonwealth or the worship of heroes and gods.

Hiram, King of Tyre, a patron of the Dionysiac flourished in Tyre and Sidon and Hiram Abiff, according to the sacred account, was himself a Grand Master of this noble order of pagan builders.

Even King Solomon, in his wisdom, accepted the services of Hiram Abiff, who was a famous craftsman of a different faith who journeyed from his own country to design and supervise the building on Mount Moriah of the everlasting house to the true God. The tools of the builders' craft were first used by the Dionysians as symbols under which they hid the mysteries of the soul and the secrets of human regeneration. They likened man to the rough ashlar, which when *trued* into a finished block through the instrument of reason, could then be fitted into the structure of that living and eternal temple built without the sound of a hammer, the voice of workmen or any tool of contention.[13] Hall in *Freemasons and Rosicrucians—The Enlightened,* states that the Roman Collegia, a branch of the Dionysiacs, had among its membership initiated artisans who fashioned the impressive monuments of the Eternal City. The adepts who trued the stones and carved their gnostic symbols on them from earlier times, initiated stonecutters and marked their perfected works with the secret emblems of their crafts and the degrees they had attained. Through this legacy, unborn generations will be able to realize that master builders of the first ages also labored toward the same goals as do men today.[14] Hall further states that the Mysteries of Egypt and Persia, had found haven in the Arabian Desert, and reached Europeans by way of the Knights Templars and the Rosicrucians and that the Temple of the Rose Cross at Damascus had preserved the secret philosophy of the Rose of Sharon.

The Mysteries from the Arabian Desert also included that of the Druses of the Lebanon Mountains, who still retained the mysticism of ancient Syria. These are the Dervishes who lean on their carved and crotched sticks, while still meditating upon the secret instruction perpetuated from the days of the four caliphs. From the far places of Irak (Iraq) and the hidden retreats of the Sufi mystics, the Ancient Wisdom found its way into Europe. The Templars had become wise in the Mysteries celebrated in Mecca thousands of years before the advent of Mohammed. They had read from the dread book of Anthropos, and had discovered parts of the Great Arcanum. It was bringing this knowledge back with them from the East to Europe, that most angered the Church, and which doomed the Templars to die. However, Truth is eternal and the so-called revelations of Truth that come in different religions are only a re-emphasis of an ever-existing doctrine whose beginning was on Sirius.[15]

It, therefore, becomes clear that Moses did not originate a new religion for Israel, but instead adapted the Mysteries of Egypt to the needs of Israel. All evidence seems to indicate that the secret doctrine of Egypt was the prototype of Israel's mystery religion. Jesus was a Rabin of the Jews and a teacher of the Holy Law who discoursed in the synagogue and interpreted the Torah according to the teaching of the sect, but brought no new messages, nor were his reformations radical. What he did was to tear away the veil from the temple, so that Pharisee, Sadducee, publican and sinner alike might together behold the glory of an ageless faith. Hall continues by saying that likewise, Buddha, in his reformation of Indian philosophy, did not reject the esoteric secrets of the Brahmins but adopted the teachings to the needs of the Indian masses. By doing so, he unlocked the mystic secrets of the Holy Vedas and disclosed them to all, regardless of caste distinction, so that everyone could partake in their wisdom and share in the common heritage of good.[16]

Mohammed, on the other hand, while in his cavern on Mount Hira, did not pray for new truths, but for the old truths to be re-stated in their original purity and simplicity, because he wanted mankind to again understand God's clear revelation to the patriarchs. What might not be known is that the Mysteries of Islam had been celebrated in the great black cube of the Caaba centuries before the holy pilgrimage. The Prophet was, in fact, the reformer of a decadent pagandom who smashed idols and purified the defiled Mysteries. [17] So, in the end, no prophet or savior ever preached a doctrine which was his own. They only re-told, in the language of their time, the Ancient Wisdom preserved within the Mysteries since the dawn of human consciousness. This is also true of the Masonic Mysteries we have today which contain the great principles of universal order, pregnant with hope and life for millions seeking to journey out of darkness into Light.

The Lodge

William L. Wilmhurst, one of the great Masons of the twentieth century in his book *The Meaning of Masonry*, says the form of the Lodge is officially described as an "oblong square' in length between East and West; in width, between North and South, and in depth, from the surface of the Earth to its center, and as high as the heavens. The interpretation of this alludes to the human individual and as Man as the Lodge. Just as the Lodge is an assemblage of brothers and fellows who meet to elucidate and expound upon the mysteries of the Craft, so is the individual man a composite being, made up of various properties and faculties assembled together in his being to achieve harmonious interaction, and the working out of the purpose of life. Everything in masonry is symbolic and figurative of Man, his human constitution and his spiritual evolution; and the Masonic Lodge is sacramental of the individual Mason. When the individual seeks admission to the Lodge and is given his first entry, it is symbolic of his first entry into the science of knowing himself. In accordance with very ancient philosophical doctrine, the number four is the arithmetic symbol of everything manifested in physical form, and Man's organism is symbolized by a four-square or four-sided building.[18]

The number three and triangle expresses Spirit, which is un-manifested and not physical. To become objective, Spirit projected itself to wear a material form or body, as denoted by the number four; the quadrangle or square, which are the cardinal points in space: east, west, north and south and are also four in number. Everything manifested is a compound of the four basic metaphysical elements, which the ancients call: fire, water, air and earth. The four-sidedness of the Lodge is a reminder that the human organism is composed of these four elements in balanced proportions, — Water represents the psychic nature; Air, the mentality; Fire, the will and nervous force, and Earth, the condensation in which the other three become stabilized and encased. The Lodge is an oblong or duplicated square because man's organism is not physical alone but consists of an ethereal counterpart in the astral body, — an extension of the physical nature and a compound of the same four elements in a more tenuous form.[19]

Furthermore, the four sides of the Lodge have the following added significance:

East — represents Man's highest and most spiritual mode of consciousness, and though very little developed in most, and still latent and slumbering, it becomes active in moments of stress and deep emotion. East also represents the way of knowledge associated with spiritual intuition.

West — is the polar-opposite of the East, representing man's normal, rational understanding and commonsense, and the consciousness he employs in the temporal affairs of his day-to-day material-minded world. The direction West belongs to that way of knowledge called reason.

South — is the mid-way point and half-way house between the extremes of East and West, between spiritual intuition and rational understanding. This point denotes abstract intellectuality, where the intellectual power develops to its highest, just as the sun reaches its meridian splendor in the South. Intellectual ideation belongs to this way of knowledge.

North — the antipode of the South is the place of intellect and morality and ignorance, symbolizing mere sense-reactions and impressions received by the lowest and least reliable mode of perception— our physical sense nature. Sense impression is, therefore, the way of knowledge associated with this direction.[20]

The degree of one's consciousness is a function of one's education, development, outlook on life and knowledge of truth, which is limited and restricted in the ordinary man. Full and perfect knowledge is possible only when man's cognitive faculties, his spiritual principle, his deep seeing vision and his consciousness have been awakened; and this state is only possible in the true Master who, like the four sides of the Lodge, is adjusted and in a state of perfect balance.

Depth —is the surface of the earth to its center, refers to the distance or difference of degree between the superficial consciousness of our earthly mentality and the supreme Divine degree of consciousness that is resident in man's spiritual center; it is only accessible when MAN opens the door of his Lodge that leads to the center, symbolically, and function from and within this Divine place.[21]

Height — "*is even as high as the heavens,*" indicates that range of consciousness possible to humanity when he has developed his potential to the fullest. Man has sprung from the earth, and has evolved through the lower kingdoms of nature to his present stage, but he is yet to complete his evolution and become the god-like being, which will be achieved once he unifies his consciousness with the Omniscient through the Initiation process. To do this, he must scale the "*height*" to attain this expansion of consciousness by the use of the ladder of many rounds, with the three principal ones being Faith, Hope and Charity or Love, being —the greatest of the three. It is important to note that all these are attainable, since every commonplace incident in one's daily life, if correctly interpreted, and its purpose in the general pattern of life eventually understood, as essential to the Plan. An explanation of these three qualifications sees *Faith* as the possibility of attaining the end in view. *Hope* as a persistent fervent desire for the fulfillment of that desire; and an unbounded *Love*, as God in all men and all things despite their outward appearances. By thinking no evil, love identifies the mind and nature in the aspirant with the ultimate Good. This enlargement of consciousness is in no way dependent upon intellectual attainment or book-knowledge and learning, even though these are lesser staves on the ladder of attainment.[22]

The Pillars — Wisdom, Strength and Beauty, the three

grand pillars that support the Lodge, relate to the triple properties resident in the soul of man. The candidate will become:

1. Conscious of an increase in the perceptive faculty and understanding;

2. Aware of having tapped into a previously unsuspected source of power, which gives him enhanced mental strength and self-confidence;

3. Conscious of developing graces of character, speech, and conduct previously foreign to him.[23]

The Floor — a checkerboard layout of black and white squares forms the groundwork of the Lodge, and indicates the dual quality of everything connected with the terrestrial life and the physical groundwork of human nature, the mortal body, its appetites and affections. It further indicates that the web of life is a mingled yarn characterized by an inextricably interblended good and evil, light and shade, joy and sorrow, positive and negative.

All the pairs of opposites are intertwined and govern our lives, and these experiences are prescribed for humanity until such time that it has outgrown the lessons they teach. When man is ready for advancement to a condition where this checker-work existence or these opposites cease to be perceived as opposites, but are realized as unity or synthesis, he enters an internal place of attainment where the peace that passes understanding is achieved. At this place of consciousness, he comes to know that the dark and the light are both alike, and those previous concepts of good and evil, joy and pain, etc., are transcended and are found to be sublimated into a condition that combines both. This is an attainment open to every Mason who can eventually walk the floor as a High Priest.[24]

The Covering —is in sharp contrast to its black and white flooring, and is described as a *celestial canopy of various colors as in the heavens.* While the flooring symbolizes the earthly sensuous nature, the ceiling typifies the properties of man's ethereal or heavenly nature, which are resident in him. Each is the reverse of, and the opposite pole of the other; the body is densely composed and visible, while the other which is tenuous and invisible, is called the aura of the human. At first the Masonic student accepts these non-physical facts provisionally, eventually coming to know them as certainties, as he realizes that he entered the craft for the following reasons:

— To receive light on the nature of his own being;

— That the Order will engage to assist him in gaining illumination regarding matters of which he is ignorant, and that the teachings and symbols were devised by wise and competent instructors, and;

— Because a humble and receptive mental attitude, rather than a critical and hostile approach toward the symbols and their meanings, will help to advance him.

The individual's aura reflects his level of conscious development. The more advanced an individual, the cleaner and brighter the colors of the sun, the moon and the stars he radiates. This radiant *clothing, covering* or *coat* of many colors, referred to in regard to Joseph, is what the science of astronomy or astrology is all about.[25]

The Letter "G"

Masonry is spoken of both as an art, founded on the principles of geometry, as well as a science dealing with the cultivation and improvement of the human mind. The customs and usages are said to be derived from the ancient Egyptians whose philosophers were unwilling to expose their mysteries to vulgar eyes and unprepared minds. They, therefore, concealed their principles of philosophy under signs and symbols, such as those we see perpetuated in the Masonic Order.

The compilers and initiates who were well versed in the secret tradition and philosophy of the mysteries, were also acutely aware of the deeper meaning and mystical sense of the Holy Scriptures. They were confronted with the dual task of giving faithful expression to esoteric doctrine and, at the same time, masking the information so that the full sense would not be understood; thus, without some effort or enlightenment, they would convey nothing to those who were unripe and unworthy for this wisdom teaching or gnosis. To the ordinary man, geometry, the art upon which the entire system of Masonry is founded, is nothing more than the branch of mathematics associated with the problems of Euclid, and unrelated to Masonic ceremonial ideals.[26] The truth is quite the reverse. Geometry was one of the seven noble arts and sciences of ancient philosophy, meaning, literally, *the science of earth measurement*. However, the Earth the ancients referred to was not the physical planet as most humans think, but the primordial substance or undifferentiated soul-stuff, out of which we humans were created, the Mother Earth from which all sprung and to which all must undoubtedly return. As the scriptures teach, man was made from the dust of the ground or earth, which is the fundamental substance of his being. It, therefore, becomes essential that this *earth substance* of which man is made be *measured* and *investigated* to understand its nature and properties. Since no competent builder constructs a building without first satisfying himself about the nature of the materials with which he plans to build, likewise, in the royal, spiritual, or speculative art of Masonry, no Mason can build the temple of his own soul without first understanding the nature of the raw materials he must work on.[27]

Geometry is synonymous with self-knowledge, and the understanding of the basic substance of one's being, its properties and its potentials. The ancient temples had the following sentence inscribed over them: *know thyself and thou shalt know the universe and God*, which implies that the uninitiated man is without knowledge of himself. Secondly, that when he attains that knowledge he will realize himself to be no longer the separate distinct individual he now supposes himself to be, but a microcosm or summary of all that is, and identified with the Being of God. Masonry, then, is the science of the attainment of this supreme knowledge based on the principles of Geometry as is defined here. It is important to understand that the earth referred to here is the corruptible, impermanent, and physical matter, which forms a temporary encasement for the imperishable true *earth* or *substance* of our souls, and allows for entry into sense-relations with the physical world.

It must be kept in mind that Masonry deals not so much with the transient outward body, but with the eternal inward being of man, though this temporal body is intimately involved with the inward man. Fundamentally, it is the understanding that the immortal soul of man is the ruined temple needing to be re-built upon the principles of spiritual science. The unruly wills and affections of the mortal body are what stand in the way of that achievement. The rubble of this ruined temple needs to be cleared before the new foundations are set and the new structure erected. However, even the rubble can be of used when re-arranged and worked into the new erection; in this same way man's outer temporal nature can be disciplined and utilized in his re-construction and regeneration. To accomplish this, Man must first have a full understanding of the material he has to work with, and upon. It is, therefore, essential that he becomes acquainted with what is called "the form of his Lodge.[28] In his book *The Masonic Letter G*, Paul Foster Case points out that it is almost impossible to have a true appreciation and understanding for Masonry without knowledge of the Qabalistic Tree of Life with its insights into the true nature of Man and the Cosmos. He goes on to develop the concept of the relationship between the geometry upon which the building and architectural symbolism of Masonry is based, and the Gematria of the Qabalists; a system of number correspondences to words and phrases that reveals the inner meanings behind the numbers, measurements and geometrical proportions prominent in both Old and New Testament.[29] He assigns the letter 'G' to the Hebrew name Gimel, the word for camel, and to the term travel, which sums up the whole work of the Craft. The camel is a symbol of that mark of the Master Mason whose ability is to *travel into foreign countries*. Masons speak of themselves as traveling East in search of Light and their quest is indicated as being a search for origins and causes.

The West is a place of sunset, the close of the day, and the end of a cycle of work or manifestation, therefore, symbolizing the things and forms produced by the Grand Architect's work in the universe. And so, to travel from West to East is to pass from these forms and appearances to their hidden causes and from those causes back to the First Cause, the Master Principle, whose location is in the East.

The Masonic lectures state that through the science of Geometry, Man is able to trace nature through her various windings to her most concealed recesses. But to accomplish this one must, of necessity:

- Move in an inward direction toward the center

- Through a winding movement, be taken from the surface to the center; in a spiral.[30]

Gimel and the letter 'G' are also assigned to the High Priestess, the woman seated between the two pillars of Solomon's Temple, in the center of which is the meeting place for King Solomon, Hiram, King of Tyre, and Hiram Abiff. This is the Sanctum Sanctorium or Holy of Holies where the Shekinah dwells.

The letter Gimel is also regarded by the wise men of Israel as the alphabetical sign of the sacred wisdom, founded on the science of geometry, and an ancient and universal symbol of the Grand Architect. The heart of Freemasonry is an esoteric doctrine founded on the science of geometry and expressed by means of geometric figures and theorems. In fact, in the old Masonic constitutions, it is specifically stated that Masonry and Geometry are one and the same.[31] That the letter G would be placed in the East of the Lodge, the direction assigned to Venus, the Divine Mother, is also no coincidence. It is the equivalent of the Greek letter gamma, and is the initial of Gaia, the Earth Mother, and Geometria, which is the science by which the powers of the Mother are measured; but the shape of the letter gamma is Γ and alludes to the Mason's square.[32]

Gimel is from the verb gawmal, which means to limit or bring to an end, and therefore to ripen, and reward with benefit or recompense. Having been measured and trued, the Craft brings Man from his crude state of ignorance to the highest possible limits of human attainment. Through this spiritual ripening process, he is raised to the sublime degree of Master Mason. He is now competent not only to travel in *foreign countries*, but also ready to receive Master's wages, as one who has completed the journey from West to East designated by the letter "G" and the number Three.[33]

The Hiram Legend

Central to the Masonic story is the Grand Architect, Hiram Abiff, who is Grand Master of the Dionysiac Architects, a Widow's son and is of no royal descent, who is said to have had no equal among the artisans of the earth. When the wise man and beloved of God, Solomon, builder of the Everlasting House, and the Grand Master of the Lodge in Jerusalem, ascended to the throne of his father David, he consecrated his life to the erection of a temple to God, and a palace for the kings of Israel.[34]

Solomon thought of no one more qualified to build this temple but Hiram Abiff, the Master Builder. The temple to be erected was no ordinary structure. It alluded to the temple not made with hands eternal in the heavens, according to a pre-ordained plan. King Solomon was assisted by the Hiram King of Tyre who supplied the building materials, the skillful artificer, Hiram Abiff, and the large companies of craftsmen and laborers. This temple, of which all material edifices are but types and symbols, is the collective body of humanity itself. A perfected Humanity was the great Temple, which in the counsels of the Most-High, was intended to be erected in the mystical Holy City.[35] The three great Master-builders, Solomon, and the two Hirams, are a triad corresponding in a manner with the Holy Trinity of the Christian religion. Hiram Abiff being the chief architect is he *by whom all things were made, and in whom the whole building fitly framed together grow-eth unto a holy habitation in the Lord.* The materials of this temple are the souls of men, as living stones are fellow craftsmen and collaborators with the divine plan and purpose. The legend of this Master-builder, Hiram Abiff, is a great allegory of Masonry, and its figurative story parallels that of Christ of the Holy Scriptures. As the story goes, CHiram (Hiram), in the building of the temple, divided his workmen into three groups:

- Entered Apprentices;
- Fellow craftsmen;
- Master Masons. [36]

To each division, CHiram gave certain passwords and signs by which their respective excellence could be easily determined. Though each was classified according to his merit, some were dissatisfied, feeling that they were entitled to a more exalted position than they were capable of filling. So finally, three of the fellow craftsmen, more daring than the rest, decided to force CHiram to reveal the password of the Master's degree.

Knowing that CHiram always went into the unfinished Sanctum Sanctorum at high noon to pray, these three ruffians, — Jubela, Jubelo, and Jubelum — lay in wait for him, one at each of the three main gates to the temple. When CHiram was about to leave the temple by the south gate, he was suddenly confronted by Jubela, who was armed with a twenty-four-inch guage. Since CHiram refused to reveal the Master's Word, the ruffian struck him on the throat with the rule, wounding him. The Master hastened to the west gate where Jubelo, armed with a square, confronted him and made a similar demand. CHiram remained silent, was struck across the breast with the square, and then staggered to the east gate, where he was met by Jubelum who was armed with a maul. When the ruffian was refused the Master's Word, he struck CHiram between the eyes with the mallet and CHiram fell dead.

The body of CHiram was then buried over the brow of Mount Moriah, and a sprig of acacia placed on his grave. The three murderers all tried to escape to Ethiopia, but the port was closed; they were finally captured, and after admitting their guilt, they were executed. King Solomon sent out a search party of three who detected the newly marked grave by the evergreen sprig. The Entered Apprentices and Fellow-craftsmen failed to resurrect their Master from the dead, but he was finally raised by the Master Mason with *the strong grip of a Lion's Paw.* [37] The story of the three ruffians also alludes to Adam and Eve's attempt to obtain prohibited knowledge, which caused their expulsion from Eden, defeating the Divine purpose until the day they and their posterity would regain the Paradise they had lost. As a result, the construction and completion of the great mystical temple was halted, until time and circumstances, according to the Divine Plan, presented itself to restore to humanity the lost and genuine secrets of his divine nature and purpose.[38]

The word CHiram Abiff signifies:

- My Father;

- Universal Spirit;

- The Mystical Christ; Hermes;

- A prototype of humanity;

- The Cosmic Martyr — based on the Egyptian rites of Osiris — whose death and resurrection figuratively portray the spiritual death and regeneration of man through initiation into the Mysteries;

- Spiritual Fire, the Kundalini of the Hindu, which when raised or lifted up through the thirty-three degrees or vertebrates of the spinal column, enters the domed chamber of the human skull, and passes into the pituitary body (Isis) where it invokes the pineal gland (Ra) and demands the Sacred Name;

- Its fullest meaning, the process by which the Eye of Horus is opened;

- The Third or incarnating part, The Master Builder, who through the ages erects living temples of flesh and blood to the Most-High.[39]

The three gates of the temple where CHiram was struck represent the three sunbursts, there being no gate in the north, since the sun never shines from the northern angle of the heavens. The north is the symbol of the physical because of its relation to crystallized water (ice) and to the body as crystallized spirit. In man, the light shines towards the north, but never from it, because the body has no light of its own, but rather shines with the reflected glory of the Divine life-particles concealed within its physical substance. It is for this reason, that the Moon is accepted as a symbol of man's physical nature. The Mysteries are the architects of civilization, and Hiram personified their power and dignity as the Master Builder, as he fell victim to the three ruffians or the recurrent trio: —the State, the Church and the Mob/ or ignorance, superstition, and fear. When the State governs, man is full of fear; when the Church governs, man is ruled by superstition; when the mob governs, man is ruled by ignorance. It is through the agencies of these three, that the Spirit of Good is murdered, a false kingdom controlled by wrong thinking, wrong feeling, and wrong action are established in its stead, and the material universe of evil appears ever victorious. The Mysteries are desecrated by the State, who is jealous of their wealth and power; by the Church, who is fearful of their wisdom, and by the rabble or soldiery, who is incited by the State and the Church.[40]

Nevertheless, the Lost Word was preserved, when CHiram was raised from his grave and whispered the Master Mason's Word, which had been lost by his untimely death. According to Philosophy, which embodies the vicissitudes of life, the re-establishment or resurrection of the Ancient Mysteries will result in the rediscovery of that secret teaching, without which civilization must continue in a state of uncertainty and confusion. Astrologically, the martyred Sun/Son is discovered by Aries, a Fellow-craftsman, where at the vernal equinox, the process of raising him begins; this is accomplished by the Lion of Judah (Leo, the sign of the Lion), who in ancient times occupied the position of the keystone of the Royal Arch of Heaven. CHiram emerges, then, as the flower that is cut down, dies at the gates of matter, is buried in the elements of creation, and like Thor, the mighty sky god, swings his mighty hammer into the fields of space, sets the primordial atoms in motion, and, establishes order out of chaos. He represents the cosmic potentiality in each human soul, waiting for man, through the elaborate ritualism of life, to transmute potentiality into divine potency.[41] However, before Mankind can live together in harmony and understanding, ignorance, must be transmuted into wisdom, superstition into illumined faith, and fear into love. Masonry, therefore, seeks to unite God and Man by elevating its initiates to that level of consciousness where they can behold a clarified vision of the workings of the Great Architect of the Universe.

The Initiations in the Blue Lodge

As the consciousness of every living individual thing dawns, it becomes aware that it is chained and so cries out with great insistence to be liberated from the binding ties which, though invisible to the mortal eyes, binds far more terribly that those of any physical prison. It is this realization that causes the candidate to aspire to seek Initiation. It is the Spirit, in fact, which cries out for the freedom to be, to express, and to manifest its true place in the great plan of cosmic unfoldment.[42] There are three grand steps in the unfoldment of the human soul before it completes "the dwelling place of the spirit." These three steps have been categorized as: youth, manhood, and old age, or in Masonic terms: the Entered Apprentice, the Fellow Craftsman, and the Master Mason, respectively. All life passes through these three stages of human consciousness; and, it is in the Blue Lodge that these three Grand Initiations take place. The Path of Life, as with all things, is governed by the laws of analogy, and just as the pilgrimage through youth, manhood and old age begins at birth, so does the spiritual consciousness of Man in his cosmic journey of unfoldment. He passes from unconsciousness to perfect consciousness in the Grand Lodge of the Universe, through a gradual, orderly, and masterful procedure of growth.[43]

The Entered Apprentice

Before this Initiation can be properly understood and appreciated, certain physical and spiritual requirements must be considered by the candidate. He must realize that true initiation is a spiritual process, not a physical ritual. That his real initiation is into the living temple of the spiritual hierarchy, which regulates Freemasonry, and that it *may* not occur until many years after he has taken the physical degree. Spiritually, he may even have been a Grand Master before he came into the world. There are few instances in the history of Freemasonry where the spiritual ordination of the candidate for initiation took place at the same time as the physical initiation. This is so because true initiation is the result of the cultivation of certain soul qualities, which are individual and personal and must be carried out alone in silence, the decision and choice being that of the mystic Mason. This degree, which is one of preparation and action, is acquired when the ***Entered Apprentice*** signifies his intent to *"take the rough ashlar, which he cuts from the quarry and prepares for the truing of the Fellow Craft."*[44]

The quarry represents the limitless power of natural resources, and symbolizes the cosmic substances from which man gathers the stones for the building of his temple. He will gather the stones he wishes to ***true*** to become a Fellow Craft, and this process symbolizes Man, who at the dawn of time gathered many blocks, cubes, and broken stones from the Great Quarry to be trued. It is important that they be gathered, for without this process they cannot be *trued*. This is a material step, dealing with material things, since all spiritual life must be raised upon a material foundation. This first step in the growth of a Master Mason is the mastering of the concrete conditions of life and the development of the sense centers, which later become the channels through which spiritual truths are expressed. No one can reach the spiritual planes of Nature without first passing through, and molding matter into the expression of spiritual power.[45] The number of the Entered Apprentice is seven, relating to the seven liberal arts and sciences. These are the powers through which he labors to reach the elevated and advanced degrees; and he does so by using them to develop his mind, to be able to receive certain impulses coming into his being, which in turn stimulate internal centers of consciousness. Action is the keynote of the Entered Apprentice, since all growth is the result of physical and mental exercise, by which the vibratory rate of the organism is intensified.

In summary, the Entered Apprentice:

- *Must have sufficient knowledge of the anatomy of the form, since the entire degree is based on the mystery of the form, of which the human body is the highest manifestation capable of analysis. Therefore, he must devote his time to the study of the complexities and mysteries of his own being;*

- *Must realize that his body is the living temple of the living God, and treat it accordingly, since when he abuses it, he breaks the sacred obligation he must assume, if he ever hopes to understand the true mysteries of the Craft. To break this pact he has with the Divine life evolving within him is to invoke the retributions of Nature;*

- *Must study the problems relating to food, dress, breathing, etc., since those who eat improperly, dress inappropriately, and only use one-third of their lung capacity, will not have the physical efficiency for full expression of the Higher Life;*

- *Must make human relationships a primary focus of his life at this stage, as part of the physical and concrete expression through which he seeks to unfold all unselfish qualities. This is necessary for a harmonious working of any Mason and his fellow men on the physical plane of nature;*

- *Must apply and study the seven liberal arts and sciences, to balance his physical and mental inequalities and to make himself ready for membership in the more advanced degrees.*[46]

The Fellow Craftman

The work of this candidate involves the work of the emotions and sentiments. He has left behind the stage of youth and has now passed into manhood or adulthood, which carries greater responsibilities.

The Fellow Craftman degree is symbolized in Masonry by a soldier, dressed in shining armor, standing on the second step of the temple. His sword is, however, sheathed and he holds a book in his hand. He is a symbol of — strength, the energy of Mars, and the spiritual unfoldment known as Fellow Craft.[47]

It is true that through each human being courses the fiery Martian rays of human emotions, a great, seething cauldron of power, which lies behind each expression of human energy. These emotional energies can be likened to spiritual horses chafing at the bit, or hounds eager for the chase, and whose emotional powers cannot be held in check, but break the walls of restraint and pour forth as fiery expressions of dynamic energy. This awesome principle of emotion we know as the second murderer of CHiram.

It is interesting to note that this fiery uncontrolled energy is the same force of spiritual light of the Cosmos we call the Fire Prince of the Dawn, which surges through the un-regenerated man and is the impulse he perverts into murder and hate. This force is the same mystic power that keeps the planets in their orbits around solar bodies, that keeps electrons spinning and whirling, and also builds the temple of God. This ceaseless power of Chaos is the seething pinwheel of perpetual motion, whose majestic cadences are the music of the spheres and is energized by the same great power that mankind uses to destroy the highest and the best. Having become a merciless slave driver, unmastered and uncurbed, this energy strikes the Compassionate One and sends him reeling backward into the darkness of his prison. Unfortunately, Humanity does not listen to the sorrowful, loving little voice of peace, imploring him in the constructive application of this energy, which he must chain if he is to master the powers of creation.[48]

King Hiram of Tyre, symbolic of the Fellow Craftman and the warrior on the second step, wearily teaches humanity the lessons of self-mastery. He does so by daily depicting the miseries of uncurbed appetites. Man is given strength, not to be used destructively, but that he would build a temple worthy for the One Life to dwell in. No one who is unable to control his emotions can expect to be entrusted with great power; he must prove his ability to use it constructively and selflessly. The lost key to the Fellow Craft degree is the mastery of the emotions, which places the energy of the universe at his disposal. The seething energy of Lucifer is now in his hands, and before he can move onward and upward, he must prove his ability to properly apply and manipulate energy. He is required to follow in the footsteps of his forefather, Tubal-Cain, who with the mighty strength of the war god, hammered his sword into a plowshare. Ancient wisdom teaches that the hand that slays must lift the fallen; the lips given to cursing must be taught to pray; the heart that hates must learn the mystery of compassion, which results from a deeper and more perfect understanding of his relation to his brother. The firm, kind hand of spirit must curb the flaming powers of emotion with an iron grip; these key principles underlie the realization and application of the Fellow Craftman degree.[49] A large percentage of humanity is now at the degree of Fellow Craft due to the intellectual and emotional development accomplished in the Age of Pisces. Mankind has learned that all the powers which his many years of need have earned for him, have come about so that through them, he may liberate himself from his bondage of ignorance. The Fellow Craft degree works with elemental fire, which must be transmuted into spiritual light, and the heart center is the center of this activity where the human side of nature with its constructive emotions must be emphasized. All these expressions of the heart must now be further transmuted into the emotionless compassion of the gods, who, in spite of, the suffering of humanity, are able to gaze down knowing that all things do work together for good, despite all appearances to the contrary.

The Fellow Craftman is the mid-point between the Entered Apprentice and the Master Mason degrees. Here, Mankind has reached a point where he has spiritually lifted up the heart sentiments of the mystic out of the cube of matter, and now realizes that his promotion to Master Mason in the spiritual lodge will come when his heart is properly attuned to a superior spiritual influx from the causal planes of consciousness. He is, however, able to manifest every energizing current and flame of fire in a constructive and balanced manner.[50]

As a Fellow Craftman, he has achieved the following:

- *Mastery over all outbreaks of emotions; poise under trying conditions; kindness in the face of unkindness; and simplicity with its accompanying power;*

- *Mastery over his animal energies; the curbing of his passion, his desires and the lower nature;*

- *An understanding and mastery of the creative forces and a consecration of them to the unfolding of his spiritual nature and a proper understanding of their physical application;*

- *Transmutation of personal affection into impersonal compassion, by understanding that all personal manifestations are governed by impersonal principles, and;*

- *Consecration of his five senses to the study of human problems, as they convey their unfolding knowledge of analogy. He then uses this material for his spiritual transmutation.[51]*

The Entered Apprentice degree is termed materialistic, the Fellow Craft, religious and mystical, while the Master Mason degree is occult and philosophical. Each is a degree in the unfoldment of an intelligent, connected life, revealing, in ever fuller expression, the gradual liberation of the individual from darkness and ignorance to light and knowledge.

The Master Mason

The Master Mason represents one who has spiritually graduated from the school of esoteric learning and stands on the upper steps of spiritual unfoldment. He is represented in the ancient symbol, as an old man leaning on a staff; this staff of life and truth upon which he leans are the years and lives of his labor. The brows of a philosopher shelter his white beard upon his chest, and his deep piercing eyes. By his wisdom and understanding, which are the true measurement of age, he is old, but not in years. It is the still small voice that speaks from the heart of his being, and not the words of others upon which he depends.[52]

From the first moment, his apprentice vision opened to a larger truth. Light from the sciences, from philosophy, from the Order itself, from friends, instructors, from helpers and light from his own *heavens* streaming through the window of intelligence of his mind, all slowly but surely guided his feet into the way of peace. Now, the last and greatest trial of his strength and commitment impose upon him the serious obligation of endurance as this kindly light is totally withdrawn from him. The time has come when all props are removed and reliance on one's natural abilities, self-will and normal rational understanding are surrendered. The aspirant must abandon himself totally to the Vital and Immortal Principle, allowing it to finish the work in total independence of his lesser faculties. He must lose his life, in order to save it. He does so by surrendering all that he has previously felt to be his life, to find life of a completely higher order. This explains why the Third or Master Mason degree is that of mystical death, and in all Mystery Systems, it is the final stage of perfection or regeneration.

This alone constitutes Masonic Initiation. In this moral way of dying, the soul is loosened from the body and the sensitive life; on becoming temporarily detached therefrom it is thus set free to enter the world of Eternal Light and Immortal Being. In this process, the candidate's liberated soul, supervised by duly qualified Masters and Adepts, is intromitted into its own interior principles, until at last, it reaches the Blazing Star or Glory at its own center. In this light, the candidate simultaneously knows itself and God, and realizes the unity and points of fellowship between them. In this instantaneous, awful and sublime experience, the initiated soul is brought back to its bodily encasement again and is re-united with *the companions of his former toils* (the cells of his body) to resume its temporal life, but with a conscious realization of Life Eternal to which are added the power and the knowledge that results. Only then is one entitled to the name of Master Mason.

In the words of the Initiate, Empedocles, he can then exclaim:

"Farewell, all earthly allies. Henceforth, Am I no mortal weight, but an immortal angel, ascending up into Divinity and reflecting upon that likeness of it, which I have found myself."[53]

The first and second degrees are in fact preparatory stages leading up to Initiation. They are not the Initiation itself, but prescribe the physical, emotional and mental purification necessary to qualify the candidate for the end which crowns the work.[54]

The Master Builder is one who has risen by labor through the thirty-three degrees of consciousness, to a position more glorious than any man can hold. On the physical plane, time is the differentiation of eternity man has devised to measure the passage of time, but on the spiritual planes of Nature, time is the space or distance between the stages of spiritual growth and, cannot therefore be measured by material means.[55] The life of a Master Mason is full, pressed down, brimming over with the experiences he has gained in his slow and steady climb up the winding stair. He embodies the power of the human mind, and the highest form of human expression. And even beyond constructive action and emotions, his power of thought soars and flies swiftly to the source of Light. The mind is the connecting link between heaven and earth, and through the fruits of reason, it is able to take him from the halls of darkness into illumination. The Heavens have opened up for him and he is bathed in the radiant celestial splendor of the Great Light, illuminating the immortal East. The ancients taught that the sun was not a source of power, light or life, but a medium through which life and light are reflected into physical substance. The Master Mason, purified by ages of preparation and the awesome power, which is the light of the lodge of the universe, is in truth a sun and a great reflector, and a spokesman for the Most-High who stands between the glorious fire-light and the world. His evolved physical body is the higher vehicle through which the nine-headed Hydra, the Great Snake passes, and out of his mouth pours forth the light of God to Man. The light he embodies and expresses is reflected to those coming behind him on the winding path.[56]

He it is who the scriptures refer to when it says: *"this is my beloved Son in whom I am well pleased."* He is the Prodigal Son who, having wandered in the regions of ignorance and darkness has now returned to the Father's House. He has passed from student to teacher, from the kingdom of those who follow, to the little group who must always lead the way. These are the glorious privileges his great wisdom and knowledge have bestowed upon him. The Master Builder has almost completed the building of the Temple, and with a sigh he lays his tools down. The last stones are in place, and as he slakes his limestone, he feels a vague regret at the sight of the dome and the minaret that rise through the power of his handiwork. Sadness weighs upon his heart as he sees the days of his labor end. Slowly, the brothers of the lodge leave him, and he stands alone on the pinnacle of the temple, as a voice from heaven then declares: *"the temple is finished and in my faithful Master is the missing stone found."* He is indeed the glorious example of God's Plan for his children. The greatest sermon he can preach and the greatest lesson he can teach is in standing as the living proof of the Eternal Plan. He is now a Knower — he knows himself — and, therefore, knows God and the Divine Plan that this *knowing* reveals to him. He knows because he is a Temple Builder, and within his own body is placed the Philosopher's Stone, the heart of the Phoenix, that strange bird, which rises from the ashes of its burned-out body with renewed youth. He has found the Lost Word because when a Master is ordained by the living hand of God, cleansed by living water, and baptized by living fire, he becomes a Priest-King after the Order of

Melchizedek, who is above the law.[57] The work of a Master Mason is the art of balance, the balance of the triple forces of the triangle. By so doing, he holds in his hand the triple keys, and wears the triple crown of the ancient Magus.

He is now King of heaven, earth and hell. Sulphur, salt and mercury are the elements of his work; and with the philosophical mercury of which he is, he blends all powers to the Divine Purpose and Plan for the liberation of Humanity. He becomes the eldest brother of the lodge and gives directions according to the Divine inspiration within himself, which his brothers are to follow. A very important fact of Masonry is that his innermost motive is the indicator of his real self. In this respect, if he allows social position, financial or business considerations, or selfish and materialistic reasons to lead him into the Masonic Brotherhood, he automatically separates himself from the true Masonic Order called the Craft.

Though they can never do any harm to Freemasonry, these individuals cannot get into the true Esoteric Lodge. But because they are ensconced within the Lodge, they feel they have deceived the Grand Master of the Universe. However, when the spiritual lodge meets to carry out the true business of the Craft, they are disqualified and are absent. Fortunately, a true Mason is not made by watch fobs, lapel badges, various insignia, or the rituals that ordain them.[58] Every true Mason comes to know that there is but one Lodge — the Universe, — and but one Universal Brotherhood, which includes the mineral, plant, animal and human kingdoms and is composed of everything that exists in every plane of Nature. He knows that behind all these diverse life-forms is the one connected Life Principle, the spark of God, and this Life can only be the measure of his brother's worth.[59] With the third degree completed, the Royal Arch degree, is its natural conclusion and fulfillment. While the Master Mason degree can be represented in Christian theology as: *he suffered, was buried and rose again*, the Royal Arch is the equivalent of the exaltation ceremony: *he ascended into heaven*. The purpose of all initiations is to lift human consciousness from lower to higher levels by quickening the latent spiritual potentialities in Man to their fullest extent through the discipline of the Initiation process.

Therefore, no higher level of attainment is possible than that in which the human merges with the Divine consciousness and knows as God knows. This is the level of the Order of Royal Arch, which is the climax and conclusion of the sacramental system of Masonry. Humanity is tired of doctrinal and dogmatic differences and quarrels, and is recognizing the need for a more intelligently presented, vital approach to God. Comparative Religion demonstrates the universality of the foundational truths which are identical in every faith. It is for this reason that the philosophic premise of Masonry is the most acceptable form of the New World Religion, in which the office, work and techniques of divine contemplation and meditation, provide the framework for the achievement of greater soul-awareness, and *eventually Christ-consciousness.*[60]

> *"Wisdom alone is the right coin with which to deal, and with it, everything of real worth is bought and sold. And for it, Temperance and Justice are achieved. Fortitude and Prudence are a kind of preliminary purification.*
>
> *And those who instituted the Mysteries for us appear to have been by no means contemptible persons, and to have intimated, in a veiled manner, that whoever descends into Hades uninitiated, and without being a partaker in the Mysteries, shall lie in the mire; but that whoever arrived there purified and initiated, shall dwell with the Gods. Yet, as said by those who preside over the Mysteries:*
>
> *'Many are the candidates seeking Initiation,*
>
> *But few are the perfected Initiates.'*
>
> *But these few are, in my judgment, true wisdom lovers; and that I may be of their number I shall leave nothing un-attempted, but shall exert myself in all possible ways."*

(Socrates in Plato's Phaedo)

CHAPTER TEN

The Science of Knowing

The Fall of Man is the descent of his soul into generation and into the Cycle of Necessity, which is described by Manly P. Hall in his book, *Lectures on Ancient Philosophy,* as that period and condition through which Man must pass in his achievement of conscious immortality, and which involves him going through the valley of the shadow of death. In this descent, a cleavage of the mind does and must occur, and so Man's assigned task is to build the bridge which will allow him to re-connect the three lower aspects of the mind to the Higher Mind or Soul and, therefore, to immortality. It is only through the science and philosophy of the process of the Antahkarana that the gift of immortality can be bestowed, and that the Above can be reflected Below. Every human soul is initially divine and incapable of dissolution; however, it cannot partake of its own permanence without the perceptions which philosophy confers.[1]

True education is, in fact, the science of building the bridge that links the integral parts of man to the environment in which he lives and, subsequently, the larger whole. Accordingly, the primary objectives of future education will be:

1. *To produce alignment between the mind and the brain through the correct understanding of the inner constitution of man, especially as it relates to his etheric body and the seven interior centers called chakras;*

2. *The construction of a bridge between the brain, the mind and the soul, to produce an integrated personality vehicle, which allows for a gradual and firm developing expression of the soul, and;*

3. *To build the bridge between the lower mind, the soul, and the higher mind to make possible the eventual illumination of the personality.*[2]

Like the spider, an occult symbol for the activity of Man, he [Man]must spin the connecting threads to bridge and make contact with his environment, and to gain experience and substance; in this way, Man repeats what God has already done, by creating both in the world of consciousness, and in life. The threads of consciousness man creates are triple in number and together with the two basic threads of the soul, they constitute the five types of energy which makes man a conscious human being.[3] This scientific experience, which constitutes the art of living, requires that the highly trained enquirer safely and soundly builds the link between the highest and lowest aspects of the mind. Three of these threads of consciousness constitute the Antahkarana and are mentally created by man, and are anchored in his solar plexus, his heart and his head. The life-thread, also referred to as the Sutratma or silver cord, is dual in nature, and is anchored in the head and the heart. The expression and employment of these five threads formed by man and the soul are responsible for the creation of the conscious man as well as the development of the major human races.

The construction of the rainbow bridge, as the Antahkarana is sometimes called, whether as it relates to Humanity or to the individual man, is synonymous with each other, and the three threads anchored in the solar plexus of both, began with the building of the first thread way back in ancient Lemuria.

This was when the dominant factor in the life expression was the Sutratma, meaning that the physical body, the animal form, and the dense outer factor were the focus of productive, exuberant vital life. In old Atlantis, the second thread of consciousness, the Antahkarana, began to emerge, as evidenced by sensitivity and awareness, which is a prelude to full consciousness. A consequence of this evolution was that *reaction* and *desire* became the essence of that cycle. Except for the evolved members of the human race, in that world cycle, mankind was considered to be *sensitives*, because their minds were very dormant, making them extremely mediumistic and psychic. They were clairvoyant and clairaudient, but lacked the ability to interpret what they contacted, and unable to distinguish between astral phenomena and ordinary physical life. They, therefore, just felt and lived due to the fact the bridge was not yet built.

In the modern Aryan race, the third and creative thread is in use and even though these three streams of energy had been present from the beginning of time, mankind has had to build the physical, emotional and mental instruments capable of expressing these energies and, therefore, he has been unaware of their existence. Recognition and use of the creative ability occurs when:

1. *The mind principle is developed and unfolded, and man then becomes a mental creature;*

2. *The personality, rather than the racial use of creativity, becomes active; and, this is a distinguishing feature of the Aryan Race.*

The impression on the mind of man through the medium of the Spiritual Hierarchy of the planet, brings about greater conscious creativity, which results in the creation of the great monuments we see throughout the planet and, at the same time, consequently leads to the conscious creation of the bridge of the Antahkarana. This vertical process is that which allows the individual and the human race to live a horizontal life of creativity.[4]

The Science of Social Evolution is the lower correspondence of the Science of the Antahkarana. And, in the future, through the Science of Magnetic Rapport, the science which lies behind all conscious awakening of the centers and their interrelation, meaning the relationships of man-to-man, group–to-group, and finally nation-to- nation will become a more established reality. In order to fulfill the individual, and the planetary goals of personal, economic, and spiritual freedom, it is important that educators and psychologists realize how absolutely important it is to bridge the gap between the different aspects of the lower self. These aspects are the physical, emotional and mental bodies, called the personality vehicle. Once the gap between them is bridged, an integrated personality emerges, which later merges with the soul and then with the spiritual triad. Only when the bridge that links these three, the Personality, the Soul and the Spirit is achieved, can there be a complete interplay of consciousness and can identification with the One Life become a reality.

It is the cleavage which occurred in the mind at the Fall of Man that is responsible for his sense of separateness from himself, his brother, and Life itself; and, therefore, his lack of a sense of self-identification. This science of bridging is the emerging psychology and the process, the knowledge and distinguishing features between the two threads, the Sutratma, the Life Thread of continuity, and the Antahkarana, the thread of consciousness and immortality will be learned and understood in the Aquarian Age. The Life-thread, the Sutratma, links and vitalizes all forms into one functioning whole, while embodying in itself the Will and the Purpose of the entity it is expressing, be it God, Man, or a crystal. The thread of consciousness, the Antahkarana, embodies in itself the response of the consciousness within the form, through a steady expanding range of contact within the total environment.

The Sutratma is the unbroken, immutable stream of life, which can be symbolically regarded as a direct stream of living energy flowing from the center of any form of life to the periphery and, likewise, from the source to outer expression or phenomenal appearance. It is, in fact, life itself and, as such, produces the evolutionary unfoldment and the individual process of all forms by being the path of life which reaches from the Spirit to the personality via the soul. It is the soul, and the indivisible thread of the soul, which exists as one and the same, that finds its anchor in the center of the human heart, it being the central focal point in all forms of Divine expression. In the beginning, a mental cleavage occurred to give the perception of differentiation in Time and Space of the One being split, only mentally, to become two. It should be noted here that the concept of

178

Space, from a spiritual perspective, refers to the field where states of being are brought to the stage of recognition. At this stage, the now *knower*, being fully aware and conscious, evokes another factor, that of Time, which affects this Space to produce a dynamic, self-directed and persistent intention. At this point in space and time, the aspirant comes to know that he is a soul, and the third Divine manifestation of a regenerated being emerges when the union of the basic dualities takes place.[5] The consciousness thread, the Antahkarana, results of the union of Life and Substance, and this differentiation in Time and Space is a result of the mental cleavage which took place in the mind of mankind at the beginning of time to produce what is also called Matter and Spirit.

The Antahkarana, then, is the weaving of the threads of the physical, emotional and mental substances of the human vehicle to connect to the monad or spirit so as to achieve *oneness* again in the mind. This process is a deeply esoteric one built through the medium of a conscious effort within consciousness itself, and although the qualities of goodwill, high aspiration, unselfishness, and intelligent understanding are essential to the process, it is far more than this, since these qualities are already considered as *givens* in the lives of those treading the Path of Return. The process involves intense mental activity, and requires the ability to visualize that which is being dramatically attempted, so as to build the Lighted Way out of mental substance.

This bridge of living light is a composite creation with the mental substance having three qualities:

- *Force that is focused and projected from the fused and blended forces of the personality;*
- *Energy drawn from the soul or egoic body by conscious effort*
- *energy abstracted from the Spiritual Triad.*

The Antahkarana is a triple thread that is woven mentally as a result of the appearance of life on the physical plane, and created and evolved as a result of this primary creation, the creation of the mental

179

substance. The aspirant works from below upwards, from without to within, and from the world of exoteric phenomena, into the world of subjective realities and meaning. Many souls in incarnation have reached this point in their evolutionary process. They have entered upon the Path of Return and are lesser adepts, facilitating the withdrawal of emphasis on the outer, as well as the beginning of the recognition and registration of that inner conscious knowledge, of the real versus phenomenal appearances. These souls have traversed the physical, the emotional, and the mental, and with the right use of the power they have gained in the process, have become efficient, thinking beings. Their beings constitute a thread of energy, colored by conscious sentient response, and a discriminating consciousness of mind, producing the internal integration, which makes for a true traveler on the Path.[6]

This Age of Aquarius will see the largest numbers of Humanity making their way onto the Path of Return, because the human family is becoming a more thinking entity, and the conscious spiritual being it was created to be. The term Human Being describes an entity capable of recognizing the ability to register contacts that are universal and subjective as well as individual and objective; this Being is a vital soul whose every expression is penetrated with individual life, radiates personality and is ultimately responsible. It is only those persons capable of responsible thinking, who are ready to apply the rules and instructions, which will enable them to make the transition necessary to come to that consciousness, which is characteristic of the illumined mystic and the intuitional knower who are qualified to enter onto the Path of Return.

From the height of supreme intellectuality, the systems of the West must now undertake the experiment to test the theories necessary to evolve and to perfect the mind faculty in man with its keenness and capacity for focus and concentration, which will lead him to full knowing. The human personality is, in actuality, a soul in form or matter, and this soul uses the three lower aspects — the composite physical, emotional, and mental bodies as vehicles for its expression. The objective, therefore, of the evolutionary process is to increase and deepen the soul's control of this personality instrument. Once this is achieved, what results is the divine incarnation of the individual. However, the aspirant must first consciously coordinate and unify these three bodies with the indwelling vital energy of the soul, for his light to begin to shine. When the light of the soul has brought the personality vehicle to the point of coordinated unity, through self-discipline, meditation and unselfish service, the consummation of this work is the conscious realization of union with the Christ, called *at-one-ment* in Christian terminology.[7]

As man moves onto the next step of the evolutionary arc, which will be the great spiritual occurrence of this age, the advancement in his mental unfoldment from intellect to intuition, and from prayer to meditation will occur. There are six stages in the process of this mental unfoldment:

- *Instinct;*

- *Intellect;*

- *Intuition;*

- *Inspiration;*

- *Illumination, and;*

- *Identification.*

The development of the intellect was a major goal and achievement of the Piscean Age, and the unfoldment of the intuitive faculty will be a primary aspect of education and psychology, a prerequisite for the major initiations to be taken in large number by humanity, in this new age. To accomplish this task, the disciple must begin to build the Antahkarana by bringing the highest aspects of the mind in the physical, emotional, mental worlds into close relationship with the Spiritual Triad. His physical brain must become a recording agent on the physical plane, demonstrating a clear alignment and a direct channel from the Spiritual Triad to his brain via the Antahkarana, which links the higher and the lower mind.

The intuitive faculty, thus developed, gives the disciple the capacity for pictorial and symbolic sensitivity, which expresses interpretively the spiritual understanding conveyed by the awakening intuition. This intuitive faculty is an agent of the Spiritual Triad, Knowledge, Wisdom and Understanding.

As this brain connection becomes stronger, the desire of the aspirant is transformed; he is now able to imagine creatively the higher order of desire, and begins to grasp the greater goal, which is the liberation of all form from the bondage to matter, through Initiation. This, Man alone is capable of achieving. It is pure and abstract reasoning that allows man to make the link into the mind of God, and thereby receive revelations of divine truths. Humanity's understanding and relationship with **God** will be transformed through *Meditation,* which is another hallmark of the Age of Aquarius. Humanity will transition from Prayer to Meditation, as a result of the development of the mind and the construction of the bridge to the higher mind. His vision will now unfold the divine plan as it is in reality to his mind and consciousness. He, Humanity, is now able to experience the glory of the knowledge committed to him as he takes his steps up on the ladder of Initiation. He is now able to grasp the great Law of Cause and Effect as it is demonstrated in the three worlds of human evolution, which expresses not only on the physical plane, but also on planes beyond.[8] By necessity, the new spiritual orientation requires that in keeping with the development of the mind, mankind acquires a clearer understanding of the concept of God through the process of Meditation, as opposed to the process of prayer that is practiced today.

Prayer, from the personality angle, is defined as the soul's desire, in which the individual asks and wrestles for the acquisition of longed for virtues, begging the listening deity to alleviate his troubles; he intercedes for those near and dear to him, and makes demands to high heaven for material or spiritual possessions he feels essential to his happiness. The individual aspires towards and longs for the qualities, circumstances and conditions that will make his life easier. He agonizes in prayer for relief from illness and disease, imploring God to answer his request for revelation; asking, expecting, and demanding are the primary characteristics of prayer, and with heartfelt desire being the dominant attribute. What must be understood here, is that it is the emotional nature and feeling part of the man, which is seeking what he feels he needs, and this can be viewed as the heart approach. Prayer has been classified into four categories with the progression correlating to the evolution of the individual's consciousness. The categories are:

1. *Prayer for material benefits and help;*

2. *Prayer for virtues and graces of character;*

3. *Prayer for others — intercessory prayer;*

4. *Prayer for illumination and for divine realization.*[9]

A study of these four types of prayer reflects that the first is rooted in the desire nature, but by the time the aspirant reaches the fourth type, prayer ends and meditation begins. At this stage, no prayer is needed except to ask for a good state of mind and wholeness of the soul. Meditation carries the work of the traveler forward into the mental realm, and desire now gives way to the practical work of preparation for divine knowledge. This individual, who began his long career and life experience with desire as the basic quality, and who reached the stage of adoration of the divine reality, though dimly seen, now passes out of the mystical world of desire into that of the intellect, reason, and eventual realization.

The mystic is produced by prayer and disciplined unselfishness, and is one who senses divine realities, contacts the mystical vision from the heights of aspiration, and longs ceaselessly for the constant repetition of the ecstatic state to which his prayer, adoration, and worship have raised him. On the other hand, through knowledge, organized disciplined service, and understanding, the illumined man produced by meditation is able to enter the kingdom of the soul and participate intelligently in its life and states of consciousness. While prayer involves the emotional nature and is based on a belief in a God who can give; meditation is based on the knowledge of the divinity of man himself and involves the mental nature, although it does not negate the mystical premise. Mysticism is actually a precursor to entry into the world of knowledge and of certainty.[10]

Meditation is the science which enables the individual to arrive at a direct experience of God in whom he lives and moves and has his being, and who he comes to know as the Eternal Cause and Source of all that is, including himself. Meditation causes one's beliefs to change into ascertained facts and one's theories into proven experience, which enables the individual to recognize the whole. The candidate becomes one with God by becoming one with himself and his own mortal soul. And when this awesome event takes place through the process of Initiation, he comes to know that the individual soul is the consciousness of the whole, and that separateness, division, distinctions, and the concept of me and them, of God, and a child of God, are now ended in the light of the knowledge and realization of unity. His integrated personality has been transcended through the ordered process of soul unfoldment, and a conscious at-one-ment between the lower personal self and the higher or divine self is realized. In other words, dualism is now replaced by unity on this Lighted Way of Union.[11]

The building of the Antahkarana is a conscious process in which certain rules must be followed correctly, if the desired results are to be inevitable and unavoidable. The student of this science must accept the following points as a working hypothesis:

I. The science of the Antahkarana is related to the entire subject of energy and how it is used and manipulated. In this regard and for clarity:

- Energy is explained as all forces pouring into the individual form, from whatever direction and source. The three major energies are usually related to the names Sutratma, life thread, or silver cord;

- Force is defined as all manipulated and concentrated

energies which are projected by an individual or group, in any direction, with many possible motives, whether they be good or selfish.12

II. It is the science of light manifestation, with the intended result being revelation and change. The qualities of light must, therefore, be properly understood, as follows:

- Light is essentially, from the angle of spirit, the sublimation or higher form of material matter;

- Light is the major characteristic and quality of the soul in its own realm, and of the etheric body, which is a reflection of the soul in the three worlds of human evolution;

- The fusion of the upper and lower light is, in fact, the object of the science of the work of building the bridge; the goal being a synthesis and shining forth of one's light in physical manifestation;

- There are technically two light bodies, the vital or etheric body, and the soul vehicle, called the personality vehicle, which is a repository of energies gathered over eons of time and through a wide range of contacts in all worlds. This soul vehicle is slowly being constructed as the third and final temple or house, not made with hands, eternal in the heavens.[13]

III. A study of the science of the Antahkarana should be made:

- Concretely, meaning in relation to the etheric body, which is a substantial, tangible form, though not universally accepted by modern science;

- Egoic-ly, meaning in relation to the soul, since the spiritual man must fuse with his etheric body in order to be a manifest divine being upon earth;

- Abstractly, the individual must develop the capacity to

think in abstract terms, without which the application of this science cannot be understood.[14]

IV. The bridge is concerned with issues related to the continuity of consciousness and those of life and death.

V. The science of the Antahkarana deals with the three-fold thread, which connects the Spirit/ Monad, the Soul and the Personality, linking all three vehicles in their aspects, while at the same time unifying the seven principles on which manifestation is established. This involves the creative expression of the personality with its total environment and includes:

- The bridge between the world of souls and the world of phenomena;

- The realm of subjective beauty, reality and the outer tangible world of nature;

- Between himself and others;

- Between group and group;

- Between the fourth and fifth kingdoms, humans and god-men, when the knowledge of Divine Plan becomes a reality to the disciple, and;

- Finally, between humanity and the hierarchy of masters.[15]

VI. This science of the triple thread, which links individual man to his spiritual source, has existed since the beginning of time. However, the recognition and conscious use of this thread as the path and means whereby ever-expanding contact is accomplished, comes later in the evolutionary process. The goal of all aspirants is to become aware of this stream of energy in all its diversifications, and to use these energies for their own self-unfoldment and in the service of the plan for Humanity.[16]

VII. The science of the bridge teaches that:

- The *life thread* comes directly from the One we call Spirit or Monad, and during incarnation is anchored in the heart, which is the seat of life;

- The *consciousness* thread comes directly from the soul and is anchored in the head, which is the seat of consciousness;

- The third thread of creative activity is initiated and constructed by the human being, and is anchored, when sufficiently constructed, in the throat. This thread is an extension or synthesis of the two basic threads —, the life thread and the consciousness thread. As man becomes truly intelligently aware, alive and desirous of full expression of consciousness, he hastens the material building process. The three lesser threads are of the personality vehicle, and connect the Physical, Emotional/Astral and Mental bodies.[17] The process involves a weaving of the following three threads and is explained below.

VIII. The Physical Body is connected to the Etheric Body by the thread which passes from the heart to the spleen, and then on to the etheric body.

IX. The Etheric Body connects to the Astral Body through the thread that passes from the solar plexus to the heart then to the Astral Body, while picking up energy from the previous thread.

X. The Emotional/Astral Body connects to the mental vehicle by passing from the ajna center (the center between the eyebrows) to the head center, then to the mind/body, while picking up energies from the other two threads. These three energies, though finally woven into one thread, remain distinct and work in tandem with the energy centers along the spinal column.[18]

XI.   The science of the Antahkarana and of the Path, therefore, deals with an entire incoming system of energies, and with the process of usage, transformation, and fusion. It also deals with the outgoing energies as well as their relationship to the environment and is the basis of the science of the energies of the force centers. In the end, these incoming and outgoing forces of energy constitute two great stations of energy, — one characterized by power and the other by love. These energies are focused toward the illumination of the individual, and humanity through the medium of the Hierarchy of Masters, which is composed of human beings.[19]

The Antahkarana is the thread of consciousness, evolved by the soul, and not the Monad or Spirit. It is one of intelligence, and is the responsive agent in all sentient reactions. It's worth noting that the soul is constructed of pure white light, while the etheric body, which is intermediary, is therefore made of golden light. The World Soul pours its ethereal thread of sentient consciousness into all forms, all body cells and all atoms. Likewise, the human soul, who is the solar angel, repeats the process on the lower arc in relation to the personality vehicle which is its shadow and reflection. In turn, the human being must repeat the process in the mental creative sense in all points of the microcosm and the kingdoms below him to reflect the macrocosm. Hence, via the life thread, the soul creates and reproduces a personality vehicle through which to function on the plane of matter. Eventually, through the building of the Antahkarana, the soul, having built sentiency on the physical plane, later bridges the gap between Spirit and Matter, Above and Below — through meditation and service. By so doing, the soul completes the creation of the Path of Return, which inevitably, must parallels the Path of Evolution.[20]

When the task of building the Antahkarana is completed, having produced perfect alignment between the Monad or Spirit on the physical plane, *the body of the soul, called the causal body*, is completely destroyed by the fire of the Monad; this fire is poured down through the Antahkarana. The head center and the center at the base of the spine will be in an unimpeded direct relation, as are Monadic Will and Personality Will. This allows for complete reciprocity between the Monad and the now fully conscious soul on the physical plane, i.e. the personality vehicle. The Divine intermediary, the soul, is no longer required because the Son of God, who is the Son of mind, dies at this point and produces the *renting of the veil of the temple in twain from top to bottom*, as spoken of in the King James Bible. This will precipitate the revelation of the Father. The aspirant will then be able to say, as Christ said, *I and the Father are one*, — He, Man, the Prodigal Son — will have now returned to his Father's House.

The final result of building this bridge is, in fact, the establishment of a line of light between Monad and personality, as a full expression of the soul. There is now a permanent tube of light between Spirit and Matter, between Father and Mother. This provides the evidence, then, that *spirit has mounted on the shoulders of matter* to that high place from whence it came; that it has gained the experience and the full knowledge of what life in matter could give, and all that conscious experience can bestow. The Son has done his work. The task of the Savior and Mediator is now complete. The aspirant knows the unity of all things as a conscious fact, and the human spirit can say, with understanding and intention: *I am that I Am*. [21]

This teaching of the Antahkarana will and must dominate what is taught in educational systems, and in the study and practice of psychology. When these stages and techniques are grasped and mastered by intelligent men or women, a new race with new capacities, new ideals, and new concepts about God and Matter, Life and Spirit, will emerge. Through this new race and the humanity of the future, not only will a new structure in the body and national system emerge, but also a soul and an entity who will manifest a nature that is love, wisdom and intelligence. Careful observation will reveal that there is uniformity among all religions and races as to the technique of entrance into the kingdom of the soul, but at a certain point on the path of evolution all ways converge and all pilgrims arrive at the same identical position on the Lighted Way. From this point of junction, they travel the same way, employ the same methods, and use the same phraseology, a fact that will become apparent when the study of comparative religion becomes more widespread.[22]

Afterword

Man is a spiritual being clothed in the garment of flesh to which he has become bound. His only hope of liberation is through the expansion of his consciousness.

Throughout the ages, the vision of a perfected civilization has been preserved as the ideal for Mankind and in this civilization a university must be established where both secular and sacred sciences concerning the mysteries of life are freely taught to all those who would seek the philosophic life.

In this institution of higher learning, there will be no place for dogma or creed and the superficial will be eliminated, leaving only the essentials. The criteria for admission will be by preliminary grades or initiations. These institutions will produce illumined minds, capable of ruling the world, with each occupying the position for which he is most admirably fitted. In these universities, mankind will be instructed in the most sacred, the most secret, and the most enduring of all Mysteries — Symbolism.

Every initiate will learn that Truth lies dormant in every atom in the Cosmos, that every form is a symbol and that every symbol is a tomb of eternal reality. Through this education, the spiritual, moral, physical and mental Man will learn to release the living truths from their lifeless shells.

Humanity cannot be preserved by the three "R's", unless the universal truths they hold are released. It was mysticism that opened up and released the secrets of religion to the world, and the time has now come for occultism to open and reveal the secrets of the sciences, since form must give up the spirit locked within it so that the seeds can grow and produce proper fruit.

Knowledge, the Great Tree, with its twelve branches, is for the healing of the nations. It is time that ignorance, superstition and fear, the three great forces opposing the essential progress of humanity, give way to knowledge and truth.

Ignorance is defined as the state of insufficient knowledge and superstition, an addiction to that which is untrue; and a fear of what one does not understand. The perfect government for this planet must eventually be patterned after that divine government by which the universe is ordered. When perfect order is re-established, peace is universal, and good is triumphant, mankind will find happiness welling up inside himself and the need to seek it will no longer be necessary.

For the establishment of this perfect government on Earth, three elements are essential. The first is the recognition of the evils defined as separation; then, the public has to be educated to assume its proper responsibility in the correction of these evils; and finally, public opinion must force the reformation of the State and curb the ambitions of the politicians.

Then, and only then, will the spirit of goodness and beauty, which has been repeatedly slain by the ignorant, become the established order. At this point sages will sit in the seats of the mighty, and gods will walk with men.

References

Chapter One

[1] Bailey, Alice A., *Esoteric Astrology*, London: Lucis Publishing Company, 1951, p. 605

[2] Ibid, p. 408

[3] Ibid, p. 409

[4] Ibid, p. 408

[5] Ibid, p. 606

[6] Bailey, Alice A., *Externalization of the Hierarchy*, London: Lucis Publishing Company, 1951, p. 89

[7] Bailey, Alice A., *Initiation Human and Solar*, London: Lucis Publishing Company, 1951, p 20

[8] Ibid, p. 21

[9] Ibid, pp. 21-22

[10] Ibid, p. 23

[11] Ibid, p. 24

[12] Ibid, p. 25

[13] Bailey, Alice A., *Esoteric Psychology vol. i*, London: Lucis Publishing Company, 1951, p. 328

[14] Ibid, pp. 311-312

[15] Ibid, p. 343

[16] Bailey, Alice A., *Initiation Human and Solar*, London: Lucis Publishing Company, 1951, pp. 42-43

[17] Bailey, Alice A., *Externalization of the Hierarchy*, London: Lucis Publishing Company, 1951, p. 658

[18]Bailey, Alice A., *Initiation Human and Solar*, London: Lucis Publishing Company, 1951, p.43

[19]Ibid, p. 44

[20]Bailey, Alice A., *Externalization of the Hierarchy*, London: Lucis Publishing Company, 1951, p. 662

[21]Bailey, Alice A., *Initiation Human and Solar*, London: Lucis Publishing Company, 1951, p. 46

[22]Bailey, Alice A., *Externalization of the Hierarchy*, London: Lucis Publishing Company, 1951, p. 508

[23]Ibid, p. 274

[24]Bailey, Alice A., The *Rays and the Initiations*, London: Lucis Publishing Company, 1951, p. 607

[25]Ibid, p. 594

[26]Ibid, pp. 592-593

[27]Ibid, p. 581

[28]Bailey, Alice A., *Initiation Human and Solar*, London: Lucis Publishing Company, 1951, p.182

[29]Bailey, Alice A., The *Rays and the Initiations*, London: Lucis Publishing Company, 1951, pp. 571-573

Chapter Two

[1]Bailey, Alice A., *Externalization of the Hierarchy*, London: Lucis Publishing Company, 1951, p. 609

[2]Ibid, p. 608

[3]Ibid, p. 609

[4]Ibid, p. 670

[5]Ibid, p. 258

[6]Ibid, pp. 256-259

[7]Ibid, p. 199

[8]Ibid, p. 110

Chapter Three

[1]Bailey, Alice A., *Education in the New Age*, London: Lucis Publishing Company, 1951, p. 116

[2]Ibid, p. 118

[3]Ibid, p. 119

[4]Ibid, p. 119

[5]Ibid, p. 120

[6]Ibid, p. 120

[7]Ibid, p. 120

[8]Ibid, p. 121

[9]Ibid, p. 122

[10]Ibid, p. 123

[11]Case, Paul Foster, *The True and Invisible Rosicrucian Order*: Builders of the Adytum, Ltd., 1989, p. 215

[12]Bailey, Alice A., *Esoteric Psychology*, London: Lucis Publishing Company, 1951, p. 400

[13]Bailey, Alice A., *Esoteric Astrology*, London: Lucis Publishing Company, 1951, p.169

[14]Bailey, Alice A., *Problems of Humanity*, London: Lucis Publishing Company, 1951, p. 90

[15]Ibid, p. 91

[16]Ibid, p. 95

[17]Ibid, p. 9

[18]Ibid, p. 10

[19]Ibid, p. 12

[20]Ibid, p. 15

[21]Ibid, p. 124

[22]Ibid, p. 135

[23]Ibid, p. 138

[24]Ibid, p. 141

[25]Ibid, p. 144

[26]Bailey, Alice A., *Education in the New Age*, London: Lucis Publishing Company, 1951, p. 81

[27]Ibid, p. 86

[28]Bailey, Alice A., *Problems of Humanity*, London: Lucis Publishing Company, 1951, p. 37

[29]Case, Paul Foster, *The True and Invisible Rosicrucian Order*: Builders of the Adytum, Ltd., 1989, p. 65

[30]Bailey, Alice A., *Problems of Humanity*, London: Lucis Publishing Company, 1951, p. 174

Chapter Four

[1]Bailey, Alice A., *Externalization of the Hierarchy*, London: Lucis Publishing Company, 1951, p. 575

[2]Case, Paul Foster, *The True and Invisible Rosicrucian Order*: Builders of the Adytum, Ltd., 1989, p.287

[3]Ibid, p. 286

[4]Ibid, p. 276

[5]Ibid, p. 272

[6]Ibid, p. 263

[7]Ibid, p. 261

[8]Ibid, p. 243

[9]Ibid, p. 223

[10]Ibid, p. 220

[11]Ibid, p. 216

[12]Ibid, p. 199

[13]Ibid, p. 198

[14]Hall, Manly P., *Secret Teachings of All Ages*, Los Angeles: The Philosophical Research Society, 1962, p. CLXXV

[15]Ibid, p. XXXIV

Chapter Five

[1]Bailey, Alice A., *Problems of Humanity*, London: Lucis Publishing Company, 1951, p. 15

[2]Ibid, p. 88

[3]Ibid, p. 28

[4]Ibid, p. 29

[5]Bailey, Alice A., *The Destiny of the Nations*, London: Lucis Publishing Company, 1951, p. 56

[6]Ibid, p. 3

[7]Ibid, p. 8

[8]Bailey, Alice A., *The Rays and the Initiations*, London: Lucis Publishing Company, 1951, p. 676

[9]Ibid, p. 581

[10]Ibid, p. 571

[11]Ibid, p. 533

[12]Bailey, Alice A., *The Destiny of the Nations*, London: Lucis Publishing Company, 1951, p. 104

[13]Ibid, p. 97

[14]Bailey, Alice A., *Problems of Humanity*, London: Lucis Publishing Company, 1951, p. 20

[15]Bailey, Alice A., *The Rays and the Initiations*, London: Lucis Publishing Company, 1951, p. 189

[16]Ibid, p. 624

[17]Case, Paul Foster, *The True and Invisible Rosicrucian Order,* Los Angles: Builders of the Adytum, Ltd., 1989, p.65

[18]Bailey, Alice A., *Problems of Humanity*, London: Lucis Publishing Company, 1951, p. 17

[19]Ibid, p. 17

[20]Bailey, Alice A., *The Destiny of the Nations*, London: Lucis Publishing Company, 1951, p. 75

[21]Bailey, Alice A., *Problems of Humanity*, London: Lucis Publishing Company, 1951, p. 26

[22]Bailey, Alice A., *The Destiny of the Nations*, London: Lucis Publishing Company, 1951, p. 61

[23]Bailey, Alice A., *Problems of Humanity*, London: Lucis Publishing Company, 1951, p. 23

[24]Ibid p. 14

Chapter Six

[1]Bailey, Alice A., *Problems of Humanity*, London: Lucis Publishing Company, 1951, p. 32

[2]Ibid, p. 35

[3]Bailey, Alice A., *Education in the New Age*, London: Lucis Publishing Company, 1951, p. 1

[4]Ibid, p. 6

[5]Ibid, p. 9

[6]Ibid, p. 70

[7]Ibid, p. 84

[8]Ibid, p. 10

[9]Ibid, p. 11

[10]Ibid, p. 19

[11]Ibid, p. 19

[12]Ibid, p. 20

[13]Ibid, p. 21

[14]Ibid, p. 21

[15]Ibid, p. 22

[16]Ibid, p. 23

[17]Bailey, Alice A., *Externalization of the Hierarchy*, London: Lucis Publishing Company, 1951, p.196

[18]Bailey, Alice A., *Problems of Humanity*, London: Lucis Publishing Company, 1951, p. 72

[19]Ibid, p. 87

[20]Bailey, Alice A., *Externalization of the Hierarchy*, London: Lucis Publishing Company, 1951, p. 328

Chapter Seven

[1]Bailey, Alice A., *Esoteric Psychology II,* London: Lucis Publishing Company, 1951, p. 120

[2]The United Nations Millennium Development Project: http://www.un.org/millenniumgoals

[3]Bailey, Alice A., *Esoteric Psychology II,* London: Lucis Publishing Company, 1951, p. 122

[4]Ibid, p. 263

[5]Ibid, p. 141

[6]Ibid, p. 141

[7]Ibid, p. 142

[8]Ibid, p. 142

[9]Ibid, p. 143

[10]Ibid, p. 143

[11]Ibid, p. 145

[12]Bailey, Alice A., *Externalization of the Hierarchy*, London: Lucis Publishing Company, 1951, p.534

[13]Ibid, p. 663

[14]Bailey, Alice A., *Esoteric Psychology I,* London: Lucis Publishing Company, 1951, p.35

[15]Bailey, Alice A., *The Light of The Soul,* London: Lucis Publishing Company, 1951, p.92

[16]Bailey, Alice A., *The Reappearance of the Christ,* London: Lucis Publishing Company, 1951, p.124

[17]Hall, Manly P., *Secret Teachings of All Ages,* Los Angeles: The Philosophical Research Society, 1962, p. XLV

[18]Bailey, Alice A., *Esoteric Psychology I,* London: Lucis Publishing Company, 1951, p. 312

Chapter Eight

[1]Hall, Manly P., *The Secret Destiny of America,* Los Angeles: The Philosophical Research Society, 1991, p. 28

[2]Ibid, p. 28

[3]Ibid, p. 32

[4]Ibid, p. 33

[5]Ibid, p. 34

[6]Case, Paul Foster, *The True and Invisible Rosicrucian Order,* Los Angles: Builders of the Adytum, Ltd., 1989, p. 88

[7]Hall, Manly P., *Secret Teachings of All Ages,* Los Angeles: The Philosophical Research Society, 1991, p. 85

[8] Ibid, p. 55

[9]Ibid, p. 130

[10] Hall, Manly P., *The Secret Destiny of America*, Los Angeles: The Philosophical Research Society, 1991, p. 57

[11] Ibid, p. 60

[12] Ibid, p. 62

[13] Ibid, p. 59

[14] Ibid, p. 63

[15] Ibid, p. 115

[16] Hall, Manly P., *Lectures on Ancient Philosophy*, Los Angeles: The Philosophical Research Society, 1991, p. 462

[17] Ibid, p. 197

[18] Ibid, p. 193

[19] Ibid, p. 194

[20] Ibid, p. 195

[21] Ibid, p. 197

[22] Hall, Manly P., *The Secret Destiny of America*, Los Angeles: The Philosophical Research Society, 1991, p.25

[23] Ibid, p. 128

[24] Case, Paul Foster, *The Great Seal of the United States,* Los Angles: Builders of the Adytum, Ltd., 1989, p. 3

[25] Hall, Manly P., *The Secret Destiny of America*, Los Angeles: The Philosophical Research Society, 1991, p.130

[26] Ibid, p. 134

[27] Ibid, p. 152

[28] Ibid, p. 154

[29] Ibid, pp. 159-161

[30] Ibid, p. 172

[31] Case, Paul Foster, *The True and Invisible Rosicrucian,* Los Angles: Builders of the Adytum, Ltd., 1989, p.150

[32]Hall, Manly P., *The Secret Destiny of America*, Los Angeles: The Philosophical Research Society, 1991, p. 172

[33]Case, Paul Foster, *The Great Seal of the United States,* Los Angles: Builders of the Adytum, Ltd., 1989, p.4

[34]Ibid, p. 4

[35]Ibid, p. 4

[36]Ibid, p. 5

[37]Ibid, p. 13

[38]Ibid, p. 15

[39]Ibid, pp. 15-16

[40]Ibid, p. 16

[41]Ibid, p. 18

[42]Ibid, pp.20-21

[43]Ibid, p. 22

[44]Ibid, p. 22

[45]Hall, Manly P., *The Secret Destiny of America*, Los Angeles: The Philosophical Research Society, 1991, pp.176-177

[46]Ibid, pp. 179-180

[47]Case, Paul Foster, *The Great Seal of the United States,* Los Angles: Builders of the Adytum, Ltd., 1989, pp. 31-32.

[48]Hall, Manly P., *Lectures on Ancient Philosophy*, Los Angeles: The Philosophical Research Society, 1991, pp.470-476

Chapter Nine

[1]Wlimshurst, W. L., The Meaning of Masonry, NuVision Publications, LLC, 2007, p. 7

[2]Ibid, p. 40

[3]Ibid, p. 35

[4] Ibid, p. 36

[5] Ibid, p. 38

[6] Ibid, p. 38

[7] Ibid, p. 39

[8] Ibid, p. 40

[9] Ibid, p. 40

[10] Bailey, Alice A., *The Rays and The Initiations*, London: Lucis Publishing Company, 1951, p. 533

[11] Ibid, p. 418

[12] Ibid, p. 533

[13] Hall, Manly P., *Lectures on Ancient Philosophy*, Los Angeles: The Philosophical Research Society, 1991, p. 437

[14] Hall, Manly P., *Freemasons and Rosicrucians—The Enlightened*, Charlottesville, VA and New Orleans, LA: Cornerstone Book Publishers, 2005, p. 6

[15] Ibid, p. 7

[16] Ibid, p. 7

[17] Ibid, p. 8

[18] Wilmshurst, W. L., *The Meaning of Masonry*, NuVision Publications, LLC, 2007, p. 55

[19] Ibid, p. 56

[20] Ibid, p. 56

[21] Ibid, p. 57

[22] Ibid, p. 57

[23] Ibid, p. 58

[24] Ibid, p. 58

[25] Ibid, p. 59

[26] Ibid, p. 53

[27]Ibid, p. 54

[28]Ibid, p. 54

[29]Case, Paul Foster, *The Masonic Letter G,* Los Angles: Builders of the Adytum, Ltd., 1989, p. *vi*

[30]Ibid, p. 45

[31]Ibid, p. 2

[32]Ibid, p. 12

[33]Ibid, p. 53

[34]Hall, Manly P., *Freemasons and Rosicrucians—The Enlightened,* Charlottesville, VA and New Orleans, LA: Cornerstone Book Publishers, 2005, p. 24

[35]Ibid, p. 25

[36]Ibid, p. 27

[37]Hall, Manly P., *Freemasons and Rosicrucians—The Enlightened,* Charlottesville, VA and New Orleans, LA: Cornerstone Book Publishers, 2005, p. 28

[38]Wilmshurst, W. L., *The Meaning of Masonry,* NuVision Publications, LLC, 2007, p. 44

[39]Ibid, p. 30

[40]Hall, Manly P., *Freemasons and Rosicrucians—The Enlightened,* Charlottesville, VA and New Orleans, LA: Cornerstone Book Publishers, 2005, p. 34

[41]Ibid, p. 37

[42]Ibid, p.58

[43]Ibid, p. 62

[44]Ibid, p. 63

[45]Ibid, p.65

[46]Ibid, p.67

[47]Ibid, p.68

[48]Ibid, p.69

[49]Ibid, p. 70

[50]Ibid, p. 70

[51]Ibid, p.72

[52]Ibid, p. 72

[53]Wilmshurst, W. L., *The Meaning of Masonry*, NuVision Publications, LLC, 2007, p.79

[54]Ibid, p. 78

[55]Hall, Manly P., *Freemasons and Rosicrucians—The Enlightened*, Charlottesville, VA and New Orleans, LA: Cornerstone Book Publishers, 2005, p. 72

[56]Ibid, p. 73

[57]Ibid, p. 75

[58]Ibid, p. 67

[59]Ibid, p. 78

[60]Bailey, Alice A., *Problems of Humanity*, London: Lucis Publishing Company, 1951, p.156

Chapter Ten

[1]Hall, Manly P., *Lectures on Ancient Philosophy*, Los Angeles: The Philosophical Research Society, 1991, p. 199

[2]Bailey, Alice A., *Education in the New Age*, London: Lucis Publishing Company, 1951, p. 6

[3]Bailey, Alice A., *The Rays and The Initiations*, London: Lucis Publishing Company, 1951, p. 450

[4]Ibid, p. 479

[5]Bailey, Alice A., *Education in the New Age*, London: Lucis Publishing Company, 1951, p.27

[6]Ibid, p. 28

[7]Bailey, Alice A., *From Intellect to Intuition*, London: Lucis Publishing Company, 1951, p. 53

[8]Bailey, Alice A., *The Rays and The Initiations*, London: Lucis Publishing Company, 1951, p.442-445

[9]Bailey, Alice A., *From Intellect to Intuition*, London: Lucis Publishing Company, 1951, p. 67

[10]Ibid, p. 65

[11]Ibid, p. 66

[12]Bailey, Alice A., *Education in the New Age*, London: Lucis Publishing Company, 1951, p. 143

[13]Ibid, p. 144

[14]Ibid, p. 145

[15]Ibid, pp. 145-146

[16]Ibid, p. 146

[17]Ibid, p. 146

[18]Ibid, p. 147

[19]Ibid, p. 148

[20]Ibid, p. 148

[21] Bailey, Alice A., *The Rays and The Initiations*, London: Lucis Publishing Company, 1951, p. 475-476

[22]Bailey, Alice A., *From Intellect to Intuition*, London: Lucis Publishing Company, 1951, pp. 183-184

Glossary

Abode of Peace: Term used to describe Jerusalem; the place from which humanity hungers for rest from strife

Abraham Lincoln: Past president of the U.S.A. during the Civil War; a racial avatar who emerged from the very soul of the people, introducing and transmitting a racial quality to be worked out later as the race unfolds

Absolute Unity: Perfect Oneness

Active Intelligence: The Third of the Divine Triad called Understanding, and assigned to Binah on the Tree of Life

Adam: A prototype of Christ; representative of the idea or pattern of the material universe designated as Eve; androgynous; a species and not a man

Adept: A human being who has traveled the path of evolution and has attained the final stage on the Path of Initiation. He has passed into the fifth kingdom and is now God-Man

Age of Occultism: Said to refer to the Age of Aquarius when the Ancient Mysteries will be revealed

Ageless Wisdom: The ancient mystery teachings, which embody the concept that all events are ordered according to a law of undeviating justice, and that every personal expression of the One Life thinks, feels, speaks and acts consciously and subconsciously through the operation of a single Life Power

Air: One of the four elements; fire, water and earth are the others.

Akhanaton: The first democratic leader; Priest-King and Pharaoh of Egypt

Alchemical Water: Regenerative, life-giving, heavenly water; the Water of Life; the Prima Materia.

Alchemical Woman: Isis; the Mother to whom the elements of Fire, Water, Air, and Earth are assigned

Alchemy: An Egyptian Art, given to the world by Hermes Trismegistus; the process of transmutation in which base metal is turned to silver and gold in the cauldron that is the human body;the process is the evolution of consciousness

Alexandria: The chief port and ancient capital of Egypt

All-Seeing Eye: A symbol of Oneness; the eye of the regenerated mind.

Amethyst: The twelfth precious stone, colored violet and adorning one of the foundations of the wall of the New City of Jerusalem

Ancient Egypt: The land from which the western mysteries emerged, and where the first democratic government functioned under the Priest-King and Pharaoh, Akhanaton

Ancient Mysteries: The Ageless Wisdom teachings of Egypt, India, Greece, China, South America, all explaining the Oneness of all life.

Ancient of Days: The innermost I AM; Melchizedek;

Animal Kingdom, The: third division of nature; the other kingdoms being the mineral, the vegetable and human kingdoms.

Annuit Coeptis: The motto on the reverse of the Great Seal of the United States of America, meaning He (God) has favored our undertakings.

Antahkarana: The path or bridge between higher and lower mind that serve as a medium of communication between the two, built by the aspirant himself in mental matter.

Aquarian Age: Our current Age and precedes the Age of Pisces; known also as the age of the unveiling of the ancient occult mysteries—that of the divine feminine.

Aquarius: Pertaining to the eleventh sign of the zodiac, with all its characteristics —Brotherhood, Revelation, and the rise of the Feminine.

Arabia: Located between the Red Sea and the Persian Gulf; also the symbolic location of the temple of Initiation, and of the Wise Men, according to the Fama Fraternitatis

Aries: The first sign of the zodiac associated with the tribe of Gad.

Armageddon: The last great struggle between light and darkness, which will be fought on the mental plane

Artisans: A skilled workman as in a member of the Masonic Craft

Aryan Age: Our present Age, which hosts the Fifth Root Race

Aryan Race: Members of the Fifth Root Race, or Fifth Life Wave, which includes all humanity

Asher: The seventh tribe of Israel associated with the sign of Libra

Ashlar: A rough-hewn block of stone; associated in masonry with the candidate of the first degree, the Entered Apprentice.

Atlantean: Inhabitant of Atlantis who made up the Fourth Root Race, or Fourth Life Wave

Atlantic Empire: The civilization of Atlantis consisting of ten islands in the Atlantic Ocean

Atlantic Charter, the: A statement and document, resulting from a meeting at sea with Churchill and Roosevelt, in which the basic aims of the Allied Nations for peace during World War II were set forth

Atlantis: The continent that was submerged in the Atlantic Ocean according to occult teachings and Plato; also the home of the Fourth Root Race

Aton: The name for God according to Akhanaton, the Egyptian Priest-King

Bacon, Francis: Author of the *New Atlantis,* and the individual who set up the Secret Order in America in the middle of the 17th century; he set up the colonization scheme for the establishment of the Philosophic Empire

Benjamin: The ninth tribe of Israel associated with the sign of Sagittarius

Benjamin Franklin: One of the signers of the Declaration of Independence

Beryl: The eighth precious stone; a vitreous, emerald-green, yellow, pink gem adorning one of the foundations of the wall of the New City of Jerusalem

Blue: One of the primary colors attributed to the vibration of the black/blue race

Blue Lodge: The Masonic Lodge in which the two preparatory initiations of Entered Apprentice, Fellow Craft, and final and true Initiation of Master Mason are taken

Bodhisattva: He whose consciousness has become intelligent

Bondage: Defined esoterically as ignorance; lack of knowledge

Book of Revelation: The last book of the King James Bible

British Empire and Commonwealth: A political association consisting of the United Kingdom, Australia, Canada, Jamaica, New Zealand, India, Nigeria, etc.

Brotherhood: Recognizes that the kingdom of God can and must appear on Earth; the members of this kingdom recognize neither rich nor poor, high nor low, labor nor capital, but are the children of one God and are all brothers; the Plan of the Hierarchy for Humanity, which is now able to grasp this fact; sharing; internationalism

Bull of Form: Related to the sign of Taurus a fixed earth sign; symbolizes matter and gold; eventually the Bull of Form will clash with the Bull of Spirit to bring about illumination in man

Calcination: The first stage in the alchemical process of the Great Work; also related to the sign of Aries

Camel: The word associated with Gimel, the High Priestess (the Uniting Intelligence) and with memory and the symbol of transportation, commerce; that which unites one point in space with another and carries news.

Cancer: The fourth sign of the zodiac concerned primarily with the world of causes; in this sign, it is said God breathed into Man the breath of Life to become a living soul, establishing the link between life and form, spirit and matter; symbolizes the tribe of Zebulon; Cancer admits the soul into the world center we call Humanity.

Capricorn: The tenth sign of the zodiac; the symbol for the tribe of Issachar; the polar opposite of the sign of Cancer; the sign under which the Christ is born and the soul is admitted into conscious participation in the life of the world center called the Hierarchy.

Ceremonial Magic and Alchemy: The Seventh Ray

Chalcedony: The third precious stone; waxy and translucent, adorning one of the foundations of the wall of the New City of Jerusalem

Chariot: The symbol for the personality vehicle, which consists of the physical, emotional and mental vehicles.

Chakras: The seven centers or vortices of energy associated with the endocrine glands

CHiram: One of the central figures of the Masonic Legend, whose Hebrew name is ChVRM ABIV, *Khurum Abiv*

Christ, the: The Regenerated Man who has reconciled the pairs of opposites, and in whom duality ends.

Christ consciousness: That stage in man's evolution where duality ends.

Chrysolite: The seventh precious stone; an olive-green transparent to translucent stone adorning one of the foundations of the wall of the New City of Jerusalem

Chrysoprase: The tenth precious stone; apple-green chalcedony, adorning one of the foundations of the wall of the New City of Jerusalem

Church, the: The multitude of ensouled images, which are the reflected ideas of Adam in the material universe called Eve

Chyle: The milky, fatty liquid substance produced in the small intestines during the process of assimilation in the Virgo region of the body; called liquid gold, this substance travels through the bloodstream and is essential in the spiritual unfoldment of the aspirant

City of the Golden Gates: The capital of the Atlantean Empire

Civilization, the Lord of: The Master Rakoczi who is regarded as the General Manager responsible for carrying out the plans of the executive council of the Christ

Compassion: The ability to identify oneself with another in all the conditions of the three worlds of matter, emotion and mind; the compassionate man is not emotional, but is mentally poised and work intelligently

Concrete Knowledge: The concretion of the individual's concepts, enabling him to build thought-forms to materialize his visions and dreams and bring ideas into being

Congelation: The second stage of the Great Work, associated with the sign of Taurus and with the tribe of Ephraim

Consciousness: The responses and reactions of the individual to the forces of the twelve constellations and the twelve planets impacting him. This leads to the development of the life of the soul toward the will-to-power, the will-to-love, and the will-to-know.

Copper: The metal associated with Venus and the direction East

Corporeal Intelligence: Body-consciousness due to transformation in the constitution of the physical bodies of the human entity; refers to the Hebrew word Qoph.

Cosmic Cycle: A period of time ca. 25, 920 years

Count St. Germanine: Also known as Master Rakozci; the Lord of Civilization; Master of the 7th Ray of Alchemy and Ceremonial Order who, who is overseer of the Aquarian Age, sponsor of the United States, Europe and Australia; is the Chief Master Mason and architect of the business and financial world in Europe and America.

Cover, the: The ceiling in the Masonic Lodge, which typifies man's ethereal or heavenly nature whose properties are resident in him

Critias: The literary work in which Plato gives a description of the Atlantean civilization

Cube: refers to the Holy city, the New Jerusalem; the personality vehicle

Cube, perfected: The Regenerated Man; the New Jerusalem

Dan: The eighth tribe of Israel associated with the sign of Scorpio

David: The father of King Solomon who gave the direction for the building of the temple in Jerusalem

Declaration of Independence, the: The manifesto of the Congressional Congress adopted on July 4th, 1776 entitled "A Declaration by the Representatives of the United States of America" giving the reasons why the colonies had declared their independence

Democracy: The realization of the unity of life; a form of government; first practiced in Egypt

Depth: Described in Masonry as the distance or difference of degree, between the superficial consciousness of our earthly mentality and the supreme nature of divine degree of consciousness at the spiritual center of man

Devil: The veiled aspect of Archangel Michael; the mental creation of mankind; the repository of mankind's fears and ignorance.

Devotion and Idealism: The sixth ray characterized by a dissatisfaction and a devotion to a desire, a personality, an ideal, or a vision until he himself becomes the ideal, which is the highest possible level for man

Digestion: The fifth stage of the Great Work and is associated with the sign of Leo

Dionysiac Artificers: Custodians of a secret and sacred knowledge of architectonics; the most celebrated of the ancient fraternities of artisans

Dissolution: Primarily a psychological process, which lifts up the energy stored in sub-consciousness into the field of conscious awareness; changes in the physical and subtle bodies of the alchemist; the eleventh stage of the Great Work, associated with the tribe of Manasseh and the sign of Aquarius

Distillation: The sixth stage of the Great Work associated with the sign of Virgo and the tribe of Naphtali

Divine Feminine: The World Mother; the Creative Principle; Venus; associated with Active Intelligence, Binah, and Understanding on the Tree of Life

Divine Plan: The blueprint of the Purpose and direction of the Hierarchial policy for manifestation of that blueprint on the physical plane

Divine Purpose: Defined by all aspects of one great law in which free will, natural law, and karma work out through the medium of humanity

Dropis: He told the story of his friend Solon, the Greek lawmaker, who visited Egypt to gain the wisdom and knowledge of ancient Atlantis; he told the story to his son, Critias

E Pluribus Unum: The motto of the United States of America meaning: "Out of Many One People." The inner Rosicrucian meaning is: "Occult wisdom leads always away from the *many-ness* of the outer world to the unity at the heart of being."

Earth: True earth is the repository of the divine energies from above, and is called Malkuth on the Tree of Life, and is held in place by the mind; the lowest and outermost manifestation of the Life Power on the physical plane

East: The direction of the Greater Light; represents Man's highest and most spiritual mode of consciousness; the direction attributed by Qabalists to Venus; East also represents the way of knowledge associated with spiritual intuition

Eden, Garden of: The three upper worlds of Atziluth, Briah, and Yetzirah; after the *Fall*, man descended into the fourth world of substance, called Assiah

Education: The science of linking up the integral parts of man, and in turn, his immediate environment, and ultimately the greater whole in which he has to play his part

Egoic: Pertaining to the soul

El Morya: Ascended Master of Wisdom who works to create a new intuitional and changing political consciousness and situation in which the family of nations will stand together for freedom of the individual, right international interplay, which will finally abolish war, and create clean political regimes, free from graft, selfish ambitions and dirty political maneuvering

Elder Brothers: The Masters of Wisdom who emerged out of the human family and who lead the way of liberation

Elixir: The Stone of the Wise is the Universal Medicine and the Elixir of Life; it is the state of conscious existence which characterize those who have passed out of the Fourth Kingdom of Humanity into the Fifth Kingdom of God-Men; truth itself

Emerald: The fourth precious beryl stone, colored bright green and adorning one of the foundations of the wall of the New City of Jerusalem

England: One of the four countries of Great Britain: Ireland, Scotland and Wales being the others

Enlightenment: The synthesis of instinct, intellect and intuition in the Pilgrim, brought about by mental unfoldment, which produces in the aspirant the final stage of mental evolution along the Path of Initiation

Entered Apprentice: The first preparatory degree in the Masonic Blue Lodge toward Initiation as a Master Mason

Ephraim: The second tribe of Israel associated with the sign of Taurus

Etheric: One of the two parts *of the* physical body, the dense physical body and the etheric body; pertains to the four highest etheric sub-planes of the physical plane

Ethiopia: A native empire of Eastern Africa, south of Egypt with Addis Ababa

Euclid: An Athenian geometer who lived about 300 B.C.

Europe: A continent comprising a vast western peninsula of the Eurasian land mass

Eve: Symbol of the mental aspect and the mind of man; attracted by the lure of knowledge to be gained through the experience of incarnation

Evil: Separation; the veil of terror hiding the beautiful countenance of truth

Fall of Man, the: Spiritual involution; like the sinking of Atlantis, which it represents; the archetype of the immersion of rational, organized consciousness into the illusionary, impermanent realm of irrational moral ignorance, which is the prerequisite to evolution

Fama Fraternitatis: The first Rosicrucian Manifesto, issued as a manuscript and circulated among German occultists ca.1610

Father's House: The center where the Will of God is known; Shamballa; the Kingdom of God where the Christ reigns

Fellow Craft, the: The second degree on the path to the Master Mason Initiation, in which the work of deep psychological self-analysis and psychic faculties of the soul begin to unfold

Fermentation: The tenth stage of the Great Work associated with the sign of Capricorn and the tribe of Issachar

Fifth Kingdom: The divine kingdom; the kingdom into which natural man evolves, when he has completed the final Initiation as Master Mason; that of the spiritual man

Fifth Life Wave: The members of the Aryan Race who make up the Fifth Root Race

Fifth Principle: The principle of mind; the faculty in man, which is the intelligent thinking principle that differentiates man from animal

Fifth Ray: The ray of Concrete Knowledge and Science, which is the concretion of the individual's concepts, enabling him to build thought-forms to materialize his visions and dreams, and bring ideas into being

Fifth Root Race: The Aryan Race representing all races and cultures, and pertains more to the development of the mental instrument where man is able to reach a point of equilibrium between the intellectual brain and Spiritual perception, crossing the meridian point of the perfect adjustment of Spirit and Matter, and is then able to understand the relationship of one to the other

Fire: There are three fires— interior, radiatory, and essential; the first primal fire responsible for the activity of a matter, its rotary motion and development of matter; the second fire is that from the cosmic mental plane and the development of mind, and the vitality of the soul; the third fire deals with the evolution of Spirit

First Cause: The Master Principle behind all forms and appearances to their hidden causes

First Matter: Heavenly Venus; Absolute Unity; the One Originating Principle

First Ray: The ray of Will and Purpose characterized as the Will of God

Fixation: The third stage of the Great Work associated with the sign of Gemini and the tribe of Simeone

The Floor: The checker-work of black and white squares, which forms the groundwork of the Masonic Lodge, and denotes the dual quality of everything connected with the terrestrial life, and the physical groundwork of human nature; the web of life of mingled yarn characterized by inextricably interblended good and evil, light and shade, joy and sorrow, positive and negative together

Founding Fathers: Those involved in the establishment of the premise, which defined the United States of America, as the New Atlantis of Francis Bacon, where the scientific and philosophic empire can flourish

Fourth Ray: The Ray of Harmony through Conflict, central to Humanity as a whole, and the challenge to transmute conflict into harmony

France: A country in Europe said to be one of the six countries to people the new nation of the United States of America; the others being England, Scotland, Ireland, Germany, and the Netherlands (Holland).

Francis Bacon: Author of the *New Atlantis*, and the individual who set up the Secret Order in America in the middle of the 17th century; he set up the colonization scheme for the establishment of the Philosophic Empire

Freemasonry: The brotherhood to which every member of the human family belongs; the largest organization in the world, which prepares candidates for the inward life

"G", the Letter: Said to be related to Geometry and was one of the seven noble arts and sciences of ancient philosophy; means literally "the science of earth measurement"; related to Gimel, Camel, of the Hebrew Qabalah; the initial of Gaia, the Earth Mother and Geometria, which is the science by which the powers of the Mother are measured

Gad: The first tribe of Israel associated with the sign Aries

Gaia: Name for the Earth Mother

Garden of Eden: The three upper worlds of Atziluth, Briah, and Yetzirah; after the *Fall*, man descended into the fourth world of substance, called Assiah.

Education: The science of linking up the integral parts of man, and in turn, his immediate environment and ultimately the greater whole in which he has to play his part

Geomatria: The science by which the powers of the Earth Mother are measured

Gemini: The third sign of the zodiac associated with the stage of the Great Work called Fixation and the tribe of Simeone

Genesis: The first book of the King James version of the Christian bible, which contains the creation story of man

Geometry: One of the seven noble arts and sciences of ancient philosophy; synonymous with self-knowledge; the understanding of the basic substances of our being, its properties, and potentialities

Germany: A country in Europe said to be one of the six countries to people the new nation of the United States of America; the others being England, Scotland, Ireland, France, and the Netherlands (Holland); the country of the noble family of Brother C.R.C. of the *Fama Fraternitatis*

Gethsemane: The place where Christ's will became submerged in the Father's Will and where Christ, representing humanity, anchored or established the Father's will on earth and made it possible for intelligent humanity to carry it out

Gimel: The Hebrew letter meaning Camel, and is connected to memory and the High Priestess

Gnostic: From the Greek word Gnosis meaning wisdom or knowledge

God-Man: The liberated man in whom the personality and the soul are fused, and is conditioned by the divine plan, and its purpose

Goethe, Johann Wolfgang, von: A great German philosopher, poet, statesman and novelist who drew the analogy between sound and form, and declared that architecture is crystallized music

Government: The authoritative direction of the affairs of men in a community; administration and rule; forms of government include Nazism, Fascism, Communism, and Democracy in which people govern, and the government represents the will of the people; this, however, is not yet a manifested fact; the ultimate goal is a spiritual government

Grand Master: Refers to one of the three Grand Masters involved in the building of the temple in Jerusalem— King Solomon, King Hiram of Tyre, and Hiram Abiff; symbolizes the triune spirit of man

Great Architect: A reference to Hiram Abiff of the Masonic Legend who was put in charge of building Solomon's Temple

Great Bear, the: The constellation influencing the first emanation of the Divine Triad, which contained the Divine Idea of the plan to be carried out in matter; the seven brothers issue from this sphere

Great Britain: The principal islands of the United Kingdom consisting of England, Scotland, Ireland and Wales

Great Illusion: Duality; the sense of separateness

Great Lakes Indians: The first League of Nations in North America created among the Indians of the American Northeast, two thousand years before the white man arrived and the democracy of 1776

Great Seal, the: An American national-coat-of-arms, which states symbolically the principles, which animate the founders of the Republic, and to the Qabalist, it exhibits the indication that with occult wisdom, it was composed under the influence of Rosicrucian doctrines transmitted through Freemasonry

Great White Lodge on Sirius: Its organized efforts are directed toward lifting the organized forces of materialism to a higher and spiritual plane.

Great Work: The spiritual process which allows the candidate for Initiation to pass out of the limitations of Time into the Freedom of Eternity, where the Past, Present and Future meet in a timeless *Now* just as any point of the circumference of a circle is at the same time the Beginning and the End, the Alpha and the Omega

Greece: One of the countries in Europe; one of the countries, together with India, Egypt and Israel, known for its contribution to philosophy, mathematics, sacred literature and scientific knowledge

Harmony through Conflict: The fourth ray related to the attribute of conflict to release its energy and power to create; the discontentment frees the latent energy in all forms to struggle, progress, and evolve to achieve union with the soul; the resultant consciousness of harmony and beauty serves to drive the journey of evolution

Height: Refers to the ceiling of the Masonic Lodge, which "is even as high as the heavens", indicating the range of consciousness possible to humanity when man has developed his potentials to the fullest

Hercules: The journey of the Sun through the twelve signs of the zodiac, which has come to be known as the Labours of Hercules

Hermes Trismegistus: The Thrice Great who is the messenger of the gods to man, and is said to have brought writing, medicine and civilization to Earth; he embodies in himself both aspects of the mental principle, the expression of the concrete and the abstract mind of God.

Hierarchy, the: A group of spiritual beings on the inner planes of the solar system who control the evolutionary processes. They are divided into twelve hierarchies. A reflection of this Hierarchy is called the occult hierarchy and is made up of adepts and initiates who are in human form.

High Priest: Symbolized by the Hierophant; e.g. Moses was the Grand Hierophant or High Priest of Jehovah

High Priestess: The Uniting Intelligence; the Female Elder of the Temple; the thirteenth Path on the Tree of Life connecting Tiphareth with the Crown

Hiram Abiff: The symbol of Masonry representing the Master-Builder and Grandmaster entrusted with the building of Solomon's Temple; he is the symbolic embodiment of the Lost Word; he has the Light and is, therefore, the Triune Self and the four elements combined; his life, death, and resurrection illustrate the story of Masonry and the destiny of humanity; he is the Master Mason who is symbolic of both Hermes and Jesus

Hiram Legend, the: According to Masonic legend, he was the Master Builder of Solomon's Temple in Jerusalem and was assailed by three villains who demanded he impart to them the Master Mason's word; a philosophic exposition of redemption of the human soul

Hiram, King of Tyre: One of the three Grand Masters of the Lodge of Jerusalem who provided the materials for the building of the temple

Holland (The Netherlands): A country in Europe said to be one of the six countries to people the new nation of the United States of America; the others being England, Scotland, Ireland, Germany, and France

Holy City: the city John saw on the isle of Patmos described in the Book of Revelation; the New Jerusalem

Holy Land: Jerusalem; the place symbolically in the individual, country, and the world, where death to separation and ignorance takes place; the Abode of Peace; the place arrived at by the regenerated consciousness; the sign of Pisces is symbolically attributed.

Holy Vedas: The body of ancient Indian sacred writings dating from the second millennium B. C., which form the Hindu scriptures

Humanity: The world disciple; symbolized by Hiram Abiff; has the capacity for freedom

Human Kingdom, the: The fourth kingdom in Nature, which has developed the mental capacity necessary for self-assessment and self-reflection and change, and the ability achieve enlightenment

Identification: The sixth stage on the path of mental development; perfect union with the divine essence, the One-Life, and a withdrawal from the Not-Self

Illumination: The synthesis of instinct, intellect and intuition in the Pilgrim brought about by mental unfoldment, which produces in him the final stage of mental evolution along the Path of Initiation

Imam Madhi: A title of a Moslem religious leader or chief

Incineration: The ninth stage of the Great Work associated with the sign of Sagittarius in which all remaining dross in the sub-conscious is burned to ashes.

Initiation: Reveals the secret of the pairs of opposites; the process of penetrating into the mysteries of the science of the Self and of the One Self in all selves; the Path of Initiation is the final stage on the evolution journey trodden by man.

Inner Teacher: The instruction of the still inner voice, which requires an active state of consciousness where the whole personal consciousness is thrown into a form of expectant receptivity

Inspiration: The fifth of the six stages of mental unfoldment; a free spiritual cooperation for the good of humanity in the work of a great spiritual Force of Being; being an agent and a soul who becomes the channel for forces, ideas and activities other than his own, but to which he gives full intuitive assent

Instinct: The first of the six stages of mental unfoldment seated in the animal nature

Intellect: The second of the six stages of mental unfoldment; the ability to express life-reason; with it, the ability to consciously create what is needed in order to bring the needed stages of manifested life into being

Intuition: The third of the six stages of mental unfoldment; inner hearing and mental vision that reveal illusory appearances; the magnetic relationship between man and the idea, which apprehended the idea

Ireland: A country in Europe said to be one of the six countries to people the new nation of the United States of America; the others being England, Scotland, Holland (the Netherlands), Germany, and France

Isis: One of the three aspects of the Virgin Mother; She symbolizes the aspect of the form of Nature called the personality vehicle, and specifically the manifestation of the Christ Child, on the emotional or astral plane

Israel: The peoples of the Earth who are descendants of the three older brothers of the Race; they are: the Arabs, Semites, Afghans, Moors, the Latin and Celtic peoples, the Teutons, the Scandinavians and the Anglo-Saxons

Issachar: The tenth tribe of Israel associated with the sign of Capricorn

Jachin and Boaz: The two pillars set up on the porch of Solomon's temple; Jachin is white and symbolizes fire and the male, and Boaz is black and symbolizes the female or earthly man and water

Jacinth: The eleventh precious stone; a reddish-orange zircon adorning one of the foundations of the wall of the New City of Jerusalem

Jasper: The first precious stone; colored red, brown or yellow and adorning one of the foundations of the wall of the New City of Jerusalem

Jerusalem: The place symbolically in the individual, country, and the world where death to separation and ignorance takes place; the Abode of Peace; the place arrived at by the regenerated consciousness; the sign of Pisces is symbolically Jerusalem

Jewish Problem: Symbolically the same as the problem of humanity, which must hold before the mind the knowledge that mankind as a whole is divine in nature, as are **all** the elections of God, and no one is chosen or lost

Joseph: One of the twelve sons of Jacob who was sold into slavery in Egypt

Jubela: Represents fear; the State; is one of the three ruffians who assailed the Master Builder, Hiram Abiff, who would not impart the last word

Jubelo: Represents superstition; the Church; one of the three ruffians who assailed the Master Builder, Hiram Abiff who would not impart the last word

Jubelum: Represents ignorance; the Mob; and is one of the three ruffians who assailed the Master Builder, Hiram Abiff, who would not impart the last word

Judah: The fifth tribe of Israel associated with the sign of Leo, and the stage of the Great Work called digestion

Jupiter: The transmitter of solar and cosmic forces designed to connect the head and the heart, the mind and love, and the will and wisdom in the human being

Karmic debt: That which condemns man to struggle for existence, both from the form and the soul side; the Lord of Karma forces man to face up to the past, and in the present, to prepare for the future

Knower: The Initiate; one who has achieved Self-knowledge

Lady Liberty: The symbol in the New York harbor of liberty, equality and enlightenment

Law of Cause and Effect: Same as the Law of Karma, Action and Reaction and the Law of Retribution, and necessitates action upon the part of the aspirant in his liberation from bondage

Law of Rebirth: The controlling and major law in all the processes of manifestation, and governs the exoteric expression of a solar, or human being, which is to bring an increasingly perfect form to the expanding service of the soul; the human family for the first is in a position to note for itself the processes of rebirth of a civilization as an expression of spiritual culture at a particular point in evolution

Lemuria: According to the Secret Doctrine, a continent which preceded Atlantis; was the home of the third root race.

Leo: The fifth sign of the zodiac associated with the fifth stage of the Great Work, and the tribe of Judah; the sign in which the aspirant finds himself

Liberal Arts and Sciences: The seven noble arts and sciences— astronomy, geometry, music, arithmetic, logic, rhetoric and grammar

Liberation: The victory and triumph, which must be experienced in all twelve signs of the zodiac

Libra: A sign of balancing and careful weighing of values to achieve the right equilibrium between the pairs of opposites; the narrow razor-edged path which runs between the pairs of opposites; one of intuitive perception

Life thread: The Sutratma, or silver cord anchored in the heart, which is symbolically a direct stream of living energy flowing from the center to the periphery, or from the source to the outer appearances

Lion's Paw: Identified with the Egyptian symbolism of the sun, and with the sign of Leo the lion

Lincoln, Abraham: A racial avatar who emerged from the very soul of the people, introducing and transmitting a racial quality to be worked out later as the race unfolds

Lodge of Masters: Custodians of the truth, as it is in Christ; those whose task it is to save the world, to impart revelation, and to demonstrate divinity

Lodge, the: As a room, it is an oblong square and represents one-half of a perfect square and the lower half of a circle. These are symbolic of the unregenerated man who is not yet "whole". Similarly, the planet Earth and the human body are considered a "Lodge" and are moving toward wholeness. When the candidate becomes a Master Mason, he has "squared the circle", and has become the perfect stone and the "chief corner stone", a cube. He is now the "Keystone".

Lodge, Blue, the: The Sirian Lodge is the true Blue Lodge, in which the candidate of this lodge has to become a lowly aspirant with all the true and full initiations awaiting him, within the sunshine of the major Sun

London: The capital city of the United Kingdom and chief city of the British Empire; located near the mouth of the Thames; one of the fives points of spiritual influx and esoteric energy centers of power in the world; the others are New York City, Geneva, Darjeeling, and Tokyo.

Lord Buddha: The perfect initiate, though having reached illumination, has not developed to perfection all the attributes of divinity

Lord of Civilization: Master Rakozi, whose work is concerned with the problems of civilization by preparing the center, called Humanity, for right reception to the stimulating, re-vitalizing, and releasing force

Lords of Compassion: The Masters of Wisdom who make up the Spiritual Hierarchy

Lords of Liberation: They are great Lives, who are themselves, expressions of the divine ideas and concepts which control human life; they note and strike, and the quality they emanate reaches out to make an impact upon the most developed of the of men found on Earth at any particular time

Lord Maitreya: He who is known in the West as the Christ; the office he holds is that of the World Teacher, and as such, he is the head of all religions, is the Master of Masters and of angels

Lost Word, the: The resurrection of the Ancient Mysteries, which reveal that man who is the "Word made Flesh", comes into the knowledge that he is both God and Man

Magus: One who has succeeded in overcoming the influence of all the pairs of opposites, and has perfectly equilibrated all the powers of the lower forces represented on the tree of Life; he is Wisdom incarnate and is beyond Master of the Temple

Mahachohan: The head of the third great department of the Hierarchy, the Lord of Civilization, and is the flowering of the principle of intelligence which he embodies

Magna Charta, the: First document of the English constitution; the Great Charter of the English liberties, delivered June 19, 1215 by King John at Runnymede on the demand of the English barons

Maitreya, Lord: He who is known in the West as the Christ, and the office he holds is that of the World Teacher, and as such, is the head of all religions, is the Master of Masters and of angels; the Bodhisattva

Manasseh: The eleventh tribe of Israel associated with the sign of Aquarius

Manu: The representative name of the great Being who is the Ruler, primal progenitor and chief of the human race

Mars: One of the seven primary planets; one of action and change; it rules the path of humanity as a whole and governs the five senses, which are the medium and basis of all human knowledge; its energies vitalizes, purifies and stimulates all aspects and organisms in the body via the bloodstream

Masonry: A veiled and cryptic expression of the difficult science of spiritual life; and the understanding of it requires special and informed guidance and a genuine and earnest desire for knowledge, as well as a great spiritual perception on the part of the aspirant seeking to be instructed

Master Architect: Hiram Abiff, the symbol for Humanity, who was put in charge of the construction of the Temple in Jerusalem

Master Dujwahl Khul: A Tibetan and very learned adept of the second ray who is called the Messenger of the Masters, and has more knowledge of the Rays than anyone else; he works with those who heal with pure altruism; he is active with those who are active in the laboratories of the world, with the great philanthropic world movements like the Red Cross and with the developing welfare movements; his work also embraces teaching and work with healing angels

Master Jesus: A distinctive leader, organizer and wise general executive; he works closely with church leaders, especially with the masses of the Christian people who inhabit western countries and those who gather in the churches; he works ceaselessly with the inner, esoteric councils of the church and with the leaders and executives; he is said to occupy a Syrian body at present and lives in a certain part of the Holy Land

Master Jupiter: The regent of India who is among the oldest in the Lodge of Masters whose task it is to guide India out of chaos and to wield her diverse peoples into an ultimate synthesis

Master Kuthumi: Master of the second ray of Love and Wisdom, and is the emerging World Teacher in charge of education and religion; he is Chief of the teaching ray, who is attempting to transmute the thought-form of religious dogma to permeate the Church with the idea of the Coming and to bring to a sorrowful world the vision of the Great Helper, the Christ; he works with the prelates of the Catholic Churches, as well as the Greek, Roman, Anglican, and leaders of the Protestant communities

Master Mason: The man or woman who has taken the final initiation and has become an adept of which Hiram Abiff is a type. S/he is the Knower and Master Builder of the Lodge

Master Morya: He acts as Inspirer of the statesmen of the world, especially those great national executives who have far vision of the international ideal; and he manipulates forces through the Lord of Civilization to bring about the conditions desired for the furthering of racial evolution

Master Rakoczi: Also known as St. Germaine; Master of the 7th Ray, Alchemy and Ceremonial Order. He is overseer of the Aquarian Age, sponsor of the United States, Europe and Australia; the Master of civilization and is the Chief Master Mason; architect of the business and financial world in Europe and America

Mercury: The Roman name for Thoth or Hermes. The name of the metal associated with the pineal gland

Messiah: The Redeemer; Gematria suggests that the numeration of the serpent who tempted Eve is identical with the numeration of the Messiach, the Messiah.

Mineral Kingdom: The first stage of the development of the Life-force through form, which produces what seems to be dead things of the inorganic world; the kingdom of stone corresponding to the alchemical element, earth

Mob, the: The third villain named Jubelum who assailed the Master Builder Hiram Abiff;

Multiplication: The twelfth stage of the Great Work represented by the sign of Pisces and is associated with the tribe of Reuben

Naphtali: The sixth tribe of Israel associated with the sign of Virgo

New Atlantis: Restated the vision of a philosophic empire in his book, written by Francis Bacon in which he describes a model of a college he named "Solomon's House", or college of the six days work

New Jerusalem: The Holy City, which represents the Regenerated Man

New World Order: The hierarchy of the Masters of Wisdom who are externalizing and will sit in positions of power in all our systems of government. They will oversee the liberation of humanity.

North: The antipode of the South, and the place of intellectual and moral ignorance in the Masonic Lodge

Novous Ordo Seclorum: Motto on the Great Seal of the United States, which in Latin means New Order of the Ages

Order of Melchizedek: The order to which Jesus belonged as a high priest

Order of the Quest: The secret philosophic order of the ancient mysteries, which formed the basis for the establishment of the New Atlantis called the United States of America

Path of Return: The path that leads to that priceless attainment, true self-knowledge

Peace: achieved through the evolution of consciousness and the resolution and synthesis of the pairs of opposites

Pharaoh: Any one of the monarchs of ancient Egypt

Philosopher's Stone: The stone that the builder refused; is associated with Mary, the Mother of the Corner Stone; the Elixir of Immortality

Phoenix: A symbol of immortality of the soul and alchemical transmutation; usually referred to in the Mysteries with the initiate or men who are born again; just as physical birth gives man consciousness in the physical world, the candidate, after nine degrees in the womb of the Mysteries, is born to a consciousness of the spiritual world.

Philosophy: The knowledge of the workings of Nature, by which knowledge, man learns to climb to those higher mountains above the limitation of sense

Pillars, the: Three grand pillars support the Lodge— Wisdom, Strength and Beauty—these relate to the triple properties resident in the soul of man

Piscean Age: The period just ended, which supervised over the gradual change in the structure, chemistry and function of the human organism, making him ready to comprehend the occult mysteries of the Aquarian Age

Pisces: The twelfth sign of the zodiac, and is associated with the twelfth stage of the Great Work and the tribe of Reuben

Pleiades: The constellation representing the third aspect of the Godhead. It is associated with Binah on the Tree of Life; called the seven sisters or the seven rays of life energy

Poseidon: The god of the sea and the island of Atlantis

Prana: The Life Principle; the Life Breath; active radiatory heat, which varies in vibration and quality according to the receiving Entity.

Prodigal Son: A symbol for humanity and the wandering Jew who left his father's house to achieve an expansion of consciousness through experiment and experience.

Putrefaction: The eighth stage of the Great Work associated with the sign of Scorpio, and with the tribe of Dan

Pyramid of Gizah: A stone emblem of the Eternal Flame, the Egyptians call "the Light".

Qabalah: The traditional Hermetic and Judaic sciences called the mathematics of human thought; the algebra of faith that solves all problems of the soul as equations by isolating the unknowns; it brings to ideas the clarity and rigorous exactitude of numbers, and its results for the mind are infallibility, relative to the sphere of human knowledge; for the heart, it provides profound peace; it is said to have its origin in Egypt.

Quarry: Represents the limitless power of natural resources, and symbolize the cosmic substances from which man gather the stones for the building of his temple

Queen Nefertiti: The wife of Akhanaton

Race: Esoterically, that which relates to the mental consciousness or state of thinking; its exponents and "race members" are found in every nation without distinction or omission; the emerging race is now being formed by members of every country and nation who are now forming the sixth root race

Reuben: The twelfth tribe of Israel associated with the sign of Pisces

Rosicrucian: A person who by the process of spiritual awakening has attained a *practical* knowledge of the secret significance of the *Rose* and the *Cross*

Royal Arch Degree: The natural fulfillment and conclusion of the Third Degree of Master Mason in which this sacramental system reaches its climax in exaltation, and the robe of blue and gold is achieved

Ruffians: The three laborers named Jubela, Jubelo, Jubelum who killed their Master, Hiram Abiff; they represent the State, the Church and the Mob, or fear, superstition, and ignorance

Sanctum Sanctorium: The Holy of Holies in Solomon's Temple

Sagittarius: The ninth sign of the zodiac in which the ninth stage of the Great Work of Incineration occurs; also associated with the tribe of Benjamin

Sapphire: The second precious stone, colored deep blue and adorning one of the foundations of the wall of the New City of Jerusalem

Sardius: The sixth precious stone;a deep brownish-red variety of chalcedony, translucent and blood-red, adorning one of the foundations of the wall of the New City of Jerusalem

Sardonyx: The fifth precious stone, an onyx with alternate layers of light-colored chalcedony and reddish carnelian, adorning one of the foundations of the wall of the New City of Jerusalem

Scorpio: The eighth sign of the zodiac, in which the eighth stage of the Great Work of Putrefaction occurs; also associated with the tribe of Dan

Scotland: A country in Europe said to be one of the six countries to people the new nation of the United States of America; the others being England, Holland (the Netherlands), Ireland, Germany, and France

Scottish Rite Freemasonry: The outgrowth of the secret orders of the middle ages, said to be founded by alchemists and Hermetic philosophers

Second Ray: That of Love-Wisdom is concerned with the unfolding of consciousness of the whole, called group consciousness; it begins with the development of self-consciousness, in which there is the realization by the soul that man is the Three-in-One and the One-in-Three

Self-consciousness: The awareness in the individual of purpose, of a self-directed life, and of a developed and definite life-plan and program. These are indicative of some measure of integration and mental perception

Seventh Ray: That of Ceremonial Order and Alchemy, which characterizes the Aquarian Age; this energy imposes an established rhythm through the development of an innate faculty to function under directed purpose and ritual

Shamballah: The city of the Gods and home of the mystical occult doctrine; the custodian of the plan for our planet

Shekinah: The mystery of God and Man, of Man in the likeness of the Elohim, and of the relation between things above and things below; the intercourse of union upon earth performed in the spirit of celestial union

Simeone: The third tribe of Israel associated with the sign of Gemini

Sirius: Called the "dog star". Vibrations from Sirius reach our planet via the cosmic mental plane. It is the Star of Sensitivity governing the Hierarchy

Sixth Ray: That of Devotion and Idealism, which grows out of and is the fruit of dissatisfaction, plus the use of the faculty of choice in devotion to a desire, personality, ideal or a vision, which is the highest possible in man

Solomon, King: The son of King David and one of the Grand Masters of the Lodge of Jerusalem who was given the charge to build the temple in Jerusalem; the temple is said to be a Biblical allegory, which was built without the sound of hammer and is more likely a spiritual than a material edifice, and is in fact *"the temple not made with hands eternal in the heavens"*

South: In the Masonic Lodge, it is the mid-way point and the half-way house between the extremes of East and West, and spiritual intuition and rational understanding

State, the: A symbol for one of three ruffians represented by Jubela, and fear, who assailed the Grand Master, Hiram Abiff

Sub-consciousness: Those forces that operate below the threshold of consciousness; one of the functions of sub-consciousness is to reproduce whatever is planted in it by acts of conscious attention

Sublimation: Purification of Matter by means of the dissolution and reduction of the same Matter into its constituents

Sulphur: The second of the three principles of the Great Work; Mercury and Salt being the others; and all three represent Father, Mother and Son

Theology: Simply, what men *think* is in the mind of God

Third Degree: The Master Mason degree of Initiation, and now able to respond to the Will of God

Third Ray: That of Active Intelligence, which is concerned with the unfolding of the creative nature of the conscious, spiritual man, and takes place through right use of the mind, with its power to intuit ideas, to respond, to impact, to translate, to analyze, and to construct forms for revelation

Thoth: The Egyptian name given to Hermes Trismegistus, the Thrice Great. (see also Hermes and Mercury)

Thunder Bird: The name used by certain of the American Indians to describe Jupiter, the God of Thunder

Timaeus: Plato's further account of Atlantis following the Critias

Topaz: The ninth precious stone; yellow sometimes green colored gem adorning one of the foundations of the wall of the New City of Jerusalem

Transfiguration: The stage upon the Path of Initiation where the personality is irradiated by the full light of the soul, and the three aspects of the personality vehicle are completely transcended.

Transformation: The evolutionary process in which man's physical body becomes obedient to the dictates of his mind, which is becoming responsive to the higher mind though the medium of the soul; the emotional nature becomes the receptacle of intuition

Transmutation: The method whereby that which is lower is absorbed by the higher, and this force is transmuted into energy so that the energy of the three lower centers ascend upward into the three higher centers of the head, heart and throat

Tree of Life: The glyph of man and the universe. This geometric symbol consists of ten Sephiroth or emanations and twenty-two secret paths, constituting the thirty-two paths of wisdom

Tubal-Cain: The first artificer; a Kabiri and instructor of every artificer in brass and iron

Unfoldment: Stages in the process of becoming a regenerated being, a God-Man

United Nations: A coalition of nations formed in early 1942 to oppose the Axis powers; an organization developed to promote right human relations essential to peace and goodwill

Uranus: The ruler of the Age of Aquarius; the producer of occult consciousness, which is the intelligent fusing condition; produces the scientific at-one-ment of the higher and lower selves through the intelligent use of the mind.

Ursa Major: The constellation of the Great Bear with its seven stars, associated with the first ray of Will and Power

Vegetable Kingdom, the: The second kingdom in Nature; the others being the mineral, the animal, the human and now the emerging fifth kingdom of spiritual man

Venus: The alter ego of the planet Earth; the mental energy of humanity that establishes the relation of man-to-man and nation-to-nation. Venus is to Earth what the Higher Self is to the Personality

Victory: The liberation from ignorance

Virginia: One of the mid-Atlantic states of the United States of America, and one of the original thirteen states of the Union; became a State June 25, 1788

Virgo: Symbolized by the weeping virgin; the constellation of Virgo also symbolizes the woman clothed with the sun

Vulcan: The esoteric ruler of Taurus. It is one of the seven sacred planets, and rules the inner man and guides his development at the first initiation or early stages of his spiritual unfoldment

Washington D.C.: The capital of the United States of America

Water: Water is the generative potency representing the union of the Father and the Mother; one of the four elements

Water-pot: A symbol for the Age of Aquarius

West: Represents man's normal rational understanding, commonsense, and the consciousness he employs in the temporal affairs of his day-to-day material-minded world; the direction West belongs to the way of knowledge called reason; the direction ones leaves in his journey to the East in search of illumination and enlightenment

Zebulon: The fourth tribe of Israel; fourth gate and foundation in the New Jerusalem associated with the sign of Cancer

Zeus: Father of the Gods who carries in his hand the thunderbolts of divine retribution, and who perceiving the arrogance, resolved to punish the arrogance of the Atlanteans by the sinking of Atlantis

Bibliography

Bailey, Alice A., *Destiny of the Nations*, London: Lucis Publishing Company, 1951

_____, *Education in the New Age*, London: Lucis Publishing Company, 1951

_____, *Esoteric Astrology*, London: Lucis Publishing Company, 1951

_____, *Esoteric Psychology vol. I*, London: Lucis Publishing Company, 1951

_____, *Esoteric Psychology vol.II*, London: Lucis Publishing Company, 1951

_____, *Externalization of the Hierarchy*, London: Lucis Publishing Company, 1951

_____, *From Intellect to Intuition, Externalization of the Hierarchy*, London: Lucis Publishing Company, 1951

_____, *Initiation Human and Solar*, London: Lucis Publishing Company, 1951

_____, *The Light of the Soul*, London: Lucis Publishing Company, 1951

_____, *Problems of Humanity*, London: Lucis Publishing Company, 1951

_____, *The Reappearance of the Christ*, London: Lucis Publishing Company, 1951

_____, *The Rays and the Initiations*, London: Lucis Publishing Company, 1951

Case, Paul Foster, *The Great Seal of the United States*, Los Angles: Builders of the Adytum, Ltd., 1935

_____, *The Masonic Letter G*, Los Angles: Builders of the Adytum, Ltd., 1981

_____, *True and Invisible Rosicrucian Order*, Los Angles: Builders of the Adytum, Ltd., 1989

Hall, Manly P., *America's Assignment with Destiny*, Los Angeles: The Philosophical Research Society, 1991

_____, *The Secret Destiny of America*, Los Angeles: The Philosophical Research Society, 1991

_____, *Freemasons and Rosicrucian— The Enlightened*, Charlottesville, VA and New Orleans, LA: Cornerstone Book Publishers, 2005

_____, *Lectures on Ancient Philosophy*, Los Angeles: The Philosophical Research Society, 1991

_____, *Secret Teachings of All Ages*, Los Angeles: The Philosophical Research Society, 1991

Wilmshurst, W.L., *The Meaning of Masonry*, NuVision Publications, LLC, 2007

Index

Manhood, 164, 167

Mankind, xiv, 3, 5, 23, 24, 25, 26, 29, 32, 33, 35, 36, 38, 40, 44, 48, 74, 77, 80, 89, 91, 92, 99, 100, 110, 111, 121, 122, 124, 147, 151, 167, 177, 179, 182, 191, 192

Manly P. Hall, 67, 68, 118, 138, 149, 175

Mantle of Peace, 53

Manu, 14, 16

Mars, 53, 54, 61, 62, 137, 167

Mars force, 54, 61, 62

Martian rays of human emotions, 167

Masonic Brotherhood, 173

Masonic Craft, 53

Masonic Legend, 52, 67

Masonic Lodge, 152

Masonic Mysteries, 151

Masonic ritual, 136, 148

Masonic secret, 11, 112

Masonic Temple, 54

Masonry, xv, 21, 30, 80, 85, 103, 112, 117, 126, 143, 144, 146, 147, 148, 149, 152, 156, 157, 158, 159, 161, 164, 167, 173, 174

Masons, 26, 68, 134, 136, 152, 159, 161

Master Builder, 160, 163, 171, 172

Master Kuthumi, 14

Master Mason, 5, 52, 54, 68, 159, 160, 162, 163, 164, 165, 169, 170, 171, 172, 173

Master Mason's Word, 163

Master of all Masters, 9

Master of Compassion, 7

Master of the Lodge, 137, 160

Master Principle, 159

Master Rakoczi, 15

Masters of Wisdom, xi, xv, 27, 75, 148

Master Souls, 25

Master's Word, 161

Materialism, 16, 17, 38, 39, 48, 53, 79, 122, 138

Material power, 85

Mathematics, 96, 157

Matrix, 62, 64

Maturity, xv, 18, 38, 42, 74

Maya, 17

Mecca, 150

Mediator, 189

Meditation, 12, 64, 93, 174, 181, 183, 184, 188

Mediumistic, 83, 177

Mental control, 45

Mental plane, 9, 18, 22, 26, 27, 80, 82, 92

Mental vehicle, 187

Mercury, 56, 59

Mercy, xiii

Messiah, 36

Mexico, 144

Middle Ages, 83, 84

Middle East, 37, 51

Military achievements, 39

Military power, 85

Milton, 146

Mineral Kingdom, 7

Mohammed, 126, 150, 151

Molten Sea, the, 68

Monad, 186, 187, 188, 189

Monarchial, 75

Monopolies, 100

Moors, the, 37

Mother Earth, 157

Mother, the, xiii, xiv, 1, 119, 157, 159

Mount Hira, 151

Mount Moriah, 67, 150, 161

Multiplication, 34

Music, x

Mysteries of Egypt and Persia, 150

Mystery Systems, 170

Mystical Christ, the, 162

Mystical Orders of Egypt, the, 126

Mystics, 89, 126, 150

N

Naphtali, 58

National Cultures, 13, 108

Nationalism, 26, 39, 41, 46, 71, 72, 82

Neptune, 57, 65, 118

Netherlands, the, 127

New Age, 26, 31, 34, 35, 53, 79, 80, 98, 103, 106, 126, 143, 149

New American Era, 134

New Atlantis, 122, 123, 127, 129, 133, 140

New Economic Order, 101

New Jerusalem, 51, 52, 54, 58, 66, 67, 68, 69, 72

New Man, 21

New Order, x, 19, 115, 132

New Order of the Ages, 115, 132

About the Author

Photo by Don Parchment

The Role of Consciousness in Governance explains how the Divine Will and Plan for humanity must be manifested on Earth, through the governments of all countries, in order for the Divine destiny of humanity to become a reality. The goal of this book is therefore to introduce to the general public some ideas regarding the trend of both destiny of nations and the world as they relate to the effectiveness of the Spiritual Hierarchy in achieving the objective of illumination in Humanity

This book is the third in a trilogy of books by Etta Jackson. The first '*Understanding Your Choice*', is a compilation of the Arcane Mysteries which she completed in 2001. The second, '*Unveiling the Secrets of the Feminine Principle*' finished in 2007 and now available, reveals the Great Mysteries of the Shekinah, the Divine Mother and Third Aspect of the Divine Triad — the Holy Ghost, the Comforter.

The *'Institute for Conscious Global Change'*, a non-profit organization dedicated to making the needs of all peoples in all countries more visible, was founded by Etta in 2007. Visibility of these needs will be accomplished through the Virtual Global Project, which virtually creates the world we envision with accurate, concrete, on-going data being provided to keep the world informed and to recommend changes in each locale. Through this virtual image of a new world and its peoples, these mental images are designed to assist mankind in precipitating those images of change into the physical world.

Etta holds a B.A. degree in Biology; M.S. degrees in Psychoanalytic Counseling and Development as well as in Administrative Leadership and Supervision and is currently a Ph.D. student in Leadership and Change.

She has a daughter and a grandson.

Made in United States
North Haven, CT
06 April 2023

35127556R00171